GENDER IN THE CLASSROOM

GENDER IN THE CLASSROOM

Power and Pedagogy

Edited by

SUSAN L. GABRIEL

and

ISAIAH SMITHSON

UNIVERSITY OF ILLINOIS PRESS
Urbana and Chicago

14.95

Illini Books edition, 1990
© 1990 by the Board of Trustees of the University of Illinois
Manufactured in the United States of America
P 5 4 3

This book is printed on acid-free paper.

The editors thank the following for generously giving permission to reprint previously published essays: *Papers on Language and Literature* for "The Feminist Teacher of Literature: Feminist or Teacher" by Nina Baym and "Woman as Oppositional Reader: Cixous on Discourse" by Robert Con Davis, both of which appeared in *PLL* 24.3 (Summer 1988). National Council of Teachers of English for "Composing as a Woman" by Elizabeth A. Flynn, from *College Composition and Communication* (December 1988). Copyright 1988 by the National Council of Teachers of English. Reprinted with permission. Carolyn G. Heilbrun for her essay "The Politics of Mind: Women, Tradition, and the University" from *PLL* 24.3 (Summer 1988). Copyright 1988 by Carolyn G. Heilbrun.

Library of Congress Cataloging-in-Publication Data

Gender in the classroom: power and pedagogy/edited by Susan L.
Gabriel and Isaiah Smithson.
    p. cm.
    Includes bibliographical references.
    ISBN 0-252-06110-1 (alk. paper)
    1. Women—Education (Higher)—United States. 2. Sex
discrimination in education—United States. 3. Sexism in education—
United States. 4. Feminist criticism—United States. 5. English
language—United States—Sex differences. I. Gabriel, Susan L.
(Susan Laine), 1950– . II. Smithson, Isaiah, 1943– .
LC1757.G46   1990
370.19'345—dc20   89-20204
                                                            CIP

CONTENTS

Gender
in the
Classroom

ISAIAH SMITHSON

Introduction: Investigating Gender, Power, and Pedagogy

Once a year I teach a graduate course called "Women and Language."[1] It draws students from sociology and philosophy as well as from English; most of them are women. I include a section on pedagogy — on language in student writing, reading, and learning — and among the several essays we read are two by Adrienne Rich, "Claiming an Education" and "Taking Women Students Seriously."[2] In "Claiming an Education," Rich admonishes women students, "You cannot afford to think of being here to *receive* an education; you will do much better to think of yourselves as being here to *claim* one" (231). The women in the seminar usually recognize the justness of Rich's advice immediately. Like thousands of other women in colleges and universities across the United States, they have experienced the obstacles and inequities Rich alludes to; they have also experienced their powerlessness.

Women now constitute a majority of undergraduate students in America's colleges and universities and are quickly becoming the majority of master's degree students.[3] Most of these women are engaged in traditionally female areas, such as education and the liberal arts. However, since the passage of Title IX in 1972 outlawed sex discrimination within education programs receiving federal funds, fields traditionally reserved for males, such as engineering and medicine, have enrolled increasing numbers of females. As women become more visible in traditional and nontraditional fields of higher education, so too do the institutionalized failures of educational institutions to respond to them.

Sex bias begins as soon as women apply for admission to college. Women students receive 28 percent less in grants and 16 percent less in loans than do males, and females are more likely to withdraw due to financial problems than are males.[4] Whereas most financial aid eligibility rules do not consider the veterans' benefits some male applicants receive as income, the food stamps and Aid to Families with Dependent Children that many women applicants receive are counted as income.[5] In spite of the repeatedly demonstrated lack of correlation between women's performance in classwork and their scoring on the Scholastic Aptitude Test, admissions boards continue to use SAT scores to deny admission to some women and to disqualify others from financial support.[6] Women students are still "counseled" by advisors who ask questions of them that they would not address to men: "How will you handle your family if you're a doctor?"[7] There are few women administrative leaders to offer role models to women students: only 10 percent of college and university presidents are women (*New Agenda* 6). Child care centers are absent from 60 percent of the campuses.[8] Most campuses fail to establish women's centers as a means of providing crucial social and intellectual networks. These are just a few of the failures students in the "Women and Language" seminar and college women in general have encountered even before they enter the classroom.

Within the college classroom, the failures are equally apparent; unfortunately, the classroom inequities female students face at college are part of a tradition begun in primary school. Many elementary school teachers still put children into groups of girls and boys when they march them from one place to another or when they organize classroom activities;[9] many textbooks still "have sexism as their subtext";[10] and many teachers and counselors continue to join with the rest of society in convincing girls in junior high and high school that math and science are especially difficult for them and in dissuading them from developing the mathematical background that most male students rely on when they get to college. Now that computers are becoming an essential part of education (and of many careers), girls are becoming as shy of computers as they have been of mathematics. Surveys of high school students in California, Maryland, and Michigan show that males make up 62.5 to 64 percent of the students in computer programming courses.[11] "Many studies documenting sex differences in the use of computers have ascertained that boys tend to be more interested in computers and use the equipment more than girls. At any given school, a lower percentage of girls than boys use computers." One explanation is "the perception that computers belong to the male domains of mathematics, science, electronics and machinery."[12]

A recent study of teachers in four states and the District of Columbia demonstrates that most teachers in fourth-, sixth-, and eighth-grade classrooms give more of their time to their male students than to their female students, ask them more challenging questions, and allow them more time to talk. "Male students received significantly more remediation, criticism, and praise than female students."[13] Since learning closely correlates with the amount and quality of interaction between students and teachers, male students often have an advantage in these lower grades. This advantage continues into college. An extension of this study at American University indicates that "the patterns established in elementary and secondary school continue in higher education. Male students receive significantly more attention, and sex bias persists" ("Sexism" 33). These negative teacher behaviors and expectations are multiplied for minority female students; earlier studies have shown that many teachers assume that poor, black, or Hispanic students are less capable than whites and that, accordingly, they are offered less encouragement.[14]

The subtle attitudes and strategies that damage children in the lower grades are continued in the college classroom. The girls who avoid mathematics, science, and computers in junior high and high school become the women who avoid physical sciences in college; in 1985, while 34 percent of America's male high school seniors planned to major in physical sciences in college, only 11 percent of America's female high school seniors had the same plan,[15] and in 1986 women made up only 13 percent of America's graduate physics students.[16] The girls who receive less attention from their teachers in elementary school become the women who receive less remediation, criticism, and praise from professors in college. Texts used in college, like texts used in lower grades, continue to "have sexism as their subtext." The most obvious example occurs in the use of the so-called generic terms.

In a 1974 study, more than 500 junior high school science students were asked to make drawings of prehistoric people based on seven statements they were given describing these people. While two groups of students were given a set of statements using gender-specific terms (e.g., *men and women*) and gender-neutral terms (e.g., *early people*), one group was given statements using supposedly generic nouns and pronouns: *early man*, *primitive man*, *mankind*, and *he*. The percentages of males and females who drew male-only figures in response to the statements containing supposedly generic terms were significantly greater than the percentages of students who drew male-only figures in response to the other sets of statements. Even a statement referring to nurturing of infants elicited male-only drawings from 49 percent of the boys and 11 percent of the girls. The researcher concludes, "Especially in science courses, where objectivity is supposedly taught by word and example, the use of such masculinely oriented terms should be abandoned."[17] In a 1972 study, 307 college students were directed to choose pictures from magazines and newspapers to illustrate the chapter titles of a sociology textbook being prepared for publication. Some of the students were assigned chapter titles such as "Political Man" and "Industrial Man." Others were instructed to work with titles such as "Political Behavior" and "Industrial Life." Among the study's findings is the fact that "about 64 percent of those students receiving 'man'-linked labels submitted pictures containing males only, whereas only about half of those receiving labels without the term submitted male-only pictures for the five labels."[18] Experiments like these demonstrate that there is no such thing as the generic *man;* almost all men and most women conceive of males when they encounter *man, mankind,* and *he.* Current research literature often substitutes the more accurate word *pseudogenerics* to denote these terms. Nevertheless, many textbooks (and teachers) continue to use the terms indiscriminately in education at all levels, deceiving their students with respect to women's contributions to the past and present.[19]

Sexual harassment is the most visible gender-based problem, especially in college education. A survey of Cornell University's upperclass and graduate women students reveals that "61 percent of the women students surveyed have been subject to unwanted sexual attention." Over 12 percent of the women report that they have avoided classes with teachers who have a reputation for sexual harassment.[20] Many campuses have initiated campaigns to make male teachers aware that making sexist remarks or telling sexist jokes in class, hanging erotic pictures of women in one's office, and touching a woman during a conference are as offensive and as illegal as trading grades for sex. Many campuses have also begun to train their administrators in the handling of sexual harassment complaints. Some schools—the University of Iowa, for example—have adopted policies that forbid amorous relationships between teachers and students "in the instructional context," even when both are consenting.[21] The extent of the educational and administrative responses to sexual harassment suggests how widespread the problem is.

These conscious and unconscious discriminations, and hundreds more like them, are harmful for an obvious reason. Women educated by America's schools and colleges are likely to graduate ill prepared to take on many professional lives they might otherwise choose. Because many women now applying for graduate programs are older than their male counterparts, have children, and attend only part-time, admissions boards, financial aid officials, and counselors who perceive them as abnormal (i.e., not twenty-two and male) can frustrate rather than encourage their attempts to gain the skills they need to pursue the careers they desire. If women do not have sufficient preparation in mathematics, science, and computer technology, they are not free to choose continued study or professional lives in these fields. If women have spent years in classrooms learning the history and achievement of *Man,* they have not become sufficiently aware of the roles women have played in the development of

America's art and technology: they are forced to develop aspirations in spite of, rather than because of, their education. If women have to avoid some teachers because they engage in sexual harassment, they miss the opportunity to gain knowledge that could prove valuable in their careers. Because women attend colleges in which only 27 percent of their teachers are women and only 10 percent of these are full professors (*New Agenda* 6), they often lack the mentors who should offer them role models as well as relationships that will enhance their continued intellectual and professional growth.

However, these discriminations are harmful for another, less obvious reason. American education does profound, lasting, psychological damage to many of its female students. Giving girls and women a woefully incomplete history of their sex, offering them literary texts considered canonical in part because of their projection of male fantasies hostile to women, insinuating that there are some subjects and some careers that are inappropriate for women, allowing males to dominate classroom interaction, responding to a woman's classroom comment with sexual harassment such as, "Well, I'm not sure what you said, but your eyes certainly lit up when you said it"—through these and thousands of similar institutional and personal gestures, universities and teachers exercise their power over female students. In so doing, they join the rest of society in attempting to undermine girls' and women's belief in themselves. It is the presence of these institutionalized abuses of power that force women to claim rather than receive their education.

I recently completed a four-year term as the director of a writing program, and each year I worked with teaching assistants who are nontraditional students—people who are over twenty-five and who have returned to college after an absence of some years. Working with these students made me especially aware of the problem of women students' faith in themselves. Over and over, I encountered intelligent, imaginative women who created excellent teaching strategies I had never thought or heard of and who wrote papers fulfilling exceptionally high standards. Yet these women did not think of themselves as intelligent and imaginative. Most of their male counterparts, whether or not they were as impressive, felt much more assured of their abilities and prospects. A study of engineering students at twenty-one American universities confirms my informal observations. The study shows that the women in the programs have higher verbal and math SAT scores and higher grade point averages than their male colleagues. Yet the "women rated themselves less strong with regard to their science, math, problem-solving and spatial abilities than did their male counterparts."[22] As Rich asks in "Taking Women Students Seriously," "How does a woman gain a sense of her *self* in a system . . . which devalues work done by women?" (239).

Both outside and inside the classroom, universities encourage women to feel inadequate to various personal and professional tasks. Universities join families and other institutions in helping to undermine the self-esteem of women students. People are becoming aware of what is called "battered woman syndrome." They are becoming aware of the complicated self-image that can develop in a woman who is cut off from any support, who is abused physically and mentally, and who underestimates her worth and power to the extent that she is as much a captive of her own lack of self-esteem as she is of her brutal partner. Universities do not batter women. However, physical and psychological abuse are part of a continuum, and in so far as education encourages women to feel inadequate to certain tasks, to feel powerless—to lack faith in themselves—it contributes to the continuum. It locks the doors to escape as surely as the battering partner does. The larger society is also responsible for this undermining, to be sure. Yet educational institutions, especially colleges and universities, are intended to lead societies, not merely to reflect their values.

Many people and elements within higher education recognize the university's failed responses to women students and wish to encourage sensitivity to women within the university and society in general. There are over 600 Women's Studies programs housed in American universities.[23] Although few are well supported by their administrations, many have been successful in creating courses, programs, women's centers, and in-service and outreach activities that inform women and men and improve the academic climate for women. At least one university, acknowledging the double burden borne by women of color, offers a "Women and Minorities Studies Concentration."[24] Women's Studies programs provide a shelter within the university in which women can gain knowledge and support and in which they can safely experiment with change and self-image. "Empowerment" may not be written on the syllabi of most Women's Studies courses, but it is necessarily the result of courses that allow women to increase their information, hone their perceptions, and share with other women their ideas and feelings with respect to the science, technology, art, and intellectual history constituting the patriarchal culture in which they find themselves.

Several Women's Studies programs have begun the vital, frustrating task of educating their colleagues in traditional disciplines. Backed sometimes by grants from organizations such as the National Endowment for the Humanities and the Fund for the Improvement of Post-Secondary Education, Women's Studies programs such as those at the University of Arizona and at Towson State University have initiated projects in "gender balancing" or "curriculum integration."[25] The intention is to make faculty outside of Women's Studies aware of some of the Women's Studies scholarship done during the last few decades and of some of the gender-based pedagogical biases built into education. The objectives of seminars and workshops dealing with these subjects are revised syllabi and teaching approaches that incorporate gender sensitivity. The hope is that professors will not only expand the range of works, people, and events included in courses, but also become aware of ways their traditional pedagogy can restrict and undermine the learning and self-concept of both women and men.

As would be expected, progress is slow and difficult. In the words of women facilitating such workshops at the University of Arizona, "Curriculum integration asks men to value the female, the very element they had unconsciously rejected in their formation of gender identity, and to relinquish traditional culture, the very construct with which they had identified in expressing and allaying their anxieties about separation, selfhood, and power."[26] Accordingly, "the project seminars functioned simultaneously on at least two levels: an intellectual, consciously rational discourse set in tension with dynamics approaching those of an encounter group. That is, the meetings had both an explicit text and a potentially explosive subtext, a communal unconscious that was often unrecognized or unacknowledged by the participants . . . " (263). Curriculum integration projects necessarily require teachers to examine themselves as well as their classrooms; they ask other teachers to come some of the distance Women's Studies teachers have come. In moving toward attitudes and behaviors that will enhance the self-esteem of women students, the male teachers are required to question some of the bases of their own self-esteem. They are required to confront many issues such as power and control in their society, their classrooms, and their own personalities. These teachers are required to grow emotionally as well as intellectually. Thus, one of the conclusions drawn from the University of Arizona workshops is that "the tools of rationality alone are inadequate to the task of intellectual change when the investments in ideas regarding gender are deep-seated and self-interested for all parties" (263).

Women's Studies and curriculum integration programs have at least two decades worth of new information to pass on to students and teachers. Women (and some men) in English, history, psychology, sociology, and many other areas have provided well-founded alternative canons, alternative versions and assessments of the past, alternative theories of women's personality development, and alternative depictions of society, power, and gender identity. This continually expanding research can be taken into Women's Studies classes and into curriculum integration work-shops and presented on its own merit. However, there is one area in which educators lack sufficient information: Women's Studies investiga-tors are far from understanding the differences in the ways women and men learn.

Males and females are obviously raised differently in American society. Anger and violence are more acceptable coming from males than from females; most women value connections with others while most males value autonomy; most males seem more comfortable with pro-fessional power than do most females; most college professors are males and most grammar school teachers are females. In thousands of equally obvious ways, American society offers roles, aspirations, and estimates of worth to women that differ from those it offers to men. It seems likely that men and women take these learned behaviors and values into the classroom with them, that gender affects the ways they learn as much as it affects the rest of their lives. It seems likely that women and men speak, write, read, think, and, therefore, learn differently. However, it is difficult both to identify the specific differences in the ways male and female students learn and to develop teaching strategies to accommodate the different gender-based learning strategies that have been identified.

There are two problems with respect to knowledge of how women and men learn: dependable information is scarce, and translating dependable information into classroom pedagogy is demanding. An issue of *College English* provides two examples of the first problem—questionable studies. In a 1979 volume featuring women and writing, the journal published three articles on female student writers. One of them is based on a teacher's observation of two women students, one at Harvard and one at Yale; it suggests that these two students are typical of many female students in that, having been raised to be "good girls," they have diffi-culty going beyond writing that seeks merely to please their audience. Thus, "Each of these women describes a lack of personality in her papers, and her sense of non-ownership, and of disappointment at not being able to make herself heard."[27] In the "Women and Language" seminar, we review and critique several examples of pedagogical research. When we read this essay, the teaching assistants in the class immediately recognize the problems of lack of personality, non-ownership, and the frustrated voice, but they recognize the problems as typical of *most* of their student writers, female and male. The rest of the seminar participants wonder whether students at Yale and Harvard are representative of students at 99 percent of America's universities and whether one can draw any useful conclusions on the basis of informal observations of two students, regardless of where they go to school. Although none of us would be surprised to find that the author's hesitant conclusion is correct— "I suspect this is a far more common problem among [women students] than it is among young men" (908)—all of us are suspicious of the study's methodology. We are not willing to classify the conclusion as dependable information.

Another of the *College English* articles describes what are termed "The Female and Male Modes of Rhetoric."[28] Female writers, the author maintains, employ a rhetoric of "indirection" in their persuasive writing. "Women who know how to use this mode well characteristically know how to lead the listener or reader through a set of experiences and/or a line of reasoning, holding off the conclusion until they have made it almost impossible to reject the validity—emotional or logical—of what they say," whereas "men more characteristically than women begin their oral or written presentations with something like their final conclusion" (909). "The 'indirection' of the female mode seems to proceed without a readily recognizable plan. The thinking represented in the female mode seems eidetic, methetic, open-ended, and generative, whereas the thinking in the male mode appears framed, contained, more pre-selected and packaged" (910). "The female mode seems at times to obfuscate the boundary between the self of the author and the subject of the discourse, as well as between the self and the audience, whereas the male mode tends to accentuate such boundaries" (910). Women use indirection, according to the article, because they write with the " 'feeling that their conclusions *are* likely to be written off, unless they can lead the audience through the line of reasoning and the felt nature of the experiences upon which they have based their conclusion' " (909).[29] After discussing advantages of both modes of rhetoric, the article suggests, among other conclusions, that "the male mode of rhetoric is probably better suited than the female mode for written discourse" (920). As evidence for his distinctions between male and female student writers, the author offers a letter from a colleague in which she says she has noted these differences among her students, his own impression that his colleague's "remarks about female and male modes of rhetorical presentation rang true to my experiences in committee, departmental, and some non-academic meetings" (910), and his analysis of passages from professional writers—two of whom, oddly enough, use both modes. The sociology graduate students in the most recent session of the "Women and Language" seminar refused to take this article seriously; they felt its methodology was so weak as to make its publication useless. An ill-defined sample, a letter from a friend, informal observations by two untrained observers, and an unexamined relation between professional and student writing simply do not constitute a sound basis for conclusions, according to these social sciences students. The English and philosophy students feel much the same way. All of us find the discussion interesting, but none of us is convinced the study is valid or reliable.

A more recent article, published in 1986, offers one other example of a questionable study; this study focuses on gender and reading.[30] The article reports on an investigation of eight subjects, four women and four men, seven of whom are students in a seminar reading works by Brontë, Dickinson, Melville, and Wordsworth, and one of whom is teaching the seminar and overseeing the investigation. The eight readers set out to determine whether "reading or literary perception varies according to the gender of the author as well as of the reader, and if perception varies as a function of literary genre...." The teacher/investigator says that, after examining five "response statements" from each of the eight readers, the eight "did not see that response varied significantly with the gender of the author.... What we did notice and generally agreed was the case was that men read prose fiction differently from the way women did, and that both sexes read lyric poetry similarly.... Men and women both perceived a strong lyric voice in the poetry, usually seeing it as the author's voice, while in the narrative, men perceived a strong narrative voice, but women experienced the narrative as a 'world,' without a particularly strong sense that this world was narrated into existence" (239). The article presents eight parts of four readers' responses, including the teacher's; these, and the teacher/investigator's interlaced comments on them, are intended to illustrate the similarities and differences discovered.

Students' opinions in my "Women and Language" seminar differ; some members think some of the passages indeed illustrate the conclusions claimed, and others think some passages contradict the claims made for them. However, all disagree with one claim. The teacher/investigator grants that a study based on four people is not "definitive," but he maintains, "On the other hand, it is not likely that chance alone is responsible for these differences" (255). The "Women and Language" participants think chance alone could very well explain the supposed differences. Further, all of the "Women and Language" participants find themselves in ironic agreement with another of the teacher/investigator's statements: "I will forego a description of the character and atmosphere of the seminar experience and of the attitudes brought into it by the members; this factor itself requires long reflection, but I omit it with the understanding that it is a salient factor that ultimately bears on the results I am claiming. All of these adjustments appear only because this is an essay and not a book" (240). The members of our seminar, discussing a study done in another seminar, agree that the character of a seminar and the attitudes brought to it by its participants are indeed salient. In fact, most members feel these factors could easily be the "chance" ingredients explaining the differences uncovered by the study. Given the effect a teacher has on the atmosphere of a seminar and given the variety of attitudes toward literature and studies of gender that teachers and students can bring to a seminar, we wonder whether the unexamined atmosphere and attitudes might not be more important than the different genders and genres in determining the study's outcome. Since the attitudes of the seminar members and the environment of the seminar affected not only the eight people's responses to the readings but also their analyses of their responses, we have been unwilling to accept the study's conclusions. We sympathize with the space constraints of the teacher/investigator; however, our examination of this study and others leads us to recognize that the study of gender and reading, like the study of gender and writing, is in an early stage and that dependable studies require thorough groundwork and extensive examination of variables, whether or not these can be reported in a single essay.

I contributed my own example of a questionable study of gender and writing in an attempt to extend some of Carol Gilligan's theories. Gilligan has published a now well-known study of how females and males make moral decisions.[31] She concludes that, when making moral decisions, males often focus on the rights of individuals and think in terms of categories or hierarchy. Females are more likely to be concerned with the responsibilities of individuals and with the relations among individuals involved in the moral dilemma; context is important for most females. According to Gilligan, "The moral imperative that emerges repeatedly in interviews with women is an injunction to care. . . . For men, the moral imperative appears rather as an injunction to respect the rights of others and thus to protect from interference the rights to life and self-fulfillment" (100).[32] Those of us in the "Women and Language" seminars often dispute Gilligan's interpretations of her interviewees' responses; when we examine the passages of conversation intended to illustrate differences in the thinking and values of male and female respondents, we often perceive both Gilligan's male and female subjects as concerned with both responsibilities and rights. Nevertheless, I decided I would like to determine whether the differences Gilligan says are evident in speech are also evident in writing. Since college writing assignments often pose moral questions, it seemed important to know whether women and men respond differently to them. If they do, the next question to be asked would be whether teachers reward one approach and undervalue the other—that is, whether an additional gender bias is built into education.

I designed an experiment relying on an assignment which requires students to make and justify a decision on euthanasia, and I attempted to insure that my results would be valid. I had colleagues who were unaware of the objectives of my research administer the writing prompt to students enrolled in sections of the first quarter of our freshman writing sequence on the first day of class (so that responses would not be prejudiced by me or by any learning done during the class itself). When the essays were given to me, each carried a numerical code instead of a student's name so that I would not know the sex of the writer. As I read each essay, I attended to whether the writer was concerned with rights or responsibilities and to whether the writer's choices were guided by attention to moral generalizations or to the relational context. After I completed my analysis, I gave sets of 10 essays to colleagues to be sure my interpretations were similar to theirs. Of the 129 essays I had gathered, 67 were written by women and 62 by men. Twenty-nine of the students exhibited both approaches. However, of the 43 who exhibited the ethic of rights exclusively, 27, or 63 percent, were men; and of the 57 who exhibited only the ethic of care, 36, or 63 percent, were women. Thus, there seemed to be a clear correspondence between gender and one's way of approaching moral decisions in writing.

Having been made wary through reading other people's gender research, I conducted a second experiment intended as a check on the first. This one required students to respond to a moral dilemma that was close to many of them. They were given a case that required them to respond to the question, "Should a twelve-year-old girl lie to her mother in order to go to a rock concert without her knowledge?" I thought this prompt would skew the results because, unlike the question of euthanasia, it is a version of a local, domestic moral issue that most college students have faced in the recent past. I thought that almost all of the writers would be so "close" to this problem that, regardless of their gender, they would respond to the dilemma's context.

I administered and analyzed the responses in the same way as I had with the first assignment. The results confirmed my suspicions. Of the 137 essays written by 74 women and 63 men, 112, or 82 percent, exhibited the ethic of care throughout: 68 women and 44 men responded to the context created by the mother-daughter relationship and the daughter's desire to go to the rock concert. Seventeen exhibited both approaches and only 8 showed a concern with rights and illustrated an hierarchal approach (though it is interesting that 7 of these were written by men.) Thus, I doubt that my first study is reliable or even valid. My studies suggest that, when students express moral decisions in writing, the particular moral situation is a more important variable than the gender of the person making the decision. Who knows what other

unexamined variables are affecting my results? I have not had the opportunity to take my own study into the "Women and Language" seminar.
When I do, though, I will treat it as I did when I presented it at a recent
professional conference—not as a source of information about gender
and writing but as another example of the difficulties involved in gathering trustworthy information about the effects of gender on learning.

Unfortunately, those of us concerned with the influence of gender on
learning, aware of the damage done by institutionalized expressions of
power, and anxious to overcome the inequities currently built into learning lack much of the research needed to support our concerns and guide
our overcoming of these inequities. Although we are informed by some
dependable studies, we await many more studies, most of which probably will be small in scale and some of which necessarily will be made
suspect by less than desirable procedures for gathering information and
by the presence of uncontrolled variables. Only when a large number of
such studies is available will we be able to inspect similar studies for
similar conclusions in order to determine which conclusions persist.
Further studies may verify that, indeed, the "good girl" syndrome does
interfere with the writing done by many women, that women are more
likely than men to be skilled in the rhetoric of "indirection," that men and
women do read prose fiction differently, and that the prose of women
written in response to assignments requiring moral choices is likely to
reflect an ethic of care. On the other hand, further studies may contradict
or effect revision of these claims. Fortunately, this process of generating
hypotheses and separating speculation from fact is underway. Some
collections dealing with gender and pedagogy are available, and each of
them contains at least some well-researched, thoughtful analyses.[33]

One claim that has already been verified by several studies has to do
with gender identity, connection, and separation. Its existence illustrates
the second problem with respect to knowledge of how women and men
learn—translating dependable information into classroom pedagogy. Nancy
Chodorow says that "in any given society, feminine personality comes to
define itself in relation and connection to other people more than masculine personality does."[34] Gilligan's study corroborates Chodorow's thesis;
Gilligan observes, "male and female voices typically speak of the importance of different truths, the former of the role of separation as it defines
and empowers the self, the latter of the ongoing process of attachment
that creates and sustains the human community" (156). Commenting on
the responses of several women and men in their late twenties, Gilligan
concludes, "in all of the women's descriptions, identity is defined in a
context of relationship and judged by a standard of responsibility and

care" (160). For men, she continues, "involvement with others is tied to a qualification of identity rather than to its realization. Instead of attachment, individual achievement rivets the male imagination, and great ideas or distinctive activity defines the standard of self-assessment and success" (163). Jean Baker Miller offers a similar description of women when she says that "women stay with, build on, and develop in a context of connections with others. Indeed, women's sense of self becomes very much organized around being able to make and then to maintain affiliations and relationships. Eventually, for many women the threat of disruption of connections is perceived not as just a loss of a relationship but as something closer to a total loss of self."[35] Mary Field Belenky, Blythe Clinchy, Nancy Goldberger, and Jill Tarule arrive at a similar judgment: "Men choose the self and women choose others."[36] These and other investigators echo a truism of gender studies: for most women in our society, identity has more to do with relations with others than with separation; for most men, identity has more to do more with separation than with relations.

Given this compelling evidence with respect to female and male gender identity, some teachers have begun the task of transforming this research into classroom strategies. Citing Chodorow and Gilligan, as well as Paulo Freire, Frances Maher describes the university as "a male-dominated hierarchy in which male professors hold social and intellectual sway" over far less powerful students who are "denied their own voices."[37] She maintains that "a pedagogy appropriate for voicing and exploring the hitherto unexpressed perspectives of women and others must be collaborative, cooperative and interactive" (30). According to Maher, such a pedagogy would feature "teaching practices which stress cooperative rather than competitive participation" (33). Nancy Schniedewind offers examples of cooperative teaching strategies. She proposes reliance on "democratic classroom processes" instead of lectures, explaining, "Many academics distrust anything that is not lecture-discussion. I once did. Yet feminism necessitates not only the development of new knowledge, but also new forms of relationships between people."[38] Citing the tradition of Paulo Freire and Jonathan Kozol, Schniedewind suggests, among other practices, that students practice communication skills that allow them to express their feelings about the class process, that students form out-of-class support groups, that a contract grading system be used to remove competition for grades, that teachers share leadership with students, and that students work in groups structured such that one student cannot succeed or fail without the other members doing the same (262–71). According to Schniedewind, "Ample research in education and social psychology points to the increased cognitive and affective learning gains of students in cooperatively structured classrooms" (266). Barrie Thorne offers additional strategies teachers can adopt to reduce their classroom power and to allow students increased learning through cooperation: relying on seating arrangements that encourage conversation, using eye contact and a tone of voice that invite participation, referring to students by name so as to authorize their comments, sharing class time among teacher, outspoken students, and quiet students, and encouraging informality and humor.[39]

Maher echoes Schniedewind's criticism of the lecture format, and in so doing she raises another issue having to do with translating research on female gender identity, relationality, and learning strategies into pedagogy. She questions the nature of knowledge itself. According to Maher, "The traditional mode of university teaching, that of the lecture, presumes that an expert will present to the students an objective, rationally derived and empirically proven set of information. This mode, no matter how complete, can only reflect one version (usually the one dominant in the culture)." The result is that students "are memorizing truths to which their own historical, cultural, and personal experience gives the lie" (30). According to Maher, traditional education in general and the lecture format in particular assume that learning consists of "the search for a single, objective, rationally derived 'right answer' that stands outside the historical source or producer of that answer." Maher's cooperative and interactive pedagogy "involves a conceptualization of knowledge as a comparison of multiple perspectives leading towards a complex and evolving view of reality" (33). With respect to the social sciences, she emphasizes the "particularistic, historical and contextual nature of all our conceptualizations of human society." With respect to the natural sciences, she quotes Helen Longino to the effect that " 'there is no independent field of facts (for recourse); scientists work within logically independent and incomparable world views determined by their paradigms' " (34). Maher concludes, "for many scholarly researchers, the study of women involves a major methodological shift. They are moving away from the traditional search for objectivity and towards a multilayered and comparative construction of social realities. In this search they acknowledge their own subjectivity, even as they try to transcend it by listening to, and drawing on, the experience of others. To go back to the classroom with this perspective is immediately to recognize its relevance to interactive pedagogies . . . " (36).

Not all teachers will respond to research about the role of relations in female gender identity in the same way. Some will propose strategies for cooperative learning different from those suggested by Maher, Thorne, and Schniedewind. Some will not feel it necessary to redefine the concept of knowledge; indeed, in my "Women and Language" seminars, several students are hesitant to accept Maher's conclusions about how knowledge is constituted.[40] Some collaborative and interactive pedagogies have already been incorporated into university education: the writing-as-process approach to composition includes prewriting to allow students to discover their own feelings and ideas, peer groups to effect cooperative revision, and a teacher who facilitates groups instead of commanding the front of the room. However, for the most part, university education thrives on competition and separation, encouraging students to learn by competing with one another, separating *A* students from *C* students, and offering professors who often dispense knowledge from their position of authority and power instead of facilitating learning. (And many students respond positively to this system.) Thus, universities are defined by many of the educational practices Maher, Thorne, and Schniedewind are attempting to change. As Maher points out, "the structure of the university, in which large lecture courses are a dominant mode, is a paradigm for the traditional concept of knowledge as a fixed store of information and expertise to be pumped into passive student minds" (45).

Educators who take feminist research seriously and who attempt to create pedagogy to match the research are likely to face profound opposition. This is true with respect to pedagogical changes intended to reflect studies of the importance of relations in female gender identity; it is also true with respect to classroom changes intended to respond to other newly gained insights into the way gender affects behavior and thought. Those who have changed the content of what is taught have done so only by overcoming resistance. Expanding the canon in literature classes, including recent studies of female personality development in psychology classes, making events such as the Seneca Falls Convention a part of American history courses, and emphasizing the Eleusinian mysteries and other Great Mother religions in religious studies classes—these changes in what students learn are occurring only after a struggle. Changing how learning is effected will often meet with similar resistance. Feminist researchers and others who undertake change in the way teaching is done (like those seeking change in the content of what is taught) require not only sound research to make their arguments compelling but also political power to gain a hearing for their ideas. Nevertheless, pedagogical change is vital. As Schniedewind cautions, "Students . . . learn as much from the process of a course—its hidden curriculum—as from the explicit content" (261).

The essays in this collection are intended to contribute to this change in how students learn and teachers teach. They are written by professors of literature, linguistics, rhetoric, and education. Most focus on reading and interpretation, some focus on composition, and all focus on teaching. Each of them approaches both of the problems discussed above—the lack of valid and reliable research on gender and learning and the difficulties of transforming gender research into classroom practices; they add studies intended to corroborate, correct, and extend already published gender research. Finally, all of them emphasize the subtle play of power within the issues of gender and pedagogy. Sometimes the power at issue is the teacher's, sometimes it's the students', sometimes it's the power of the text or of the society, and in one instance it's the power of federal statutes to affect gender-based pedagogy. Throughout the collection, though, the problem of power is interwoven with the problems of generating reliable research and of transforming available research into classroom pedagogy.

Carolyn Heilbrun's opening essay, "The Politics of Mind: Women, Tradition, and the University," offers an overview of women's experience as teachers and students in the university. Heilbrun's essay introduces many topics that are elaborated in the collection's following essays. A revision of a presentation originally given at Columbia University, Heilbrun's essay draws upon one of Lionel Trilling's famous phrases, "the life of the mind." Heilbrun explores some of the ways in which the supposedly neutral "life of the mind" is "organized to reflect the politics of mind, particularly the politics of a wholly male-centered culture and university." She analyzes higher education's reaction toward both the intrusion of feminist criticism into the university's life of the mind and the invasion of increasing numbers of female students and professors into the university's classrooms. She argues that "women particularly have a great deal to contribute to the life of the mind in the University, but that they have been prevented from doing so because much of what passes for the life of the mind is, in fact, no more than the politics of mind." Heilbrun argues that universities "resist the broader implications of feminist theory," insisting instead on the traditional, unexamined "phallocentric values of our universities." While resisting the power of feminist theory, universities also restrict the power of their increasing number of female students: "like [Jane Austen's] Mr. Knightley, having taken the young women to its institutional bosom, it wishes to confine the energies it found so attractive to the already designated duties of a girlfriend or co-ed, or eventually of a consort." Heilbrun illustrates several ways in which both men and women could be empowered if resistance were replaced by a reaction encouraging both men and women to define and participate in the university's life of the mind.

The three following essays focus on power in the classroom—on the unconscious use of power by traditional teachers and on problems encountered by feminist teachers consciously attempting to allow for the power inherent in their positions. "Power Relationships in the Classroom," by Cheris Kramarae and Paula A. Treichler, describes and analyzes male and female students' different perceptions of the ways three teachers exercise power over discussion of a literary text in a graduate seminar they are team-teaching. Kramarae and Treichler note that "women are seemingly more concerned than are the men with the teaching-learning process," that "women are more likely to report enjoyment of classes in which students and teacher talk in a collaborative manner," and that, in the classroom under investigation as well as in classrooms in general, "there is a nonproductive tension between the traditional academic class-room management and revolutionary, nontraditional topics."

While Kramarae and Treichler concentrate on traditional teachers and traditional class settings, Nina Baym and Patrocinio Schweickart deal with feminist teachers and the environments they attempt to create. Baym's "The Feminist Teacher of Literature: Feminist or Teacher?" and Schweickart's "Reading, Teaching, and the Ethic of Care" probe the complex issue of how the feminist teacher is to reconcile her power as a teacher with her principles as a feminist. Baym acknowledges that "the issue of power is assuredly among the most difficult that feminists face. Power is most often experienced as oppression and hence the desire for it is frequently disavowed. Yet, insofar as power is the energy and control that get things done, it is not only an ineluctable dimension of any situation, it is something that feminists require." Baym continues, "I take it that whenever there is teaching, there is a power relationship. . . . " A feminist teacher is acutely aware of the unequal distribution of power in the classroom and often relies on some form of interactive or collabora-tive exchange as a means of balancing this power. A feminist teacher of literature is also aware of another source of pedagogical power: her students are the victims of a male-dominated literary canon and of the traditional male-originated interpretations that accompany the canon. Given the presence of these unavoidable sources of power in classroom discussions and in judgments of students' work, how does a feminist teacher avoid occupying the position of yet another powerful force pressing yet another authorized interpretation onto her students? Baym asks with respect to students, "Are they more silenced, or less silenced, in the classroom of a woman teacher? Of a feminist teacher?"

Baym's essay offers some answers to her question. Schweickart's offers another. Drawing on the work of Norman Holland, Jürgen Habermas, Gilligan, and Nel Noddings, Schweickart takes the first steps in transforming an ethic of care into a theory of reading and a way of teaching. Analyzing not only the scenario in which the student reads a literary text but also the situation in which the teacher reads a student's text, Schweickart offers a theory of reading that addresses the unequal distributions of power among reader, writer, and text in these different situations. She advances a theory that emphasizes the similarities between reading, on the one hand, and speaking and listening, on the other—a theory that offers a reciprocity of care in place of domination by either reader or writer. Schweickart's article offers interesting insights on reader-response theory and discourse theory and combines these into a feminist approach to reading and teaching that does not silence the student.

Whereas the preceding essays focus on specific methods and problems of opposing particular expressions of institutionalized patriarchal power, Robert Con Davis's essay, "Woman as Oppositional Reader: Cixous on Discourse," considers not specific instances of power and opposition but the very concept of opposition to power. Using the career of Hélène Cixous as exemplary of oppositional criticism, he considers the extent to which political opposition is able to escape and move beyond that which it opposes. According to Davis, Cixous "reads the discourses of contemporary culture to expose crucial . . . binarities . . . that govern the exercise of power." Davis (along with other critics) argues, however, that Cixous's opposition to the binary logic which constitutes patriarchy remains trapped in that same logic. He maintains that Cixous's thought, like the thought of any critic intent on analyzing and changing the dominant interpretations of a culture, is necessarily defined by the ideology opposed. According to Davis, Cixous's work and criticism of it by later feminists "raises disturbing questions . . . about the potential to subvert and change culture from within." Exploring a theory of oppositionalism developed by thinkers such as Aristotle, A. J. Greimas, and Fredric Jameson, Davis's article attempts to respond to these disturbing questions and to show that resistance to power, though necessarily circumscribed, can be effective. Since Davis considers Cixous in all three of her capacities—as writer, teacher, and reader—his concerns are closely related to those of Heilbrun, Kramarae and Treichler, Baym, and Schweickart. That is, Davis's analysis of opposition to power applies not only to large-scale cultural criticism carried out by literary critics but also to less inclusive dissenting readings applied to texts by feminist teachers and their students in the classroom.

The three essays by Elizabeth A. Flynn, Susan Gabriel, and Linda Laube Barnes differ from the preceding essays in their emphasis. Whereas the preceding essays deal primarily with gender-based issues concerning students as readers and teachers as sources of alternative readings, these essays deal primarily with student writers and with teachers as judges of their writing. However, as would be expected, reading and writing are never wholly separate in these essays. These three essays differ from most of their predecessors in another way: they are quantitative in approach. Whereas the essays by Heilbrun, Baym, Schweickart, and Davis depend on reasoning based on their authors' informal classroom observations and on their engagement with other scholars' theories, these three essays are similar to Kramarae and Treichler's in that they rely primarily on information-gathering methods and data developed and gathered specifically for these essays.

Flynn's "Composing as a Woman" continues the work begun by Schniedewind and Maher (discussed above). Like them, Flynn attempts to translate recent research on gender identity into classroom pedagogy. Acknowledging that "for the most part, . . . the fields of feminist studies and composition studies have not engaged each other in a serious or systematic way," Flynn draws on Chodorow, Gilligan, and Belenky and her colleagues to suggest the outlines of a writing pedagogy intent on "empowering developing writers and readers." Flynn analyzes samples of student writing for signs of the differences in gender identity described by Chodorow, Gilligan, and Belenky and her colleagues. Her objective is to illustrate that "the questions raised by feminist researchers and theorists do have a bearing on composition studies and should be pursued" and to offer some "pedagogical strategies" in response to this feminist research. She maintains that "we must encourage" women students "to become self-consciously aware of what their experience in the world has been and how this experience is related to the politics of gender." And she concludes that writing teachers have "an obligation" to encourage "women students to write from the power of that experience."

Gabriel's and Barnes's essays also emphasize the issue of women's writing out of their own experience. Concerned that "female students are continually asked to identify with feelings and experiences which are not consistent with their experiences as women," Gabriel's "Gender, Reading, and Writing: Assignments, Expectations, and Responses" offers a study in which male and female students in a writing class respond to short stories by creating journal entries in which they assume the identities of the male and female fictional characters and by writing commentaries on the difficulties they encounter in assuming those identities. The objective of the study is to build on the research of Anne Selley McKillop, Mary Crawford and Roger Chaffin, Patrocinio Schweickart, and Judith Fetterley by gaining information about how and to what extent female (and male) students identify with fictional characters of the same and other sex. Gabriel's sample suggests that most women students read texts differently than most men do (sometimes in ways consistent with the findings of Miller, Chodorow, and Gilligan); that their writing about these texts reflects these differences; and that teachers should be aware that their reading and writing assignments, as well as their judgments of them, are seldom gender neutral.

Gabriel's and Flynn's essays include emphases on the need for female students to develop a writing voice that reflects their own experience. Gabriel's and Schweickart's essays include considerations of the effects of gender on teachers' responses to students' work. Barnes's essay, "Teachers' Responses to Gender Stereotypes," extends both of these concerns. After surveying recent research on gender and language, Barnes reports on a study in which she analyzes writing teachers' responses to gender-based stereotypes in student writing. Among her conclusions are the following: "male and female students have different academic experiences"; male and female teachers accord greater respect to what is identified as the "masculine" voice than they do to the "feminine"; and some of the characteristics of the female student's writing voice are mirrored in the responses of the female teachers. Barnes joins Flynn in illustrating the relative powerlessness of the female writing student — a powerlessness exhibited in the writing voice developed by many female students — and she joins Gabriel and Schweickart in calling attention to the destructive power of the gender bias built into many teachers' responses to student writing.

The final two essays deal with direct means for overcoming sexism in education. "Sexism, Legislative Power, and Vocational Education," by Penny L. Burge and Steven M. Culver, describes how federal legislation, a feminist perspective, and vocational education combine to offer educational programs designed to train and support women in the workplace. Vocational education has always been closely connected to federal legislative mandates, and it has in recent years become involved with a variety of gender equity programs. Burge and Culver's essay describes several gender equity programs intended to empower women students by training, recruiting, and supporting them in nontraditional fields and by offering them guidance for adjusting to the changes in family structure that accompany working women. Burge and Culver's essay illustrates how the power of the federal government and feminist principles can be used by educators to improve gender equity.

Myra and David Sadker also focus on programs to improve gender equity. However, their essay, "Confronting Sexism in the College Classroom," emphasizes programs designed for teachers rather than for students, and programs intended to confront sexism in the classroom rather than in the workplace. After documenting the existence of several modes of gender bias at all educational levels, Sadker and Sadker describe a training program that is effective in making professors aware of their gender-based biases and in helping them change their attitudes and practices. The Sadkers' comparison of experimental and control groups illustrates that gender equity workshops can have a dramatic effect. In the classes of teachers who have participated in the gender equity workshops, more teachers are sufficiently responsive, fewer female students are silent, and fewer male students dominate discussion. Power is better distributed in these classrooms.

The essays by Burge and Culver and by Sadker and Sadker join the preceding essays in providing dependable research on gender and pedagogy, in describing some of the problems involved in translating this research into teaching methods, and in analyzing the roles played by several types of power within the field of gender and higher education. Of course, this collection of essays does not deal with all significant groups and issues. The gender-based educational problems specific to Native American, Asian, Hispanic, black, and other minority women are not approached, though gender studies and education in general would surely profit from research into the experiences of these students and teachers. The subjects of sexual harassment, women's college athletics, and the imbalance in academic administration are also omitted, though these are important areas. Although necessarily the ten essays in this collection cannot do justice to all relevant groups and issues, they form an important part of the ongoing, wider dialogue respecting gender and pedagogy— responding to some of the questions raised in earlier research and posing additional questions for research still to come.

Reading a collection of essays emphasizing the gender-based deficiencies of university education can be oppressive. In spite of acknowledgments of improvements and suggestions for change that are included in the essays, the situation can seem hopeless—so many educators need to be educated. Certainly those of us in the "Women and Language" seminar have felt that frustration as we have read article after article detailing the biases built into language, learning, and teaching. Often we have had to reflect on the past in order to maintain our perspective on the present.

Women did not even begin to receive a university education similar to that received by men until 1837, when Oberlin College accepted four women—over 200 years after Harvard was established to educate America's men.[41] Discussions of gender and education were far more frustrating then and in earlier decades than they are now. Benjamin Rush, a member of the board of directors at Andrew Brown's Philadelphia Academy for Young Ladies, had the following to say *in favor* of "female education" in 1787: "The state of property in America, renders it necessary for the greatest part of our citizens to employ themselves, in different occupations, for the advancement of their fortunes. This cannot be done without the assistance of the female members of the community. They must be the stewards, and guardians of their husbands' property. That education, therefore, will be most proper for our women, which teaches them to discharge the duties of those offices with the most success and reputation." This advocate of women's education continues, "a principal share of the instruction of children naturally devolves upon the women. It becomes us therefore to prepare them by a suitable education, for the discharge of this most important duty of mothers." In addition, "the servants in this country possess less knowledge and subordination than are required from them; and hence, our ladies are obliged to attend more to the private affairs of their families. . . . " As to the content of female education, "Pleasure and interest conspire to make the writing of a fair and legible hand, a necessary branch of a lady's education. For this purpose she should be taught not only to shape every letter properly, but to pay the strictest regard to points and capitals." "Some knowledge of figures and book-keeping is absolutely necessary to qualify a young lady for the duties which await her in this country. There are certain occupations in which she may assist her husband with this knowledge." A knowledge of "history, biography and travels" will "qualify her not only for a general intercourse with the world, but to be an agreeable companion for a sensible man."[42] Benjamin Rush was one of the "enlightened" men of his time, but he saw the ends of women's education primarily as preparing women to assist their husbands, teach their children, supplement ill-trained servants, and write legibly. The only nondomestic role he envisioned for the educated woman was as a public school teacher. After all, male teachers commanded a salary at least twice that of female teachers (Newcomer 15).

Given these hostile and patronizing beginnings in the eighteenth and nineteenth centuries, there is as much hope as there is frustration in figures demonstrating that in 1985 women received 30 percent of America's humanities Ph.D. degrees, that in 1986 49 percent of America's veterinary school students were women, that in 1987 women made up 33 percent of America's medical school enrollment, and that in 1988 24 percent of Stanford University's engineering students were women.[43] There is as much hope as frustration in the realization that some researchers are now documenting the obstacles and inequities that Rich and others allude to, that other investigators are studying gender-based learning differences, and that Women's Studies programs are offering gender-balance workshops to help teachers integrate this research into their teaching. There is reason to believe that American universities of the late twentieth century are being forced to take women students seriously —

partially because universities are the site of this expanding research on gender and education, and partially because a majority of their tuition fees now come from first-time and returning women students. Thus, there is reason to hope that universities will become institutions which empower rather than undermine women.[44]

NOTES

1. The bibliography on women and language and the field itself are extensive; the following offer useful introductions: Deborah Cameron, *Feminism and Linguistic Theory* (London: Macmillan, 1985); Francine Wattman Frank and Paula A. Treichler, eds., *Language, Gender, and Professional Writing: Theoretical Approaches and Guidelines for Nonsexist Usage* (New York: MLA, 1989); Alette Olin Hill, *Mother Tongue, Father Time: A Decade of Linguistic Revolt* (Bloomington: Indiana UP, 1986); Cheris Kramarae, *Women and Men Speaking: Frameworks for Analysis* (Rowley: Newbury House, 1981); Dale Spender, *Man Made Language*, 2nd ed. (Boston: Routledge & Kegan Paul, 1985); Barrie Thorne, Cheris Kramarae, and Nancy Henley, eds., *Language, Gender, and Society* (Rowley: Newbury House, 1983); and Barrie Thorne and Nancy Henley, eds., *Language and Sex: Difference and Dominance* (Rowley: Newbury House, 1975).

2. Adrienne Rich, "Claiming an Education" and "Taking Women Students Seriously," *On Lies, Secrets, and Silence: Selected Prose 1966–1978* (New York: Norton, 1979).

3. *The New Agenda of Women for Higher Education: Report of the ACE Commission on Women in Higher Education* (Washington, D.C.: American Council on Education, 1987) v.

4. Myra Sadker, "Sex Bias in Colleges and Universities," *The Report Card, no. 2* (Washington, D.C.: Mid-Atlantic Center for Sex Equity and Project EFFECT, American University, 1984).

5. "Women Face Uphill Fight for Student Aid," *On Campus with Women*, Project on the Status and Education of Women (Washington, D.C.: Association of American Colleges) 17.1 (1987): 5.

6. Phyllis Rosser, "Girls, Boys, and the SAT: Can We Even the Score?" *NEA Today* 6.6 (1988): 48–53. According to Rosser, although females get higher average grades than boys in high school and college, males score higher in both the verbal and math sections of the Scholastic Aptitude Test (48), and "the SAT is the only standardized test in which girls are receiving lower verbal scores" (50). According to another study, the Educational Testing Service "recently admitted that the SAT *under*predicts the grades women can expect to earn in college." See *The 1986 PEER Report Card: A State-by-State Survey of the Status of Women and Girls in America's Schools*, Policy Paper no. 5 (Washington, D.C.: Project on Equal Education Rights, NOW Legal Defense and Education Fund, 1986) 3.

7. Roberta Hall and Bernice Sandler, *Out of the Classroom: A Chilly Climate for Women?* (Washington, D.C.: Project on the Status and Education of Women, 1984) 6.

8. "What's Happening with Child Care on Campus?" *On Campus with Women* 16.1 (1986): 2.

9. The practice is so widespread that the Mid-Atlantic Equity Center at American University offers a poster for teachers titled "101 Ways to Line Up."

10. Letty Cottin Pogrebin, *Growing Up Free: Raising Your Child in the 80's* (New York: McGraw-Hill, 1980) 492.

11. "Sex Bias at the Computer Terminal—How Schools Program Girls," *Computer Equity Report* (Washington, D.C.: Project on Equal Education Rights, NOW Legal Defense and Education Fund, 1984) 2.

12. Preston K. Jones, "The Relative Effectiveness of Computer-Assisted Remediation with Male and Female Students," *T.H.E. Journal* (March 1987): 61.

13. Myra Sadker and David Sadker, "Sexism in the Classroom: From Grade School to Graduate School," *Phi Delta Kappan* 67.7 (March 1986): 32.

14. Jerome B. Dusek, "Do Teachers Bias Children's Learning?" *Review of Educational Research* 45 (1975): 661–84; Geneva Gay, "Teachers' Achievement Expectations of and Interactions with Ethnically Different Students," *Contemporary Education* 46 (1975): 166–72; and Gregg Jackson and Cecilia Cosca, "The Inequality of Educational Opportunity in the Southwest: An Observational Study of Ethnically Mixed Classrooms," *American Educational Research Journal* 11 (1974): 219–29. These studies and supporting research are discussed in DeAnna Banks Beane, *Mathematics and Sciences for the Future of Minority Students* (Washington, D.C.: Mid-Atlantic Center for Race Equity, American University, 1985).

15. "Physical Science: Intended Area of Study for Male and Female High School Seniors," *1986 PEER Report Card* 14.

16. Susanne D. Ellis, "1985–86 Graduate Student Survey," *AIP Report* (New York: American Institute of Physics, 1987) 2.

17. Linda Harrison, "Cro-Magnon Woman—In Eclipse," *The Science Teacher*, April 1975, 11.

18. Joseph W. Schneider and Sally L. Hacker, "Sex Role Imagery and Use of the Generic 'Man' in Introductory Texts: A Case in the Sociology of Sociology," *American Sociologist* 8 (1973): 14. Both the Harrison and the Schneider and Hacker studies are summarized by Casey Miller and Kate Swift, *Words and Women: New Language in New Times* (New York: Anchor, 1977) 22.

19. A useful discussion of the generic *he* is contained in Wendy Martyna, "Beyond the He/Man Approach: The Case for Nonsexist Language," in Thorne, Kramarae, and Henley, eds., *Language, Gender and Society*, 25–37.

20. Cornell Institute for Social and Economic Research, *Assessing Sexual Harassment and Public Safety: A Survey of Cornell Women* (Ithaca: Office of Equal Opportunity of Cornell University, 1986) 3, 2.

21. *The University of Iowa Policy on Sexual Harassment and Consensual Relationships* (Iowa City, IA: Office of Affirmative Action of the University of Iowa).

22. Kathryn W. Linden et al., "Predicting Engineering Retention for Undergraduate Women and Men," *U.S. Women Engineers* (November/December 1985): 36.

23. "Women's Studies Programs," *PMLA* 102 (1988): 640–47.

24. This interdisciplinary program is offered by Xavier University (Ohio). "New Major in Women and Minorities Studies," *On Campus with Women* 18.1 (1988): 1.

25. For information about the program at Towson State University, see *On Our Minds*, the newsletter published by the Women Studies Program at Towson State University, Baltimore. For information about the program at the University of Arizona, see Susan Hardy Aiken et al., "Trying Transformations: Curriculum Integration and the Problem of Resistance," *Signs* 12 (1987): 255–75. Other useful resources dealing with gender balancing are Diane L. Fowlkes and Charlotte S. McClure, eds., *Feminist Visions: Toward a Transformation of the Liberal Arts Curriculum* (University: U of Alabama P, 1984); Marilyn R. Schuster and Susan R. Van Dyne, eds., *Women's Place in the Academy: Transforming the Liberal Arts Curriculum* (Totowa: Rowman & Allanheld, 1985); Peggy McIntosh et al., comps., "Transforming the Liberal Arts Curriculum through Incorporation of the New Scholarship on Women," *Women's Studies Quarterly* 11.2 (1983): 23–29; Betty Schmitz, "Women's Studies and Projects to Transform the Curriculum: A Current Status Report," *Women's Studies Quarterly* 11.3 (1983): 17–19; and *The Study of Women in the Liberal Arts Curriculum*, special issue of *Forum for Liberal Education* 4 (October 1981).

26. Aiken et al., "Trying Transformations," 271.

27. Joan Bolker, "Teaching Griselda to Write," *College English* 40 (1979): 906.

28. Thomas Farrell, "The Female and Male Modes of Rhetoric," *College English* 40 (1979): 909–21.

29. Farrell is quoting from a letter sent to him by a Sarah d'Eloia.

30. David Bleich, "Gender Interests in Reading and Language," *Gender and Reading: Essays on Readers, Texts, and Contexts*, ed. Elizabeth A. Flynn and Patrocinio P. Schweickart (Baltimore: Johns Hopkins UP, 1986) 234–66.

31. Carol Gilligan, *In a Different Voice: Psychological Theory and Women's Development* (Cambridge: Harvard UP, 1982).

32. Although Gilligan offers several generalizations about how males and females approach moral decisions, she maintains that "the contrasts between male and female voices are presented here to highlight a distinction between two modes of thought and to focus a problem of interpretation rather than to represent a generalization about either sex" (2).

33. In addition to the resources cited in note 16, the following collections are useful: Charlotte Bunch and Sandra Pollack, eds., *Learning Our Way: Essays in Feminist Education* (Trumansburg: Crossing Press, 1983); Cynthia L. Caywood and Gillian R. Overing, eds., *Teaching Writing: Pedagogy, Gender, and Equity* (Albany: State U of New York P, 1987); Margo Culley and Catherine Portuges, eds., *Gendered Subjects: The Dynamics of Feminist Education* (Boston: Routledge & Kegan Paul, 1985); Elizabeth Langland and Walter Gove, *A Feminist Perspective in the Academy: The Difference It Makes* (Chicago: U of Chicago P, 1981); Christie Farnham, ed., *The Impact of Feminist Research in the Academy*

(Bloomington: Indiana UP, 1987); Elizabeth A. Flynn and Patrocinio P. Schweickart, eds., *Gender and Reading: Essays on Readers, Texts, and Contexts* (Baltimore: Johns Hopkins UP, 1986); Jean F. O'Barr, ed., *Reconstructing the Academy*, special issue of *Signs* 12 (1987); Sharon Lee Rich and Ariel Phillips, eds., *Women's Experience and Education*, Harvard Educational Review Reprint Series no. 17 (Cambridge: Harvard UP, 1985); and Nancy Schniedewind and Frances Maher, eds., *Feminist Pedagogy*, special feature of *Women's Studies Quarterly* 15 (1987).

34. Nancy Chodorow, "Family Structure and Feminine Personality," *Woman, Culture, and Society*, ed. Michelle Zimbalist Rosaldo and Louise Lamphere (Stanford: Stanford UP, 1974) 44. Chodorow develops this theme also in *The Reproduction of Mothering: Psychoanalysis and the Sociology of Gender* (Berkeley: U of California P, 1978).

35. Jean Baker Miller, *Toward a New Psychology of Women*, 2nd ed. (Boston: Beacon, 1986) 83.

36. Mary Field Belenky et al., *Women's Ways of Knowing: The Development of Self, Voice, and Mind* (New York: Basic Books, 1986) 46.

37. Frances Maher, "Classroom Pedagogy and the New Scholarship on Women," *Gendered Subjects: The Dynamics of Feminist Teaching*, ed. Margo Culley and Catherine Portuges (Boston: Routledge & Kegan Paul, 1985) 31.

38. Nancy Schniedewind, "Feminist Values: Guidelines for Teaching Methodology in Women's Studies," *Learning Our Way*, ed. Bunch and Pollack, 262.

39. Barrie Thorne, "Rethinking the Ways We Teach," speech reported in *Women and Language News* 7 (1983): 15. Roberta Hall's *The Classroom Climate: A Chilly One for Women* contains additional analyses and suggestions. (Washington, D.C.: Project on the Status and Education of Women, Association of American Colleges, 1984).

40. Interesting discussions of objectivity and knowledge occur in Elizabeth Fee, "Women's Nature and Scientific Objectivity," *Women's Nature: Rationalizations of Inequality*, ed. Marian Lowe and Ruth Hubbard (New York: Pergamon, 1983); Sandra Harding, *The Science Question in Feminism* (Ithaca: Cornell UP, 1986); Ruth Hubbard, "Science, Facts, and Feminism," *Hypatia* 3 (1988): 5–17; Evelyn Fox Keller, "Feminism and Science," *Sex and Scientific Inquiry*, ed. Sandra Harding and Jean F. O'Barr (Chicago: U of Chicago P, 1987) 233–46.

41. Mabel Newcomer, *A Century of Higher Education for American Women* (New York: Harper, 1959) 5.

42. Benjamin Rush, quoted in Shirley Nelson Kersey, *Classics in the Education of Girls and Women* (Metuchen: Scarecrow Press, 1981) 170–72.

43. "Who's Getting What Doctorates?" *On Campus with Women* 17.3 (1988): 7; "More Women Vets!" 17.2 (1987): 5; "Nursing Down, Medicine Up," and "Women Like Engineering at Stanford," 17.3 (1988): 7, 2.

44. I am thankful to Twana Biram, Jean Kittrell, and Nancy Ruff, all of Southern Illinois University at Edwardsville, for offering me critical readings of drafts of this essay.

CAROLYN G. HEILBRUN

The Politics of Mind:
Women, Tradition, and the University

I have been a member of the Columbia University community for more than thirty-five years, and I cannot but consider myself to be speaking as what Lionel Trilling called an opposing self,[1] opposed to culture—in this case the culture of the university. Lionel Trilling was the most powerful and honored presence during most of my years at Columbia; as much as anyone, he defined, both for his department and for the wider community beyond it, what he honored as the life of the mind. But history has moved, times have changed, the politics inherent in that phrase "the life of the mind" have emerged. We have come to recognize the degree to which the life of the mind is organized to reflect the politics of mind, particularly the politics of a wholly male-centered culture and university. The numbers of women in universities today, and the whole question of the canon, has come under a scrutiny which Trilling could scarcely have foreseen. It is unfortunate that the very phrase "the life of the mind," which has for so long represented all that was desired from education and all that women, excluded from education, had come to cherish as an ideal, what Virginia Woolf called "the strange bright fruits of art and knowledge," has become a kind of "buzz word" for something disembodied, unconnected with gender or race or the differing cultures and aspirations in our rapidly changing world.

In 1971 at the Library of Congress, Trilling delivered the first Jefferson Lecture in the Humanities, entitled "Mind in the Modern World." He spoke of the marvelous "life of the mind" and of how that proud concept was being undermined by, among other things, affirmative action. His deep concern with the threat to the "life of the mind" from affirmative action was phrased in his usually forthright and vigorous way. He called attention to

> the silence of our colleges and universities about what is implied for their
> continuing life by the particular means our society has chosen to remedy

the injustice [of inequality]. I have in view the posture toward colleges and universities which of recent years has been taken by the Department of Health, Education, and Welfare. [It] has responded with its directive that institutions of higher education which receive government funds shall move at once toward bringing about a statistically adequate representation on their faculties of ethnic minority groups and women. The directive does not pretend that this purpose is to be accomplished without a change in the standards of excellence of the academic profession.[2]

Trilling does not deny the importance of the goals inherent in affirmative action; his point is only "that the academic profession does not debate it." "Surely," he continues, "it says much about the status of mind in our society that the profession which is consecrated to its protection and furtherance should stand silent under the assault, as if suddenly deprived of all right to use the powers of mind in its own defense" (29).

Trilling could hardly have anticipated the direction events have taken in this decade: reactionary forces have attempted to consolidate the defense of "the life of the mind" with other objectives, including the promotion of "old-fashioned values" and the protection of a narrowly demarked "legacy" or "intellectual heritage," in ways that, I think, he would not have welcomed. Trilling was right in observing that it is the reluctance of the academic community to debate these points which most threatens the life of the mind.

My thesis, then, is that women particularly have a great deal to contribute to the life of the mind in the University but that they have been prevented from doing so because much of what passes for the life of the mind is, in fact, no more than the politics of mind. The life of the mind is a synonym for what is referred to as the universal—treated, revered, accepted as though it had been engraved somewhere as eternal and unchanging truth. But we must ask what is lost to this "life of the mind"—to mind itself, to colleges and universities, to that proud contemplation of texts and culture to which Lionel Trilling devoted his life—when women are excluded from taking their full part?

There are additional reasons for considering at this time the importance of women to the essential life of a university, to its life of the mind in the most creative and vital sense. One is the extraordinary fact that there are almost no all-male colleges or universities left in the United States or, for that matter, in England. (That all the original, all-male, colleges at Oxford now have women undergraduates is a phenomenon little noticed or commented upon in this country. The loss to these colleges has not been to the life of the mind but to the life of the playing fields. The athletic, hearty, and rather mindless young men who made up about a third of these famous colleges are no longer there, their absence fundamentally affecting the quality of undergraduate life, though probably not the quality of the life of the mind.) Many women, on the other hand, for reasons faculties of coeducational institutions ought to take more seriously than they do, still prefer to attend all-women colleges. This has a great deal to do with the life of the mind.

Feminism has now reached a retrospective stage. We are very far from the early years when rather unsophisticated methods started feminist literary critics on the heady road toward reinterpretation. Feminism itself has developed new critical strategies for reading literature and has elaborated theoretical models which place literature and cultural forms within a complex set of ideological and social arrangements. Despite this, often the most sophisticated male readers of cultural texts, even those who in their own work underscore the material and symbolic conditions that produce a politics of mind, resist the broader implications of feminist theory. Thus we discover these words from a prominent male scholar—my colleague, Edward Said: "Nearly everyone producing literary or cultural studies makes no allowance for the truth that all intellectual or cultural work occurs somewhere, at some time, on some very precisely mapped-out and permissible terrain, which is ultimately contained by the State. Feminist critics have opened this question part of the way, but they have not gone the whole distance."[3] Women, it seems, are likely to be condemned both if they do go all the way, and if they don't.

We must recognize the unique force of feminist criticism in revising the assumptions and deflating the platitudes of our cultural and literary life, in or out of universities, but particularly within them. More than a few male academics, however, remain fearful of what they conceive to be a feminist threat. That is, I think, most unfortunate, for men in the university have everything to gain and little to lose from feminist criticism. Of course, they must put aside the fear of feminization in a profession that has always risked appearing effete and in which the codes and flourishes of masculinity have long been fetishistically clung to.

Why are men so afraid? "I think the answer to this question," Christine Froula, a young feminist critic, writes, "has to do with the fact that woman's voice threatens to discredit that masculinist culture upon which [men have] modeled their identity."[4] Many works of the canon have constructed their "speech on the bedrock of woman's silence." "Men very commonly express the fear that feminist criticism will invert that hierarchy in which they have invested so much—will, in other words, silence *them* as patriarchal discourse has silenced women. . . . But woman speaking does not reverse the conditions of her own silencing. She does not demand that men be silent; she only asks that men cease speaking in such a way as to silence her" (178).

All the jokes in literature about women-dominated marriages, all the horrible wives in Dickens, Trollope, and others speak to the male fear of hierarchical reversal. If men are not boss, women will be. But this is what men fear, not what women want. Women ask men only to "grant women's voices an equal position with male discourse, rescuing it from the now inevitable reactive position of either assimilation or opposition."[5] Women do not ask for a new harmony with the major theme always in the soprano range, but for counterpoint.

Feminist criticism is another way of knowing. Uniquely, it addresses the longest established binarism of our culture, a binarism seen as most in need of protection by those who fear change, new ideas, and the loss of power and control. It is no accident that the new Right, here and around the world, and the religious fundamentalists with whom they are almost coextensive, are driven first of all by the need to return women to their traditional place of powerlessness in society.

What men have to gain by reconstituting the category of woman is not only the risk and excitement that is the reward of challenging long-held convictions or the satisfaction of declining to dismiss them because they are discomforting. What men have to gain is the heady sense of encountering the future; what they lose is the heavy sense of insisting upon the unexamined rectitude of the past. We may all gain a way to conceive difference without opposition; we may, with equal daring, challenge the ancient male-female binarism as an intellectual imperative.[6] Nor should we allow this challenge to be met by the accusation that it overturns old "values," old morality. Old values and old morality are most often defended by those who benefit from them and fear to share those benefits.

All women who have ever read a classic or undertaken an intellectual pursuit have imagined themselves as men. What alternative was there? Women in universities and outside of them have always "read with a double consciousness—both as women and as the masculine reader they have been taught to be."[7] Might not men gain now by learning to read, not with a double consciousness but consciously as men in relation to women? The male establishment at universities might consider that the discomfort they feel before women's texts is the discomfort women have long lived with and have never quite learned to take for granted, though some have been more thoroughly trained to this, as to restrictive clothing, than others. In literature and out, femininity has existed only as a representation of masculine desire: "Men appear unwilling to address the issues placed on the critical agenda by women unless those issues have first been neutralized . . . to the already known, the already written . . . " (Owens 62). Women challenge the degree to which all male modern texts are narratives of mastery; women may suggest other narratives, other modes of relationship.

Yet we live in a time when the already read and the already written are being hailed as revitalizing our "legacy," when men like Secretary of Education William Bennett and retired Yale President A. Bartlett Giamatti bemoan the loss of some fetishized tradition. We may notice that men in fundamentalist societies fear the loss of virginity in unmarried women: sexual experience for women, like the not-already-read books written by women or with women as their protagonists, seem horribly to threaten the male claim on paternity and authorship. Virgins are held sacred, and terribly fragile; and female writings are declared ephemeral, charming, but altogether too sensitive for the manly business of literary authority. Lynn Sukenick quotes Hugh Kenner, who writes: "Lady novelists have always claimed the privilege of transcending mere plausibilities. It's up to men to arrange such things. . . . Your bag is sensitivity, which means, knowing what to put into this year's novels . . . the with-it cat's cradling of lady novelists."[8] Other men broach the matter more forthrightly: Anthony Burgess finds Jane Austen's novels to be failures because she "lacks a strong male thrust," and for William Gass women writers "lack that blood congested genital drive which energizes all great style." Norman Mailer says a good writer must have balls.[9] These gentlemen express with clarity the phallocentric values of our universities—a set of assumptions which we have not sufficiently debated and which Bennett and Giamatti would have us take for granted, marking all debate as destructive.

"What characterizes good teaching in the humanities?" Bennett asks, and triumphantly answers himself: "First, and foremost, a teacher must have achieved mastery of the material."[10] Bennett does not mean only that the teacher should have read the material but that he should have incorporated it into his conception of the universe. More importantly, mastery means that one knows what questions to ask and, more important still, what questions not to ask. Giamatti is in no doubt about this last criterion. He says that today "students of literature are increasingly talking only to ourselves and no one else is paying any attention."[11] We are hardly surprised to learn that the two villains are feminism and theory, which are largely to blame for the failure of the many eager students of literature to come properly to love what has, by theorists, feminists, and their ilk, been snatched from them. It does not occur to either of these gentlemen that what marks the immortality of the literature we all love and cherish is precisely that it continues to require new questions. We love what we are in dialogue with; the rest we endure, or protect out of fear. Universities are not, or should not be, merely museums for the display of culture. They ought to be theaters for its ongoing creation and re-creation.

Blaming feminists, new-fangled theorists, and women writers are all ploys in the oldest game in town—older than Hawthorne, who bewailed the scribbling women who stole his audience, older than Aristotle, who classed women with slaves and animals. What is surprising is that, in an age when youth is most notably responsive to inspiration electronically conveyed, the life of the mind seems to consist in asking the same canonical questions of the same canon. Bennett is not loath to tell us what that canon includes: his list, ranging from Homer to Faulkner, embraces, with a nod toward the second half of this century, the Birmingham speech of Martin Luther King, Jr., and the works of Jane Austen and George Eliot. The devoted canonists, forced by some pressure they see as faddish but must reluctantly pretend to acknowledge, will always choose Jane Austen or George Eliot if they must include a woman writer. The unthreatening aspect of these two writers is, of course, a delusion: but it requires a more probing and indeed theoretical reading to discover the not-already-read in these apparently conventional novelists. Once permitted, albeit reluctantly, to enter the canon, such new arrivals deserve to be met with new non-canonical questions. But, of course, they probably will not be. Who is prepared to suggest that Elizabeth Bennet in *Pride and Prejudice* did not absolutely triumph in capturing Darcy and Pemberley?

There is a scene in *The Mill on the Floss* when Maggie visits her brother Tom at his school, run by Mr. and Mrs. Stelling. Tom has said to her: "*you'll* be a woman some day," and Maggie, not much liking the crossness of the women she knows, answers: "But I shall be a *clever* woman." "O, I dare say," Tom responds, "and a nasty conceited thing. Everybody'll hate you."[12]

They were presently fetched to spend the rest of the evening in the drawing-room, and Maggie became so animated with Mr. Stelling, who, she felt sure, admired her cleverness, that Tom was rather amazed and alarmed at her audacity. . . .

"What a very odd little girl that must be!" said Mrs. Stelling, meaning to be playful, but a playfulness that turned on her supposed oddity was not at all to Maggie's taste. She feared Mr. Stelling, after all, did not think much of her, and went to bed in rather low spirits. Mrs. Stelling, she felt, looked at her as if she thought her hair was very ugly because it hung down straight behind.

Nevertheless it was a very happy fortnight to Maggie—this visit to Tom. She was allowed to be in the study while he had his lessons, and in her various readings got very deep into the examples in the Latin Grammar. The astronomer who hated women generally caused her so much puzzling speculation that she one day asked Mr. Stelling if all astronomers hated women, or whether it was only this particular astonomer. But, forestalling his answer, she said:

"I suppose it's all astonomers: because you know, they live up in high towers, and if the women came there, they might talk and hinder them from looking at the stars."

Mr. Stelling liked her prattle immensely. (123)

What Maggie is puzzling about, as the literary critics Mary Jacobus and Nancy Miller have observed, is "the maxims that pass for the truth of human experience." These maxims, and the encoding of that experience in literature, are organizations, when they are not fantasies, of the dominant culture.[13] George Eliot herself tells us this later in the novel, describing, one cannot but feel, those who insist that to rescue women from the generalities that have confined them is to work against time-ratified "values." The "man of maxims," Eliot writes, "is the popular representative of the minds that are guided in their moral judgment solely by general rules, thinking that these will lead them to justice by a ready-made patent method, without the trouble of exerting patience, discrimination, impartiality, without any care to assure themselves whether they have the insight that comes from a hardly-earned estimate of temptation, or from a life vivid and intense enough to have created a wide fellow-feeling with all that is human" (435).

The historian Joan Scott recently observed at a celebration at Smith College that "there is in [the literature about higher education for women] a persistent and striking undercurrent of concern with sex and gender, with the impact education will have on the sexuality of women and on that system of gender relations deemed 'natural' to human society." She quotes a doctor who, in 1873, attributed those cases of "female degeneration" he had seen to co-education: "Put a boy and girl together upon the same course of study, and with the same lofty ideal before them . . . and there will be awakened within them a stimulus unknown before, and that separate study does not excite. The unconscious fires that have their seat deep down in the recesses of the sexual organization will flame up through every tissue, permeate every vessel, burn every nerve, flash from the eye, tingle in the brain, and work the whole machine at highest pressure."[14] This sounds fine to me; the worried doctor, however, was concerned with the fate of the womb. We in universities today seem more concerned with the fate of the legacy, which threatens to dissolve or disintegrate under this "highest pressure." We no longer worry, as President Eliot of Harvard did, about the dangers "of bringing scores or hundreds of young men and women into intimate relations in the same institution at the excitable ages of eighteen to twenty-two." But having so widely accomplished these "intimate relations in the same institution," for the salvation, we might note, of the male institutions, we now worry, not that mental and physical exertion will desex women, but that the exertion of female questions may desex our legacy.

The questions women wish to ask of the canon are certainly not questions only about women. We women within the university wish to examine not only the exclusion of women from culture—although that should not be forgotten—but those less obvious "exclusions that keep us outside the desire for theory and the theory of desire."[15] Diana Trilling has noted that "it is when we close the book on Emma Woodhouse's marriage that we let ourselves be fully aware of the pleasure we took in the energies that will probably no longer be exercised: the wise Mr. Knightley will curb them as unsuited to a wife, attractive as he found them before marriage."[16]

The university is not unlike Mr. Knightley: it has found attractive the energies of the young women who will increase its pool of intelligent applicants and who will encourage young men to choose that college where such intelligent young women are to be found. But, like Mr. Knightley, having taken the young women to its institutional bosom, it wishes to confine the energies it found so attractive to the already designated duties of a girl-friend or co-ed, or eventually of a consort. Where the university must change is in allowing the energy of women to be exercised fully and to its own ends. Nothing is perhaps so wasted in our culture as the energies of its women; Diana Trilling wisely pointed to "the cruel disparity there has been in literature, as in life, between female promise and female fulfillment" (506). If we look back over all the women in the literature in the established canon, including what Mr. Bennett sees as imperative for a student of the humanities, we cannot fail to notice that female energy is the least prized and the most wasted resource, even, perhaps especially, in the novels of Jane Austen and George Eliot. Yet how often is that question of blunted energy raised in a course like a survey course in literature, or a graduate course in Victorian prose writers, or a course on the Romantics? Women who are at the margin of the society and of the university no longer wish only to examine that marginality; rather, they profoundly desire to alter the nature of discourse that defines margins and centers, to make the condition of the oppressed not merely a fact in the study of domination but a living part of the legacy of western civilization.

Women within the university need not only to pass from the margin to the center of intellectual life, they need help from the university in confronting the problems of being female in our culture and especially in the culture of the university at this time. There is a sign in my local newspaper store reading: "By the time you know all the rules you're too old to play the game." Men in today's university might well complain that, by the time they know the rules, women have changed the game. But rules always change with time, and women, like men, need help from one another as these rules inevitably change.

Women need help in the university in other ways besides challenging the canon or daring to see our heritage as other than male centered (or other than racist or classist, since it also comes to that). The woman student faces special problems. As likely as her male counterpart—perhaps likelier—to have mixed feelings about a female authority figure, she is at the same time eager to show herself worthy of the club she has been allowed to join. Deliberately or not, women are raised to be untroublesome, and to many women, young and old, it seems profoundly boorish to question the nice gentlemen who have let them into their university. As E. M. Forster put it, it is hard, after accepting six cups of tea from your hostess, to throw the seventh in her face.[17] Women fought for a century or more to gain a university education, and they are slow to realize that they are no longer pounding on the doors but, on the contrary, finding that the door they lean on gives way so readily that they collapse across the threshold. There is, furthermore, a tendency for an accomplished woman to think of herself as a special case, not as a member of a group called "women"—a situation intensified by the unfortunate fact that, in any revolution, those who fight are seldom those who win. The young women who now receive the rewards scarcely understand what the struggle was all about. How could they, for they will never find themselves so equal as they seem in college. Unfortunately that makes it difficult for the college to prepare them to cope with the inevitable inequalities of work, marriage, child-rearing, and aging.[18] If the men who teach them refuse to bring openly into discussion the place of females in our culture, the young women will rest in an attitude of gracious appreciation, bathed in the comforts of male authority, marvelously unprepared for the life that awaits them, including the life of the mind. To this might be added that young men themselves would benefit from knowing what the female destiny has been and may be, and from questioning not so much their attitude toward women as their attitude toward themselves and the presumptions of their maleness.

Women in the university would welcome from devotees of the legacy an enlightened understanding of why non-canonical texts must be read and canonized texts approached with new questions. Here I can offer a personal example. The period, as we say, that I specialize in is modern British literature. When I was in graduate school thirty years ago, that was a totally male literature and has largely remained so. In earlier years, the peculiarity of this never occurred to me. That I was forbidden to teach Virginia Woolf or even mention her without fear of raucous laughter struck me as in the nature of things. In American literature, similarly, Gertrude Stein was a joke, or part of a limerick I remember finding particularly funny: There are geniuses three named Stein/ There's Gertrude there's Ep and there's Ein;/ Gertrude's writing is junk/ Ep's statues are punk/ And nobody understands Ein.

More recently I heard this joke from about the same time: a critic was asked to review *A Skeleton Key to Finnegans Wake*, and he refused, saying that what Joyce needed was a lock, not a key. I don't agree with the sentiment here expressed, but I noticed it because it is the only joke I can remember hearing about the proliferation of studies of Joyce. When Woolf began to be studied and written about, and to have her letters and other writings published, the result was a howl of laughter that echoed from *New Yorker* cartoons to newspaper articles discussing the "cult" of Virginia Woolf. (We have also, of course, had "cults" of contemporary women poets like Sylvia Plath.) It is the usual no-win situation: either a woman author isn't studied, or studying her is reduced to an act of misplaced religious fanaticism. All these are gambits to ensure non-recognition of women authors. We must read Gertrude Stein and Virginia Woolf because they are writers of the first importance for an understanding of our world: it is really that simple. Tender buttons as well as phalluses can organize a vision.

I well remember the love I felt for modern British literature in all my early academic years. The period was close to contemporary then, and it spoke exactly of the way we felt: it spoke us. Taught to read as a man, I did not notice that I was nowhere in most of the texts by which I believed myself gloriously empowered. Neither bird-girl with feathers nor arrogant young sinner among prostitutes, I read as I had been taught to read, failing to identify myself as other than a reader, male, of texts also male, but pretending to be neuter, universal. Today I find the same literature equally compelling, but I can perceive not only that words like *collegiality* camouflage the inevitable maleness of our university culture but also certain connections, like those between the fear of women and the attraction of fascism, the disdain of women and the ease of imperialism. Hugh Kenner, who has called my period the Pound era, has also said that *Ulysses*, like *Paradise Lost*, is the pivotal work of its time.[19] I believe this last to be true, including in the sense that the important voices are those that have turned from Joyce as T. S. Eliot turned from Milton. This is not to say that Joyce and Milton are not among the greatest writers we have in our legacy. It is to say that we must learn to ask new questions of them.

It is to say, further, that Virginia Woolf and Gertrude Stein have asked those questions in ways that soon reveal themselves when they are read with the same intensity with which Kenner and his colleagues have read Joyce and Pound and Eliot.

If we look back over the history of the English novel, we cannot but be struck by the centrality of women within it. Most of the women who study the English novel feel empowered by this fact. Simply to name Richardson, Defoe, Thackeray, Collins, Meredith, Hardy, Gissing, James, Lawrence, Forster is to perceive that woman's grip upon the imagination of most male English novelists is intense — almost, one might guess, as though the limited condition of women, their inability to fulfill, in James's words, the demands of their imagination, spoke to male novelists of something close to their own experience, to their own fears. Yet how often is the English novel studied from that perspective? Similarly, the most cursory study of nineteenth-century literature indicates that George Sand was perhaps the greatest single influence upon many of the major male English authors. But how many courses in the Victorian age even mention George Sand, let alone study her writings and her life?

Down to this very day, women's place in culture has been what might be called a Lacanian "contained spectacle," existing only as an embodiment or representation of male desire. Because half our student population is female, but not only because of this, reclaiming and restoring the life of the mind requires us to confront that central cultural fact, as yet unexamined in the legacy that men like Bennett and Giamatti would hand on to us. Their legacy, their literature, has served men well. Yet we often fail to notice in the texts we study how much they embody both fear of women and the need to protect conventional masculinity. Feminist criticism provides the essential analytic methods to use if one wishes seriously to engage the gender basis of our culture. Yet how infrequently has such analysis been admitted in the discourse of the university. Courses in history that deal at length with the Scientific Revolution, the Industrial Revolution, the French and Russian Revolutions, and the Revolutions of 1848 scarcely touch upon the revolution in the status of women. If the universities neglected to debate affirmative action when it was first imposed upon them, they have declined to debate the assumptions about gender which they have accepted far longer and more readily.

So today, each time we take up — and often enough we do not even bother to take up — Milton's Eve, or Shakespeare's Lady Macbeth, or Jane Austen's Emma, or George Eliot's Maggie Tulliver, or Charlotte Brontë's Lucy Snowe, or Henry James's Isabel Archer, or D. H. Lawrence's Lady Chatterley, we do not ask them to speak themselves: we do not ask of them what we ask of the Underground Man, or Pip, or Tom Jones, or Lear, or Beowulf.

And we must ask women within the university to speak for themselves also. We must permit women, without shaming them as foolish, or strident, or shrill, or unsexed, to enter, with respect, the ancient discourses. Carlyle met Margaret Fuller with certain assumptions, upon which he later commented. She is, he wrote, "a strange lilting, lean old maid, not nearly such a bore as I expected."[20] When he said this of her, Margaret Fuller was thirty-six; she would be dead at forty. We know how much Carlyle was amused when she told him wearily that she had decided to accept the universe. "She'd better," he said (87). But in the end we shall learn that she need not accept the universe he took for granted; we may even hope that her appearance, her marital status, and her age will not be the primary aspects with which we engage, that the ways she questions the universe will come to seem as essential to understanding the humanist legacy as the questions of Plato, Augustine, Joyce, and T. S. Eliot have always seemed.

NOTES

1. Lionel Trilling, *The Opposing Self* (New York: Viking, 1955).

2. Lionel Trilling, *Mind in the Modern World: The 1972 Jefferson Lecture in the Humanities* (New York: Viking, 1972) 27.

3. Edward Said, *The World, the Text, and the Critic* (Cambridge: Harvard UP, 1983) 169.

4. Christine Froula, "Pechter's Specter: Milton's Bogey Writ Small; or, Why Is He Afraid of Virginia Woolf?" *Critical Inquiry* 11 (1984): 178.

5. Kristen Kann, student paper, fall 1986.

6. Craig Owens, "The Discourse of Others: Feminists and Postmodernism," *The Anti-Aesthetic: Essays on Postmodern Culture*, ed. Hal Foster (Port Townsend: Bay Press, 1983) 57–82.

7. Judith Fetterley, *The Resisting Reader: A Feminist Approach to American Fiction* (Bloomington: Indiana UP, 1978) xii.

8. Hugh Kenner, quoted in Lynn Sukenick, "On Women and Fiction," *The Authority of Experience: Essays in Feminist Criticism*, ed. Arlyn Diamond and Lee R. Edwards (Amherst: U of Massachusetts P, 1977) 28–44.

9. Burgess and Gass, quoted in Sandra Gilbert and Susan Gubar, *The Madwoman in the Attic* (New Haven: Yale UP, 1979) 9.

10. William J. Bennett, *To Reclaim a Legacy: A Report on the Humanities in Higher Education* (Washington, D.C.: National Endowment for the Humanities, 1984).

11. A. Bartlett Giamatti, speech before the Signet Society, 94th Annual Dinner, Harvard University, 11 Apr. 1985.

12. George Eliot, *The Mill on the Floss* (Cambridge: Riverside P, 1961) 130.

13. Nancy K. Miller, "Emphasis Added: Plots and Plausibilities in Women's Fiction," *PMLA* 96 (1981): 36–48.

14. Joan Scott, "Women's History as Women's Education," address, Smith College, 17 Apr. 1985.

15. Elaine Marks, "Breaking the Bread: Gestures toward Other Structures, Other Discourses," *Bulletin of the MMLA* 13.1 (1980): 55.

16. Diana Trilling, "The Liberated Heroine," address, Columbia University, April 1978; published in *Partisan Review* 45.4 (1978): 501–22.

17. E. M. Forster, *The Longest Journey* (New York: Knopf, 1961) 75.

18. This is a remark I heard Gloria Steinem make. If it is printed, I do not know where.

19. Hugh Kenner, *Joyce's Voices* (Berkeley: U of California P, 1978) xii.

20. Paula Blanchard, *Margaret Fuller: From Transcendentalism to Revolution* (New York: Addison-Wesley, 1978) 257.

CHERIS KRAMARAE & PAULA A. TREICHLER

Power Relationships in
the Classroom

Interesting, amorphous, combative, nice, tense, responsive, productive, useless, paternalistic, supportive, formidable, chaotic, sermonish —teachers and students used these adjectives to describe university classroom interactions. In fact, they used these different adjectives to describe the *same* classroom interaction. As a continuation of work done by others with elementary and secondary school students, we designed the following study to focus on what women and men say about their experiences in university classrooms. Our work is prompted by continuing reports from female university students suggesting not only that their classroom experiences are different from males' but also that their experiences are often unsatisfactory in ways that are not recognized by most university teachers and critics of educational policy. These women's reports occur in a variety of places which are, for many people, invisible and inaudible— government publications, feminist journals, and feminist conferences. They include information on many problematic areas of educational policy, such as the curriculum and its epistemological underpinnings, the history of women's place in pedagogy, and the relation of gender to work status and income. These reports have transformative possibilities for education, including a reconceptualization of how classroom interaction could better serve its participants. Yet they exist in relative isolation from other analyses of educational theory and practice and from research on language and gender.[1]

Drawing from the literature in these areas, we propose the following argument. The reasons women experience a "chilly climate" in academic settings are several, and they include curricula which largely exclude the experiences of females, professional advising that restricts their options, and male control of classroom talk.[2] Remedies proposed by critics who challenge the present system include changing the behavior of women, establishing segregated classes, or retraining teachers to help women adapt to traditional classroom interaction. We identify the structure of classroom interaction as a major reason many women find the classroom inhospitable, and we offer alternative solutions.[3]

In designing an initial study to test the analytic value of our argument, we wanted to explore in a vigorous but flexible way women's and men's reflections on classroom interaction; we also wished to enlarge our understanding of student and teacher concerns, and to explore paths for continuing research. We began by observing a graduate humanities course at the University of Illinois; at the end of the term, we asked 19 students (volunteers from the 34 enrolled students and 18 auditors) and the 3 (white, male) co-teachers to participate in a multilayered study. We thought these students (11 white males and 8 white females, aged 22–35) were likely to be more articulate when discussing academic structures than many undergraduates would be; we were aware, however, that their very presence at this academic level suggests they may have become more accommodated to the expectations and structures of the university than have undergraduates.

In individually scheduled sessions, we collected information in three ways. First we asked participants to listen, one at a time, to a tape of approximately five minutes of talk from one of their class sessions and to stop the tape when they had comments to make about the interaction; these comments were also taped. This part of the study, then, was not highly structured by us. The five-minute sequence was chosen after three people listened to the tape and indicated what they thought to be a cohesive segment of talk; it included talk by three students (two female, one male) and the three teachers in the class. Second, after we had elicited their perceptions of the characteristics of the taped interaction, participants were asked to complete a written questionnaire containing questions about the specific sequence and about classroom interaction in general. The questionnaires also asked them to rank the relative importance of forty features of classroom interaction.[4] Finally, during sessions after they finished the questionnaires, the students and teachers were encouraged to ask questions about the study and to offer additional comments about their classroom experiences. These conversations (conducted and taped primarily by a student, Sally Green, working with us) were initially planned as brief talks to provide each participant a chance to comment on the study. But we soon discovered that most participants had many things to say about the class in particular and about classroom interaction in general; most of these sessions continued for more than half an hour, and some were longer than an hour.[5]

The material gathered from the three phases of these individual sessions (which resulted in approximately twenty-two hours of tape) could be examined and discussed in a rich variety of ways. In the sections that follow, we focus on the ways these men and women conceptualize their place in the processes of giving and gaining knowledge and in the structure of power relationships in the classroom. We argue that we can learn about the structure of power in classrooms by listening to students and teachers talk about their rights, duties, privileges, and problems. One of the things we discover is that women and men perceive these in very different ways.

In this multilayered analysis, we examine the classroom context from which the taped interaction was taken; we look at responses to the interaction—particularly how respondents characterized the interaction, the individual speakers, and the relationship between this segment of interaction and their other classroom experiences. In addition, we look at students' characterizations of and responses to classrooms in general; here we draw upon both numerical measures and comments made in the interviews.

General Observations on Seminar Interaction

FEMALE STUDENT: There is a bit of a "head hunter" style—that is, the profs come to the work with a great deal of background and a developed reading or position—and as people try to discuss more inchoate positions, the same criteria of completeness get applied. In other words, if you stick your interpretive neck out, you get it chopped off.

MALE STUDENT: [I like] heated discussion between students or between student[s] and professor. It bores the hell out of me when we refuse to argue with one another to save face.

MALE STUDENT: Don't show the world that you're an ignorant ass. Much better to be a silent ass.

The course we studied was an interdisciplinary postgraduate seminar in critical theory called Basic Issues in Interpretation; it was team-taught by three white male faculty members from the departments of English, philosophy, and speech communication. Because of its size, the class was held in an amphitheater-type classroom, with the mostly white students sitting in five tiers of fixed seats facing the teachers, who sat at the front of the room, behind a desk on a raised dais. The three teachers were relatively young (mid-thirties), and fairly well known to a number of the students; the teachers were typically addressed by their first names. Classroom observation suggested that, despite such collegial and egalitarian aspects of the class, classroom interaction, for the most part, was hierarchical. The instructors controlled topics, format, and sequence of class sessions, guided discussion firmly, and did most of the talking. The size and seating arrangement reinforced these tendencies. One or more of the instructors presented a formal lecture each week, with class discussion occurring in the time remaining. Students almost invariably addressed comments and questions to one or more of the instructors, rather than to other students; the instructors almost always gave "answers" rather than, say, inviting discussion. Interaction among the three instructors centered around the demarcation of their differing intellectual positions—an explicit goal of their co-teaching format—and took a variety of forms, including responding formally to each other's presentations, explicitly challenging a statement or position, needling or bantering, and deferring to one another's expertise.

This was very much a graduate course. For many of the students, it represented an intellectual milieu compatible with their intellectual and professional achievements and aspirations. It was seen as a *serious* course. According to one woman, "People who spoke seemed to have a commitment to what they said. The interactions were quite serious." Said another, "I do feel I'm a participating scholar." There was also competition and considerable awareness of "polished" verbal style. Several students expressed discomfort with this. "The class is dominated by 'little professor' discussion by students," one woman wrote. But others commended such discussion; one of the instructors described verbal interaction in his own field (philosophy) as "duelling" and emphasized, for graduate students, the necessity of "taking a side and defending it." The size and the team-teaching structure were seen as inhibiting class discussion which, in one male student's words, tended to be dominated by "four or five classic, aggressive males," which he defined, when asked, as "someone who's very sure of his position, doesn't think that what he has to say might be in any way considered ridiculous, and thinks that other people necessarily do want to hear about his particular position."

Students emphasized the importance of a teacher's behavior in structuring class discussion and saw the three teachers clearly as authority figures, well versed in the frequently "esoteric" and difficult subject matter. For some students, this expertise provided a formidable obstacle to participation. The women students seemed especially aware of this:

> The professors dominate the scene, sort of not making students want to speak and interact unless the students feel very secure; and there are some students . . . who do feel very certain of themselves and want to make a show of themselves.

> [I felt] the professors [were] just judging your viewpoint, you know, standing there like the tribunal, making you feel like a moron.

> There was a lot of competition among students for the floor depending on how confident they were and on how prepared they were—who had the floor was controlled by the instructors—and there's really no chance for a spirited interchange between peers.

> The impression was, at least for me, that everybody in that room had so much more knowledge of the subject that I couldn't possibly stand up to it, you know—that people were always talking about Foucault.

In the class sessions we observed, the teachers tended to talk more frequently than students and for longer periods of time. In addition, they interacted freely with each other, something the students did not for the most part feel they had the right to do. Thus, virtually all talk by class members flowed through one or more of the teachers. In the class session from which the taped interaction was taken, for example, teachers talked through just over two-thirds of the session; this included their lectures. Though during the discussion period teachers and students divided floor time about equally, the 3 teachers talked more frequently and took longer turns at talk. They also talked to each other (though sometimes looking at the class or into some middle distance rather than making eye contact with each other). What is most striking is that, of the 43 class members and auditors in attendance that day, only 9 participated actively, talking 28 times in 3 hours: 6 men talked a total of 11 times; 3 women talked 17 times. This overall 3:1 ratio of teacher-to-student talk is typical for this class and for college classrooms in the United States in general (Treichler and Kramarae); the women's talk time here is atypically high and occurs almost exclusively in the taped exchange selected for microanalysis (selected because it *did* include women talking). That teachers control talk is borne out also by the fact that, out of the 130 total utterances that occurred during the discussion, only 2 utterances (1 interchange) did *not* involve 1 or more of the 3 teachers. This occurred, significantly, when a male student directed a question to a male faculty member who was sitting in on this class session. This teacher responded to the student (turning in his seat to do so) rather than to the other teachers or to the room at large.

In sum, this seminar, while different from some graduate seminars in the humanities by virtue of size and interdisciplinary emphasis, seemed to embody, in high relief so to speak, a number of features probably characteristic of many university classrooms: teacher control of class structure and flow of talk; perception among students that authorization to talk depended on certain credentials, including the quality of the product (*what* was said, *how* it was said), expertise, disciplinary training, and ability to comfortably engage in "little professor" talk; domination of discussion by a small group of (predominately male) students; little explicit attention to classroom process; and discussion structured around intellectual challenge and confrontation rather than collaboration. Some female students perceived this last characteristic as typical of male talk:

> I felt that women were more prone to support one another.

> The men tended to be more combative or something. . . . I just found that women after class or during break would more easily strike up discussion with one another about what was going on whereas men didn't seem to do that.

> Three men at one time with difficult material. I wondered at one point what it would be like if there would have been one female faculty member among them. . . . I don't know why, but I think it would have been different.

It is significant that, although classroom process was rarely addressed explicitly, our interviews and earlier research make it clear that class participants tend to be keenly aware of process issues and other aspects of classroom life.[6] This becomes very clear in the next section.

Students' Comments on Taped Interaction

Students and instructors were asked to listen to and comment on a five-minute segment of taped class discussion from the third class session. During a part of the segment, a woman student and a teacher discuss a critic's psychoanalytic approach to *King Lear* which features the theme of incest:

FEMALE STUDENT: There is something about the, uh, the presence of that kind of a of a sexual feeling for someone that ()[7] expresses itself even in most superficial kinds of relationships () and () would express itself even in the () plain love of father for daughter. If it wasn't present. And if it wasn't present it wouldn't matter, so I think that that may be why he he says well it doesn't matter whether we're considering actual incest or not. (1 sec.) Um () I don't know. Um () It's just sort of an intuition [laughs] I have () about that. (2 sec.) So it wouldn't () really matter if it if there was actual incest () if he was actually thinking of incest, but if he had () I'm not making myself at all clear. Sorry about that (laughs).

MALE TEACHER: I'm not sure () quite () I think in a way () the fact that he wants to say () almost by putting it into a condition—if he resisted the idea—which he is clearly doing—I mean, uh, and making it seem as if it doesn't therefore matter if it's, uh, conditional—that's precisely his way of sort of resisting it. To make it into an option that we have available rather than something which it seems to me at this point in his reading just thrusts itself upon you. Obviously, Lear cannot demand this at this context given the forbidden nature of the () I mean the type of nature of the act desired.

SAME FEMALE STUDENT: That's why I think—well, even if the last alternative— the thing about its incompatible [inaudible] other levels.[8]

SAME MALE TEACHER: <u>Yes.</u>

SAME FEMALE STUDENT: Still in a sense it's applicable to Cordelia, because she reciprocates this love, can have no other love out—outside of Lear because of it. And yet can't () fulfill () that love.

SECOND MALE INSTRUCTOR: It did strike me when she said that in order to, uh, in order to give her love to her husband as well she cuts herself in two.

(The discussion continues with additional comments from male and female students.)

Individual respondents varied widely in their overall judgments of the "effectiveness" and "success" of the interaction. In general, the women seemed particularly alive to the interaction as an interpersonal event. Though some of the male students also commented favorably on "the collaborative nature of the interaction" and on the student's initiative and persistence in making her point, they commented less frequently on interpersonal process.

In the one case where a male did mention interpersonal interaction, he considered the emotional aspects of the exchange to have "thwarted any potential for developing a coherent line of argumentation." Process, in other words, was noticed because it compromised product.

Other men also saw discussion as building a viable "product"—positive to the extent that it succeeded, negative to the extent that it failed:

The interaction seemed to lack *clear* direction and purpose.

[I liked] the student's persistence in establishing her presence even when she had a hard time finding her focus, and the instructor's tone in taking off from the student's comments.

The discussion went as far as it could go in the absence of a *detailed* psychoanalytic interpretation of the play.

While one point was followed through upon, it was not related to more general issues.

Men students were most critical of the interaction when they felt it had not led to "clear statements" and when ideas had been "ill conceived or unclearly expressed." The women students, on the other hand, were put off by their sense that the women speakers in the interaction had been uncomfortable:

There wasn't much attempt on the part of the profs to help the student clarify her position before they started challenging it. They [could have] facilitated her argument in order to make the 'best case' for her position.

The student, in her initial comments, didn't feel that her comments were being picked up and felt she had to apologize. She didn't seem comfortable. There is a lot of tension.

Asked whether they remembered this brief interaction from the third class session, it is interesting that almost all students remembered it. Recalling their thoughts at the time, most men had docketed the discussion according to its content:

It raised questions of specific interest to me.

For a class on interpretive theory, there was no attempt to connect discussion of the text to basic issues in interpretive theory, e.g., the relevance of psychoanalysis to interpretation.

[I remembered] that it did not reach any concluding moment.

Seemed to get off onto vague, tangential issues and not relate to the general content of Cavell's essay or his interpretive practices.

None of the women recalled the discussion in terms of content alone:

It exemplified the tendency for the female students to put forward amorphous, heavily disclaimed positions that were subsequently eviscerated.

I was wondering why I was not comfortable.

It was one of the many times when I felt relieved that someone else [was] speaking.

I was *quite* uncomfortable.

Two of the instructors commented favorably on the interaction. One felt that "different points of view were expressed, and a variety of people got the topic opened up from many perspectives." Another instructor felt his task had been to "flail" the first speaker verbally for not formulating the position clearly enough. For this instructor, discussion involves "taking sides" and being able to defend a position. Some of the tension perceived by some students in this interaction derived from this sense of what one student termed "the level of accountability one had to consider before speaking."

Finally, we asked students to comment on their actual or potential participation in this discussion: at what points might they have joined in and why? Many made clear they had not participated and/or would not have participated. Males were likely to attribute their not speaking to an unfamiliarity with the material or the topic, thus, to an inability to contribute substantively to the discussion:

I certainly would have [spoken] if I had had anything substantial to say. Would have waited rather than speak uncertainly.

I have my own views about Freudian or psychoanalytic criticism. . . .

To be perfectly frank, I had not read the particular article involved.

One of the women who did speak indicated that intellectual curiosity ("I wanted to see what others had seen in the sexual motif") had overcome the "safety and security" of silence. Most of the women attributed their nonparticipation to a perception of the classroom process:

Particularly early in the semester, I felt I could not make my ideas clearly understood: part of that resulted from newness of the material; yet . . . I always had trouble assessing who I was talking to.

Because the discussion tends to occur on two levels, I find it cautionary not to join in. At a surface level there is a call to interact freely and openly, but there seems to be an underlying tension or competition over which reading will emerge victorious. . . . Students don't explore each other's positions on ideas so much as they vie for attention and *compete* to get their own ideas to be heard.

Students' General Comments on Classroom Interaction

We encouraged participants to discuss further their perceptions of how talk is managed in classrooms. From many hours of taped responses, we can here include only some illustrations from men and women about (1) the amount of student talk in classrooms; (2) power plays between professor and student; and (3) power relations among students.[9]

Amount of Student Talk

The women had a lot to say about their experiences in this course, experiences which, their responses to our questionnaire indicated, were sometimes traumatic in ways that they did not seem to be for the males; the women also had more to say about talk in other classrooms than the men did. Women thought men have more freedom to talk in classrooms:

Men seem to talk for a long time and say a lot, and women say shorter things and get to the point. I'm not sure how much women talk in classes in general; I don't think they talk too much.

Women eventually talk as much as the men, but I think it takes some time to get the response. . . . I think it takes them some time to warm up.

I've noticed again and again in most classes the students, the male students, seem, perhaps it's a fallacy on my part, seem to speak up more easily while women hesitate.

I've talked with other women. They say, "Before I can speak I have to be doubly sure of what I am saying. And my heart races and my stomach ties itself in knots. But at least I spoke." Other women will say, "Oh, I made no sense, did I? I really didn't make any sense." I wish more women would speak up in class, and I wish I could.

[Commenting on a woman who spoke up in a seminar] And I think she wanted to quit because she was feeling stupid, but then the instructor didn't say anything so she had to get herself going again and had to say something else.

[In classes with "authoritarian" teachers] I remind myself not to say anything in class, no matter what, since otherwise I leave class feeling foolish.

The men did not offer many statements about the relative amount of talk from men and women. One male said:

If a female student is aggressive [and talks a lot], the the instructor finds it much more interesting; it sort of registers, you see, a certain interest, perhaps a sympathetic interest, perhaps not, which a male student might not get. I mean there may be much more impatience with a male student who is aggressive and articulate.

Power Plays between Teacher and Student

Many students remarked on the ways teachers establish and maintain power or control. The women talked about teachers who "stand there like the judge," who "field questions but don't really entertain them," who "make fun of what people say," who refer to texts not assigned, and who force a student "to defend her position" against the teacher's perspective. One woman thought that many teachers wield power in part by embarrassing female students:

This can happen in various ways: a harmless reference [by a female student] to "three points or levels in the narrative" could call up a remark such as, "Oh, we have triplets here" by a male teacher. [Asked whether a woman teacher would as likely say that, the student said:] I've very often wondered how men feel in classes [with women teachers]. Of course I haven't noticed any embarrassment such as I've noticed with male teachers.

Some comments connected male teachers' power in the classroom to the "legitimate" power men have in general. For example:

I think that male teachers just like to hold forth and see that as another arena where they can talk freely, and are paid to do this. How are you going to break the circle? . . . I would like to see them not distant, not overbearing, not protecting their space . . . [But they seem, from what I sense, almost terrified of giving up some of this authority.]

[If students express uncertainty] teachers come back with a tone that is typically male, typically professor. It's assured. It almost feels authoritarian to me.

Some women talked about the position of "competent authority" or "superior knowledge" continually established by some teachers even if they asked for discussion. For example:

It's very hard to come in with your own suggestions when the teacher has his preformulated ideas and you don't have time to examine them but you are expected to react to them, and then you react in a "short-sighted" way and then you get dumped on.

[The men] are affirmed, given credence and credibility in a way I never [am]. . . . Part of the dilemma I have with this is that it [is seldom talked about]. I think I must be inventing this problem, that it exists only in my mind . . . I'm not saying that male instructors don't also sometimes dismiss the males and dismiss them abruptly at times. But it is not as consistent, it is not as profound.

[It is clear that teachers' comments should be considered] their own little sermonettes. [You might be called on to take another stand] but if you take it, you're going to have to defend it even if you don't want to.

The men initially seemed to us to be more interested in the specific content of the course; they did not report as much unease with power relationships between students and teacher. However, listening to the tapes, we realized that they also mentioned the kind of process they enjoyed, even if they usually put the emphasis on "ideas." One reported that he enjoyed classes in which students "punched and jabbed" at the teacher's comments. Another example:

[I enjoy classes when] I attack the teacher's ideas and the teacher attacks mine, without any sense of ill feeling.

A few males said they were conscious that being a male made their interaction with teachers different.

Power Relationships among Students

It was sort of clear to me when I came here as a grad student that certain people accepted me as having something worthwhile to say. . . . A lot of that is just due to the fact that I'm male and I'm prejudged in certain ways.

The women were more likely than were the men to object to the "loneliness" of making comments in the classroom and to the lack of what they thought of as collaborative work. (The men may well have heard the "battling over ideas" as collaborative work although they didn't speak of it in that way.) From women:

> Students don't try to integrate others' ideas into their own; they just blow off other ideas when they present their own.

> Ideas from intuition, experience (not interpretation grounded in the text) don't elicit very much feedback from the instructors or weren't paid much attention to by the other students.

> The teachers dominate the scene, sort of not making the students want to talk and interact unless the students feel very secure. There are some students in classes who do feel very certain of themselves and want to make a show of themselves.

Several of the men talked about "the burden of proof" placed on a student who talked in class, but they were more accepting of this. One said:

> [I talked] when it was something that really concerned me, or I maybe had a point I wanted to make or there are times, I think, I have something I need explained, not much, and that's all it is, just that I didn't understand something. And I guess there are also times when I want to get others arguing or at least sort of get them talking about something.

Students who discussed sex-related differences in classroom interaction were asked to suggest reasons for their existence. The males were more likely to discuss women's reluctance to mention "touchy subjects" in class, or women's shyness:

> Generally female students are more shy about expressing themselves, less strident in the give-and-take of, you know, heated arguments. Whereas a male student might, might, might not be as sensitive, might not register certain power plays, a female student might register it more, might be much more sensitive to certain power plays.

> [Discussing the "inarticulate responses" of some female students:] Some students just don't do a good job of communicating real well.

However, most of the explanations the women offered concerned the behavior of the teachers, the differing status of women and men in the classroom, and the differing concerns of women and men.

Many of the problems they experience in the classroom could be alleviated, some of the women said, if talk were more collaborative. Discussing a classroom situation she had enjoyed, one woman said:

> It was just wonderful. There were integrated, reciprocal, co-existing dialogues happening most of the time. There were people interrupting people and there were all kinds of things happening. The dialogues, the interaction, was in sync so I was very comfortable. But some people told

me they were confused and one man said, "Look, at least in other class-rooms I know what is right and I know what is wrong, and I can't deal with this." He just didn't show up anymore. I [think] it is okay to enter into a dialogue and be confused and go through it. But our educational system doesn't allow this.

Responses to Questionnaire

We include here, as possible guides to future research, information gained from our questions about classroom interaction in general. Because of the small number of students interviewed (nineteen), we do not argue that their answers tell us all we need to know about graduate students' relationships to each other, their teachers, and the pursuit of knowledge. We do think, though, that these responses, along with other indications that women and men have different experiences in the classroom (Treichler and Kramarae), raise important questions for those of us concerned about university education.

Most of the women wrote about their enjoyment of open discussion, commenting positively on "natural discussion with people addressing one another's points," on "being able to question informally and inter-rupt if something is unclear (though interrupts would be few)," and on having "student discussion with instructor input equal to explore the topic." In contrast, most of the men wrote about the importance of a "structured discussion."

Men and women offered different responses to the question "Under what conditions are you *most* comfortable about talking in class?" The men indicated more concern with their own preparation and feeling of control; the women showed more concern with the behavior of the teacher. Similar differences occurred in answer to the question "Under what conditions are you *least* comfortable about talking in class?" Again, the women were more likely to show concern with the teacher's behavior.

We asked students to give numerical evaluations for forty features of classroom interactions, teacher behavior, and physical aspects of classrooms. For several questions for which it was possible to make predictions, the following t-tests were significant at $< .05$ or better for 1-tailed test.[10] Women reported themselves more motivated than the men to talk in class in order to support friends who had spoken ($t = -2.23$; $df = 15$). Women gave more importance than did men to the following: to the teacher's trying to insure that class members feel good about each other ($t = -1.81$; $df = 17$); to students' introduction of personal experience as explanation/example ($t = -2.07$; $df = 17$); and to the presence of windows in the classroom ($t = -2.70$; $df = 15$). Men gave more importance than did women to the teacher's organizing most of the class content through lectures (t = 2.01; df = 17).[11]

Discussion

One female student commented:

> I do see gender differences . . . in the classroom. I probably see it more than other people do because I tend to focus on it. For example, I was in a seminar this semester and there were more women in it than men and I felt a whole lot more empowered—I felt a whole lot more listened to—I felt like I had a whole lot more credibility than has been my general experience in the seminars I've gone to because traditionally they've neither been led by a female instructor nor have women been encouraged to dominate. I don't know if *dominate* is the word—I mean to feel comfortable with having a dominant role in the interaction. And I guess it would be my desire for someone to consciously take that into consideration when they're leading a seminar. I like instructors who try to pay attention to everybody participating and seeking out and encouraging the quiet ones, and I try to do it myself when I teach. And it's interesting that if you don't just let the eager people who want to talk but you encourage other people, you get a whole different sort of classroom discussion going.

The comments of graduate students about a taped segment of their humanities seminar and their responses to questions about talk in the classroom indicate that these women and men have different feelings of esteem and power in the classroom. As in a study of power relationships in French universities,[12] the males are more likely to talk as individual beings, while the women talk with an awareness of their gender and the subordinate social standing of women.

The women are more interested than are the men in talking in class to support friends, and in spirited shared discussion; they also feel more at ease with teachers who do not impose their views on others. Women are seemingly more concerned than are the men with the teaching-learning process and attend more to the personal experiences of other students (both as discussed in the class and shared in the classroom interaction). They consider the openness and supportiveness of the instructor the salient factor in determining whether they feel comfortable about talking in class and give more importance than do men to the teacher's attempts to insure that class members feel good about each other. Women are more likely to report enjoyment of classes in which students and teacher talk in a collaborative manner, rather than in student-to-teacher and teacher-to-student monologues. The women are more apt to report feeling engulfed by the different perceptions of male teachers.

The men are more interested than are the women in the content of the learning, with the cognitive and nonpersonal aspects of classroom interaction. They report more concern than do the women with their own active participation in class and more interest in teacher control over classroom discussion; they express more interest in teachers who organize most of the class content through lectures and who encourage questions and comments from individual students. Men are more likely than women to attribute the amount and kind of their class talk to their interests and ideas, rather than to the teacher's behavior.

While the women make more explicit statements about the structure of the learning process than do the men, the men's focus on the importance of debates about ideas suggests a priority on interaction based on individual expertise and presentation and elaboration of abstract concepts. The valuing of this kind of knowledge acquisition is compatible with a commitment to relatively nonpersonal, hierarchical classroom interaction. The responses of the men and women in the class indicate it is a circular process: how participants in the classroom talk shapes the kind of discovery and invention processes that occur.

In an earlier paper which served as the theoretical backdrop for this study, we reviewed literature on classroom interaction, other descriptions of university life, pedagogical alternatives developed in Women's Studies programs, and research on female and male interaction patterns and power relationships in childhood and adulthood (Treichler and Kramarae). Girls and women are made to experience many types of social, political, and economic discrimination, in educational settings and in other institutions which affect our daily lives.[13] It seems indeed likely that the different classroom interaction patterns are due in part to the different societal constraints and privileges females and males experience. Adrienne Rich makes a useful distinction between "claiming" and "receiving" an education.[14]

Of course, women and men typically also spend a good deal of time in mixed-sex company in school, in businesses, and in the family, and they certainly share *some* of the same ideas about how to get meanings established. We have focused here on differences because most studies of academe have paid little attention to the reasons for the differences or to the type, scope, or implications of these differences and hierarchies.[15] Furthermore, these hierarchical differences may influence the ways meaning is socially created.[16] As almost all teachers and students of Women's Studies realize, there is a nonproductive tension between the traditional academic classroom management and revolutionary, nontraditional topics. Some of the essays in the collection *All the Women Are White, All the Blacks Are Men, but Some of Us Are Brave* point to the relationship of the types of women's interaction and their contributions to knowledge;[17]

Johnella Butler notes that reductionist classroom material and teaching methods (composed, conducted, and critiqued in the U.S. primarily by white, middle-class males) make teaching about plurality very difficult.[18]

With this focus on differences and hierarchies, what we have found is that the women in this exploratory study, like the women in related studies,[19] report more ease and more discovery in settings where learning is a communal activity shared fairly equally by students and teacher. Men seem more satisfied with authoritarian educational settings. These varying student and teacher preferences are important in helping us understand not only how power relationships function in the classroom and how knowledge is created but also what knowledge is and who can create it.

There are potential solutions for some of the conflicts and tensions caused by, and causing, the differences discussed here. Students and teachers could discuss these issues and make explicit their expectations and wishes. A variety of approaches to classroom structure and process could be used throughout a course, incorporating several modes of interaction familiar to women and men of differing classes and racial and ethnic groups. But this is not simply a matter of encouraging more classroom discussion now and then. Incorporating these and other values and ideas of women will bring new questions and experiences to the classroom and may redefine what constitutes knowledge and processes of discovery. If education is to serve both women and men, we need to continue to attend to the particulars of their perceptions and experiences, for the comments of the women participating in our study suggest that male dominance may be taught in part by the structure of the classroom itself.[20]

NOTES

1. Paula A. Treichler and Cheris Kramarae, "Women's Talk in the Ivory Tower," *Communication Quarterly* 31.2 (1983).

2. See Roberta M. Hall and Bernice Sandler, *The Classroom Climate: A Chilly One for Women*, Project on the Status and Education of Women (Washington, D.C.: Association of American Colleges, 1982), and *Reconstructing the Academy*, special issue of *Signs* 12.2 (Winter 1987): 203–418.

3. The university is a subculture which typically fosters interaction patterns compatible with white men's established ways of behaving. This argument, and the review of literature on which it is based, is discussed in our essay "Women's Talk in the Ivory Tower."

4. The items on the questionnaire were derived from studies reviewed in our classroom interaction essay "Women's Talk," from student comments and reports, and from language and gender research such as Cheris Kramarae, Barrie Thorne,

and Nancy Henley, "Sex Differences in Language, Speech, and Nonverbal Communication: An Annotated Bibliography," *Language, Gender, and Society* (Rowley, MA: Newbury House, 1983) Section V–F-2.

5. This procedure caused some problems, illustrating some of the potential difficulties of studying classroom interaction, where research questions may seem uncomfortably close to evaluative issues. We selected this particular class to study because it was team taught and because we wanted to look at a graduate seminar large enough to make anonymity possible. But as many of the students were aware, we knew the three professors and some of the students. Despite our guarantee of confidentiality, some students were understandably uneasy about making certain comments (we were also deliberately carrying out these interviews before they received a final grade). Further, we were encouraging them to speak unguardedly about the interactions of students and professors with whom they would, in many cases, have a continuing relationship. It is thus possible that some students responded more cautiously than they would have in another kind of situation. On the other hand, many students were deeply interested in this topic and had given it considerable thought; many made intensely critical statements about classroom interaction in general which surprised us in their vehemence. Some of them expressed the hope that we would talk with teachers about our findings. Some of the women students said they were glad to have an opportunity to speak with women researchers about this topic and indicated they would have been less open had the researchers been male. Some of the men may, conversely, have been less open because we were not male.

Many researchers avoid studying the daily environment of academe simply because it raises so many problems of this kind, but this avoidance does not seem a satisfactory solution. We believe it is crucial to look at actual classroom interaction, yet equally important not to exploit students as a captive population of passive objects (a characteristic of some classroom interactions many of them deplore). We should therefore continue to seek ways to study the academic environment that are genuinely meaningful yet do not create distrust or cynicism. See Pauline Bart, "What's a Nice Feminist Like Me Doing in a Place Like This," *For Alma Mater: Theory and Practice in Feminist Scholarship*, ed. Paula A. Treichler, Cheris Kramarae, and Beth Stafford (Urbana: U of Illinois P, 1985) 73–86; and Nancy M. Porter and Margaret T. Eileenchild, *The Effectiveness of Women's Studies Teaching*, Women's Studies Monograph Series (Washington, DC: GPO) for commentary on this subject.

6. For example, see David A. Karp and William C. Yoels, "The College Classroom: Some Observations on the Meanings of Student Participation," *Sociology and Social Research* 60 (1976): 412–39.

7. This sign () indicates a pause of less than one second.

8. The underlining indicates simultaneous speaking.

9. We have not included in this essay detailed discussion about students' differing expectations of female and male teachers. The evidence that students are less tolerant of female teachers in a number of respects and expect more interpersonal support from them suggests that this is also an important topic for research. See Sheila Kishler Bennett, "Student Perceptions of and Expectations for Male

and Female Instructors: Evidence Relating to the Question of Gender Bias in Teaching Evaluation," *Journal of Educational Psychology* 74.2 (1982): 170–79; Sarah Hall Sternglanz and Shirley Lyberger-Ficek, "Sex Differences in Student-Teacher Interactions in the College Classroom," *Sex Roles* 3 (1977): 345–52; Kramarae, Thorne, and Henley, *Language, Gender, and Society,* Sec. V–F-2; and Lawrence B. Rosenfeld and Mary W. Jarrard, "The Effects of Perceived Sexism in Female and Male College Professors on Students' Description of Classroom Climate," *Communication Education* 34 (1985): 205–13.

10. For some tests the variances of the two groups were unequal, so we had to use the separate variance t-test. See Marija J. Norusis, *SPSS* (New York: McGraw-Hill, 1982).

11. Given the relatively small sample size and the exploratory nature of the study, we also looked for results which, although not significant, were trends. Thus, we looked at tests significant up to the .10 level. For 1-tailed tests we found that women tended to give more importance than did men to the teacher's organizing most of the class content through discussion ($t = -1.28$; $df = 15$) and to the use in the classroom of movable seats ($t = -1.31$; $df = 17$). In a study with a greater number of participants, these may well be significant differences.

For other items, where there was no reason to predict directionality, these 2-tailed t-tests were significant at .05 or better. The men, when considering the reasons they were most likely to want to talk in class, reported as more important than did the women the desire to be considered an "active, involved" student ($t = 2.78$; $df = 10.8$); the women reported as more important the desire to contradict the instructor ($t = -2.14$; $df = 15$). Women thought the lighting in the classroom more important than did the men ($t = -2.02$; $df = 17$). Men reported as more important than did the women the teacher's encouraging of questions and comments from individual students ($t = 1.75$; $df = 17$).

12. Noelle Bisseret, *Education, Class, Language, and Ideology* (London: Routledge & Kegan Paul, 1979).

13. Andrew Fishel and Janice Pottler, *National Politics and Sex in Education* (Lexington, MA: Heath, 1977).

14. Adrienne Rich, "Toward a Woman-Centered University," *Lies, Secrets, and Silences* (New York: Norton, 1979) 237–45.

15. See Marilyn J. Boxer, "The Theory and Practice of Women's Studies in the United States," *Signs* 7.4 (1982): 661–95; Fishel and Pottler, *National Politics and Sex in Education;* Malcolm R. Lacey, "The Seminar—Experiences and Reflections," *Universities Quarterly* 37.1 (1982–83): 57–70; and Bernice Sandler, *Women on Campus: A Ten-Year Retrospective,* Project on the Status and Education of Women no. 26 (Washington DC: Association of American Colleges, 1980).

16. See Sally McConnell-Ginet, "The Origins of Sexist Language in Discourse," *Discourses in Reading and Linguistics,* ed. Sheila White and Virginia Teller, special issue of the *Annals of the New York Academy of Sciences* 433 (1984): 123–35; and Margo Culley and Catherine Portuges, eds., *Gendered Subjects: The Dynamics of Feminist Teaching* (Boston: Routledge & Kegan Paul, 1985).

17. Gloria Hull, Barbara Smith, and Patricia Bell Scott, eds., *All the Women*

Are White, All the Blacks Are Men, but Some of Us Are Brave (New York: Feminist P, 1983).

18. Johnella Butler, "Complicating the Question: Black Studies and Women's Studies," *Women's Place in the Academy: Transforming the Liberal Arts Curriculum,* ed. Marilyn Schuster and Susan Van Dyne (Totowa, NJ: Rowman & Allanheld, 1985) 73–86.

19. For example, see Hall, "Chilly Climate," and Laurel Walum Richardson, Judith Cook, and Anne Statham Macke, "Classroom Management Strategies of Male and Female University Professors," *Issues in Sex, Gender, and Society,* ed. Laurel Richardson and Verta Taylor (Lexington, MA: Heath, 1981).

20. We thank Sally Green, Victoria Leto, Judy Page, M. Scott Poole, and Kathleen Zoppi for their contributions to this project. We are also appreciative of the time and thoughtfulness of the students and professors who participated in the study.

NINA BAYM

The Feminist Teacher of Literature: Feminist or Teacher?

The new women's movement has revealed to us how thoroughly our social arrangements and our inner lives are pervaded by gender inequities that we have been taught to think of as "natural." As a social and political movement with practical goals, feminism necessarily emphasizes the destructive results of such gender teachings on those humans who are biologically female. As Simone de Beauvoir wrote in the originary text of the new feminist movement, *The Second Sex*, "one is not born a woman, but becomes one."

In attempting to redress the injustices that follow from, and depend on, acceptance of gender inequity, feminists have developed two different, not always compatible, practical goals. One is to revalue such traditionally denigrated female attributes as compassion, empathy, nurturance; the other is to remove the barriers that have kept women from the sources of power, property, and pleasure in our culture.[1] Neither aim directly addresses the fate of men. But feminists usually assume that in a society that values the "female" qualities while giving biological females access to the full range of human choices available in the culture, life will be better for all.

To move from the large social and political goals of the women's movement to the protected artifice of the literature classroom is to narrow one's aims dramatically. But there is no ground to till except what we stand on; only by learning to apply feminist principles in particular instances does one make change occur. Feminist teachers have invented a variety of women-centered courses for undergraduate and graduate students over the last fifteen years. Some of these courses consider works written by both men and women, others works by women only. Feminist teachers have also attempted to open mainstream classes to feminist insights.

In her teaching the feminist generally sets herself one of two tasks: she calls attention to "new" texts—that is, texts not traditionally taught—and she develops "new readings" of old texts, readings that make visible their gender markings.[2] In work by women authors, the teacher usually looks for the signs of a specific female writing presence—sometimes called the "signature"—which may be revealed directly through accounts of gender-specific experience or, more problematically, through particular stylistic habits.[3] The feminist teacher may interpret such habits as learned strategies, or as the natural expression of the female; and she may take them to represent the woman writer's resistance to, or her unwitting revelation of, patriarchal pressures.[4]

In considering work by a male author, the feminist teacher often tries to show how it complacently accepts or vigorously defends the biased social structure that gives dominance to males and devalues women. The various strategies of devaluation become the primary focus of her teaching. From this perspective, the male-authored text (and by extension the male author himself) is of feminist interest only in relation to women (and, until recently, only the strikingly, almost parodically misogynist texts were considered useful for such purposes). Another approach to male authors, however, tries to discover covert feminist sympathies. Hence a given author—Hemingway, for example—may be attacked for his male supremacism or valued for his sympathetic representations of women under patriarchy, according to the particular feminist reading.

Therefore, for academic feminists—those who study women within various disciplinary practices and who come together under the rubric of "Women's Studies"—to consider gender in relation to biologically sexed men is both logical and, for some projects, necessary. To discuss gender as though it pertained to women only is inadvertently to replicate the dangerous cultural fiction that men are not gendered, that they are the disembodied mentality of the human while women are irrevocably embodied in their biological sex: as Beauvoir put it, men equal the transcendent, women the immanent. Feminism, in going beyond women to query the concept of the transcendent male, also queries claims central to our traditional way of teaching literature and justifying that teaching: claims that literature is important because it contains themes, that there is a hierarchy of themes from the local and parochial to the "universal," and that literature containing "universal" themes is the most valuable. Feminism proposes that the concept of the "universal" theme is a delusion and implies that literature, and the teaching of literature, need some other justification. At the same time, it asks us to look again at the specific strategies that critics and teachers have used to elevate particular works to the status of masterpieces, and it makes ludicrously evident the masculine bias of traditional literary canons.[5] It is perhaps a measure of the importance of these activities that feminism is constantly singled out as the greatest enemy of traditional humanism; whereas, it could be argued— I would want to argue—that feminism represents a logical and inevitable expansion of humanistic principles.

Thus feminist studies have something to gain (though perhaps also something to lose) from an enlargement of their focus to include gender effect per se. To the extent, in fact, that inequities or differences between the genders form the basis of any feminist's argument, she actually cannot confine herself to the study of women since she will then have no grounds to assert the existence of whatever difference it is she wishes to analyze or alter.

While feminist pedagogical activities have, in the view of many, "made decisive and permanent changes in the way literature is studied," they also point to unfinished business and disclose boundaries of their own.[6] One such boundary is the limit of gender itself as an explanatory category. Gender is only one of many factors that constitute individuals and their interior lives, and it is an assumption rather than a certainty that it is the most important of them. Feminism per se does not require that gender be the most important factor; feminism is ultimately a practical decision about where to direct one's limited energies and powers in the effort to make a more livable world.

Additionally, gender is a concept, a social norm, imperfectly transmitted at best, so that most particular individuals will only approximate it. Women's and men's relation to their assigned social gender can only be partial. Moreover, though for every time, place, and social stratum there are two and only two gender norms—that is what gender is all about— these vary in history and across class, ethnic, and national lines. Therefore, uninstructed attempts to read any particular man or woman by means of a particular gender code may be far off the mark.

Moreover, with whatever degree of success socialization manages to control experience and shape behavior, it succeeds far less in its attempts to control subjectivity, where writing originates. Conversely, subjectivity is not a good tool for recognizing oneself as the product of social, economic, and political forces; it is the nature of subjectivity to experience oneself as a source, not as an effect. Therefore, the fit between any particular woman writer and the gender taken as a whole is always at best partial, even when—perhaps especially when—a writer offers herself as representative of her gender.

A second boundary involves the fact that feminist teachers of literature are teachers, necessarily conveying perceptions within the classroom setting and the conventions of teaching literature. College literature is an institutionally defined subject whose conventions remain—as the examples which follow are meant to suggest—largely unexamined "second nature" to even the most dedicated of feminist teachers.[7] These unexamined settings and conventions may be necessary to achieve our aims, which means that our aims may be internally conflicted. For a long time the literature classroom has been the place where one produces interpretations, interpretations which, it is anticipated, undergraduate students would not have been capable of producing on their own. The feminist teacher has no more reason than any other teacher to expect an unguided student to see what the teacher sees in the text. In fact, students unfamiliar with feminist approaches to literature are apt to find the interpretive strategies of a feminist teacher strange, perhaps counterintuitive. As several critics have observed in other contexts, "reading like a woman," by which the feminist really means "reading like a feminist woman," is an acquired skill even for women.[8]

And since different feminisms may lead to different interpretations of the same literary work, since (for example) a particular work may be read either as resisting or succumbing to patriarchy, the feminist teacher carrying out her objectives may find herself imposing an interpretation on her students. Such an activity requires her to interpret the students as defective readers and then to reconstruct them as the kind of reader required by her kind of feminism. It is this possibility, indeed probability, that the two examples developed at length below are meant to investigate.

My first example, which involves women readers only, shows how a teacher who constructs "a" woman reader may have to override the female subjectivities from which this construction is, presumably, derived. The event is a faculty colloquium on theories of the woman reader held on my campus in December 1986. Everyone attending agrees that, whether male or female, readers demand pleasure; at issue therefore are questions of whether, and how, women might read various specific works pleasurably. The worrisome problem for most at this psychoanalytically weighted meeting rises from the presumption that literary works are structured by male psychological imperatives and convey a male thematics, so that women can find pleasure in them only by assuming the male stance (what feminist film critics in particular call the position of the transvestite) or by accepting and transvaluing a relegation to the position of the narcissist-masochist, delighting in being made the object of oppressive, even murderous, attention, as, for example, in the films of Alfred Hitchcock.[9]

Traditional "women's" texts seem to offer no alternative, because in a system of unexamined gender inequalities—as ours has until recently been and still largely remains—such writing will reflect only the dominant value system and, by reflection, seem to substantiate it. No hope here, except for a future in which an as yet unimaginable sort of woman's writing is to be created. Such reasoning leads to the conclusion that a woman's reading pleasure in any patriarchal society must be a product of false consciousness—that is, of one's having been successfully indoctrinated in ideas hostile to one's true interests. It leaves the teacher with the thankless task of instructing women students in the displeasures of the text.

Evidently this task involves denying and overriding the testimony of women readers themselves. The project contains the powerful, unexamined assumption that there is "a" way of reading proper to women, which it is the job of feminist literary theory and criticism to find and of feminist teachers to implement. This assumption accounts for the neglect, at this gathering, of texts like those that "real" women readers—that is, non-academic women—choose to read, when they do read.[10] A focus on texts typically found in English and American literature courses, and a concern with how properly to read them, revealed that by "women readers" this colloquium actually meant women *student* readers, women dealing with assigned texts to which they might respond inappropriately if left unguided, whether by failing to enjoy feminist texts or by taking pleasure in works that reinforce traditional patterns of male-female relationships. The woman student reader implied here is thus the reconstructed woman student who reads in the manner of her teacher. Ultimately, then, this gathering was about *teachers*.

This approach correctly understands that no mere expansion of the canon, in and of itself, can guarantee any particular kind of reading. The expanded canon is a potential that can be implemented in a variety of ways. The existence of a broader canon can guarantee, to be sure—and this is no small thing—that students of the future need not perceive "literature" as a fixed, given, eternal storehouse of works created entirely by men. An American literature anthology that includes works by Margaret Fuller and Elizabeth Stoddard and Harriet Beecher Stowe as well as Henry David Thoreau and Ralph Waldo Emerson clearly creates a teachers' tool for presenting students with a more diverse literary history than the reductive "eight major authors" textbooks of yesteryear. But this is literary history; in the literature class that is about interpretation, about doing things with and to texts, literary history is only the inert background against which specific literary works are incarnated in the teacher's readings. At the moment that the feminist teacher's readings become the content of the course, the woman student is in precisely the same relationship to that teacher as she stands to any other teacher. As feminism becomes another variety of interpretation, the feminist is overriden by the teacher.

Associating women with pleasure is deeply inscribed in the ideologies of Western cultures (perhaps non-Western as well), and implicates us in a far-reaching system of invidious oppositions wherein terms associated with the female are always devalued. "Pleasure" is set over against "duty" or "virtue." This configuration exists in a powerful historical line antedating Virgil and continuing to Roland Barthes and Jacques Derrida. (By appropriating the Barthian/Derridean term "jouissance," some literary feminists have even planted it in the heart of feminist theory.[11]) To these dualisms are added "body" and "mind," "populace" and "elite," "retrogression" and "progress," "delusion" and "enlightenment," "youth" and "maturity," and (since the nineteenth century) "popular culture" and "high art."[12]

A thinker who wants to rescue a denigrated term must detach it from the female. The writer who would celebrate the body associates it with male prowess and stresses female weakness. If popular culture is the critic's domain, he points out that the field is dominated by male display. To recuperate pleasure, he calls women prigs. (Priggishness is especially in evidence when women fail to derive pleasure from manifestly misogynist, often scatological texts.) But never, under any circumstances, does he deploy a dualism that associates mind with the female, because, for thinkers, mind is the most valuable term. The critical dualism in literary academe, then, is that between mind and pleasure, or between intellectual and sensual pleasure. Interpretive analytic procedures deliberately distance the student from immediate reading pleasure by conceiving of texts as coded artifacts decipherable only through the acquisition of difficult techniques. Pleasure becomes the manipulation of the text into an interpretation.

Since the future of literature lies in the classroom, these dichotomies would be pernicious for their simplification of literature itself, even if they did not also have an effect on how actual gendered human beings are treated. The elevation of interpretation as "the" only appropriate reader activity means the triumph of a term imagined to be masculine; it is therefore deeply implicated in establishment attempts to define and secure literary study and literary production as masculine preserves.[13]

A first response to this dilemma might be to restructure the classroom so that power is less concentrated in the figure of the teacher, thereby to counteract the inadvertent effects of her expectations.[14] Attempts to dismantle the teacher's role have been undertaken by a variety of educational liberationist movements. Almost none of the pedagogical innovations that flourished between the late 1960s and mid-1970s has survived the pressures of the institutions within which they were allowed to develop, not only because institutional inertia is both powerful and co-optive but also because teaching cannot be other than an intervention.

An imbalance of power in the form of an imbalance of knowledge is what makes teaching necessary.

The issue of power is assuredly among the most difficult that feminists face. Power is most often experienced as oppression, and hence the desire for it is frequently disavowed. Yet, insofar as power is the energy and control that get things done, it is not only an ineluctable dimension of any situation, it is something that feminists require. I take it that whenever there is teaching, there is a power relationship; the question is what is produced by and through that relation. Equalization of power is not to be achieved except by the equalization of knowledge, which is not to be arrived at except by the teacher's effective transmitting of knowledge to the student, and this typically has not occurred—if it occurs at all—until the course is over. One problem then is how to empower students in a situation where the ultimate power must remain with the teacher; a second problem is what comprises knowledge in the literature classroom. A possible solution to both problems, it seems to me, is for the feminist teacher to relinquish her interpretation. Or, at least, to hold it more lightly.

We all know that there are writers or works whose blatant sexism, once highlighted, can galvanize even the most complacent victim of false consciousness, and at the colloquium which forms my occasion here—and to which I now return—the chief exhibit of this sort was D. H. Lawrence. According to one who spoke on behalf of a woman unfortunate enough to find herself reading *Lady Chatterley's Lover,* the novel was so thoroughly contaminated by sexism that no woman could possibly derive pleasure of any sort from it. Even the fallback position of female masochist was denied, because the heroine gets what she wants during most of the book as well as at the conclusion.

We were asked therefore to think about this ludicrous conclusion—or rather, asked to assent to the proposition that the conclusion was so ludicrous as to remove the book from any serious consideration as a candidate for female pleasure. The rhetorical conjunction of the word *serious* with the word *pleasure* seemed to me to raise a possibility that the speaker was not confronting—the possibility that she was less interested in pleasure than she thought, was even, perhaps, suspicious of pleasure. An odd position for a speaker devoting herself to the pleasures of the text.

Catching myself thinking these thoughts, I noted that I was evolving, in response to the discourse, into a resisting reader[15]—not, alas, resisting D. H. Lawrence, but resisting a feminist resisting Lawrence. It occurred to me to wonder about my own readings of *Lady Chatterley's Lover.* An inexperienced fifteen-year-old when I read it for the first time, I found it, unquestionably, sexually exciting beyond anything I had ever encountered. Along with several high school friends, I pored over the explicit scenes, which combined for me, in exactly the right proportions, descriptions of the physical with a heady romanticism conveyed in what struck me at the time as wonderful writing. By situating the sexual passages in a love story and describing them in "literary" language, Lawrence created a safe space for a teenaged female to enjoy the erotic. This adolescent reading of *Lady Chatterley's Lover* was not gender aberrant for my time and social class (since the book was being passed around from friend to friend, and all testified to its delightful effect); nor is it now. For, now that video recorders have led to the increasing production of pornographic films for showing at home to heterosexual couples, to women as well as men, filmmakers are finding that they must situate the repetitious, organ-centered moments of traditional male pornography within a romantic story line that decouples sex from violence; pay more attention to setting, character development, and human emotion; and put more "art" into the films. Which is what D. H. Lawrence did in his novel.

That female-centered heterosexual pornography takes this form means that one common idea about gender difference between women's and men's texts is probably wrong. I refer to the frequently encountered feminist belief that all conventional, or "classical," texts are structurally male; that traditional Aristotelian narrativity—with beginnings, rising action, middles, climaxes, ends, and agents who are characters—is uncongenial to women because we are suited by nature or culture to produce and enjoy open, repetitive, static, or circular structures. It appears indeed that it is men who like repetitious, static pornography. Thus, we must question the division of pleasure into two types, one for each gender—a division I have already objected to on theoretical grounds. One might suggest that association of the nonlinear with women is a simplistic product of the very structures of thought that one wishes to escape. In fact, even to define Aristotelian structures as male and therefore antagonistic to women, and then to develop the utopian story of eventually triumphing over them through the creation, after struggle, of a truly woman-centered literature, is actually to cast the issue in Aristotelian terms. Story, then, is a basic human way of making structure that transcends gender. Women readers as well as men will recognize that I have paused in my story to make this important point.

To return now to that story: it was clear that my first reading of *Lady Chatterley's Lover* was immensely pleasurable. Why should I deny this or apologize for it? When next I read *Lady Chatterley's Lover* I was a graduate student in my early twenties, preparing for Ph.D. preliminary examinations. My aim was to fit the novel into Lawrence's development.

Comparing it to works like *The Rainbow* and *Women in Love*, I identified it as the moment when Lawrence's "realism"—that is, his attention to complexity, specificity, and unpredictability of character—was giving way to a quasi-fascist populism making intellectuals a target by representing them as aristocracy. A nasty strategy, given the middle-class or working-class origins of most intellectuals throughout history. I "read" *Lady Chatterley's Lover*, then, as incipient right-wing political allegory, as the point when (for my taste) Lawrence's work began to decline. Though I was hardly seeking pleasure in the novel, I certainly derived satisfaction from "mastering" an uncongenial text, thereby escaping Lawrence's designs on me.

These designs on me, however, seemed to have less to do with my being a woman than with my being or becoming an intellectual. In fact, Lawrence's use of Connie's choice as the sign of worth seemed to elevate her status. In my first reading, her choice had appeared to designate the worthier man; it was expanded now to ratify the worthier cause. And, though diminished and intellectualized, the book's earlier sexual power was not entirely absent for me in this second reading. As a respectable graduate student properly married to another respectable graduate student, I was reminded by the book of certain brief dalliances with appealing young men who were, for various reasons, entirely "unsuitable" for a serious young woman like myself. If, in the first reading, *Lady Chatterley's Lover* had been a perfect instance of female pornography, it had now become a perfect instance of a female escape fantasy, in which the impossible romance is safely realized within the covers of a book that ends before the actual consequences of running away with the wrong man begin.

I want to emphasize the note of safety in both these readings. In the first instance, I was provided a safe space to enjoy the erotic; in the second, to enjoy alternative romances. At least one problem with the approach of the speaker at this gathering, then, could be understood as its negation of the fantasy component of literature.

This second reading of *Lady Chatterley's Lover* was also my last. Lawrence's writing now seems shrill and clumsy; his pontificating tedious; his social programs dangerous; his ignorance immense. I rejoice that, as an Americanist, I have no responsibility to teach him. But to follow the speaker's argument, I attempted an imaginary reading of *Lady Chatterley's Lover*. The middle-aged woman I now am, veteran of feminism and many other life events, viewed with interest the spectacle of a novel with a female protagonist whose chief helper (to use Proppian terminology)[16] is characterized affirmatively by attributing to him the ability and desire to give sexual pleasure to a woman.

One might choose to read the stress on Mellors's sexuality biographically, as evidence of Lawrence's defensive insecurity in his relationship with a woman more sexually experienced than he. Or one might refer it to a socially asymmetric world outside the novel—the reader's world wherein women's provision of pleasure to men is the norm, men's to women exceptional. Either way, it seemed significant that Mellors seeks the approval of one woman only, displaying himself as sexual object within a scenario of fidelity.

To pursue this line: *Lady Chatterley's Lover* might be taken as a novel whose main male character is secondary to a woman from whose point of view the male is seen. This male has, as chief attributes: a desire to pledge himself to one woman; the will and ability to give sexual pleasure to that woman; and a readiness to display himself as sexual object for her approval. (True, he talks a lot, but his talk is part of his sexual display. Charlotte Brontë and a host of other women writers have made clear how appealing to bookish women is the scenario of the male teacher submitting to the woman student. And only bookish women, one assumes, would be reading work by D. H. Lawrence.) Mellors, then, might be a male character who is configured solely with reference to the woman's desire. This makes the novel one that reverses the traditional social positions of male and female. One could read it as Utopian fantasy or escapist daydream. One might also search for moments in "real life" that permit a reversal of the norms of sexual politics, allotting power to the woman and requiring the man to display himself as the object of her possible choice. Of course such moments exist in pockets of Western (and perhaps other) cultures: they are called courtship.

Lady Chatterley's Lover then might be named a comedy of courtship. And if, during courtship, the positions of male and female are (temporarily) reversed, it can only be that, in a novel about courtship presented from the woman's point of view, the reader positions are also reversed, which means that the implied reader of this novel is a woman. Then, one hazards, the novel itself enacts the courting of a woman reader by means of a male heterosexual display. Lawrence, in sum, is wooing women readers. In my reverie I could easily imagine using this perception (if it were confirmed by a careful rereading of the novel) to initiate a variety of classroom discussions in which formalism, feminism, and historicism— does courtship of this sort exist any longer among our youth?—might all be brought together.

Returning at this point from my meditative excursion, I reencountered the speaker in the process of iterating her insistence that, absolutely, no woman could derive pleasure of any kind whatsoever from this book. It was not difficult now to see why she took this position. She was urging her women auditors to resist the seductions of the text because its promises did not fit the realities of a hard world. Women were being asked to bring their extra-textual knowledge of courtship as fraud to their reading and to condemn the book for its lack of "realism." Precisely because *Lady Chatterley's Lover* did *not* work as a "traditional" classic narrative allowing women only the reader positions of transvestite or masochist, and precisely because it gave the reading woman, for the duration of her reading, a power that in "real life" she has only during the brief deception of courtship, the book was deemed particularly dangerous. It was the task of a feminist teacher to uncover the deadly hook beneath the beguiling surface, to create distrustful, resisting readers.

As a member of the audience at this presentation, I was a target for this speaker. I could, of course, recognize and understand her didactic motives. She was the teacher as rescuer, a crusader arming the defenseless innocent against the aggressive sallies of the immoral text. Her stance was, simply, that of Victorian moral realism. This is a common pedagogical position, though until recently not deployed against "canonical" texts; in fact, canonical texts, historically, have been chosen in some large measure for their ability to counteract the dangerous wiles of popular literature. Indeed, in my view the very idea of a canon, the sense of a need for it, has risen historically as part of the campaign to organize, routinize, scrutinize, and *school* the behavior of marginal populations.[17] What is aimed for here is both to rupture the blissful connection between reader and text, and also to obliterate the reader's memory of her previous pleasure by enforcing a new, unpleasurable interpretation. The aim is to create, through interpretation, a new kind of person. For the feminist, it is to create a new kind of woman. In saying that no woman could take pleasure from *Lady Chatterley's Lover*, the speaker was instructing her audience in womanhood.

But wasn't that previous, unschooled reader also a woman? Wasn't I, occupying the student position in this event, actually a plurality of women, producing a plurality of readings, no one either more right or more wrong than any other, each exactly congruent with the moment of my life that called it forth? And, too, didn't the very intensity of the speaker's insistence that no woman could take pleasure from *Lady Chatterley's Lover* betray the real intention: to make women renounce the unenlightened pleasure they *had* taken from the book? That is, did not her very position call for a prior pleasure as its ground?

Deferring to the speaker's seriousness, I decided not to ask these questions at that time. And therefore, acquiescing to the force of a presentation informing me that I had erred in enjoying *Lady Chatterley's Lover*, I became a silenced woman. And this is what happens to women students all the time. The silenced, perhaps resisting—but how are we to know?—readers are after all typical. Are they more silenced, or less silenced, in the classroom of a woman teacher? Of a feminist teacher? My point is really not to criticize the particular woman who was occupying the teacher's position, but to underscore how the position of certified interpreter is a political position, constraining those who occupy it in a manner that overrides their gender.

In a recently published essay, Robert Scholes writes that "more than any other critical approach feminism has forced us to see the folly of thinking about reading in terms of a Transcendental subject: the ideal reader reading a text that is the same for all. This does not happen. Readers are constituted differently and different readers perceive different features of the same texts."[18] Little is gained by substituting two gendered Transcendental readers for the one that we had before.

I turn from this example of a teacher constructing (unsuccessfully, in my case) a Transcendental, resisting, woman reader to an example of a teacher constructing two gendered Transcendental readers. In a fascinating essay called "Gender and Reading," Elizabeth A. Flynn reports on differences between men and women students writing about three short stories—James Joyce's "Araby," Ernest Hemingway's "Hills like White Elephants," and Virginia Woolf's "Kew Gardens."[19] Flynn's thesis is that men and women read (i.e., interpret) differently in ways that accord with gender socialization: men are aggressive, women are cooperative.

In order to analyze her student's responses Flynn develops theoretical descriptions of three kinds of reading, two bad and one good. She names one bad kind "dominant" or "resisting": the reader rejects the alien text "and so remains essentially unchanged by the reading experience." This kind of reading, she finds, is unique to the men in her sample. A second kind of bad reading is called "submissive": here "the text overpowers the reader and so eliminates the reader's powers of discernment." This sort of reading is produced by both men and women—indeed, by a majority of them. A third response in which "reader and text interact with a degree of mutuality" (268) is called "interactive" and represents Flynn's ideal, an ideal that she finds more often attained by the women in her sample than the men. On the basis of these findings, Flynn proposes that men tend to be dominant readers and that women tend to be better readers than men. This is because women possess "a willingness to listen, a sensitivity to emotional nuance, an ability to empathize with and yet judge."[20]

It is difficult to use this experiment to draw such conclusions (and Flynn presents them merely as hypotheses) since the experimenter already knew the genders of the authors and of her respondents as she read and interpreted.[21] The hypotheses are also put in question because differences among the men's responses are greater than any differences between the two genders; men turn up as all three kinds of readers while women do not. "Scientifically" speaking, when differences within a group are greater than differences between two groups, no particular difference between the two groups is significant. If men as a group are much more various in their readings than women as a group, the significant finding with respect to "difference" might be that men are, feel free to be, more "individualistic" readers than women. That Flynn neglects the finding of variability and concentrates on her interpretation of men as resisting readers is probably attributable to the system of gender differences with which she approaches her material. In brief, the experiment was motivated by the *desire* to find two kinds of response which would fall out along stereotypical gender lines.

Note that the colloquium speaker in my first example has a different idea from this teacher about what constitutes a good reader. The anti-Lawrentian's ideal is the very resisting reader rejected by Flynn. Too, while the opponent of *Lady Chatterley's Lover* imagines that novel as an aggressive male from whom a female reader could only protect herself by counteraggression, Flynn appears to imagine her stories as distressed clients needing female ministrations. In effect, these two teachers implement the two different feminist goals—allowing women to act like men, praising traditional female qualities.

The interpretive work that the teacher performed as she decided how to classify particular responses bears investigating. Following Iser rather than Bakhtin, she defines a good interactive reading as one that develops a "consistent pattern of meaning from among the seemingly incompatible stimuli" present in the work; "meaning is finally achieved only when tensions are resolved."[22] In other words, a good reading is an interpretation, a thematization of the story organizing it as a single expository voice. A student who declines to advance an interpretation, or who finds elements of a story to be unassimilable to a single reading, is characterized as a "dominant" reader who rejects the text.

Here is how this teacher reads "Hills like White Elephants." The story "focuses on a conversation between an American man and a young woman" which is "tense" because the couple are in conflict. The conflict "is resolved through the young woman's denial of her feelings and the man's assertion of his will." She goes on to say that "this is a story, then, about female vulnerability and defeat. The imagery suggests that the woman's position is life-affirming and that renewal is possible only through her victory over the man. The ending of the story, though, suggests that she is powerless to change the nature of the relationship" (276–77).

This is certainly not a bad reading of the story, although its assumption that the situation applies to all men and women makes "Hills like White Elephants" into an allegory of gender. One can imagine alternative readings, well argued and well documented. If more men than women did *not* produce this particular interpretation—if more men than women declined to produce interpretations altogether—the explanation could as well lie in the interactions between students and teacher as in that between students and text. For various reasons the women might have been more attentive to the teacher's signals and have produced, not a reading of the story, but a reading of the teacher: the Clever Hans phenomenon. For it is of course the teacher who decided that reading "Hills like White Elephants" well is equivalent to producing the particular reading she has set forth. It could be, then, that our rejecting student is rejecting either the call for interpretation as the appropriate reading activity, or the expectation that a good reading is one that makes unitary sense of every element in a text, or the one particular interpretation that, to the teacher, amounts to the best reading. The gender difference here might be that men are more willing to risk the teacher's displeasure—but this in turn could be a situational matter, since the teacher was a female. And a feminist.

Interestingly, the student most hostile to the man in "Hills like White Elephants" is a male. The teacher calls his response "overly judgmental." He uses two items—the man's detailed knowledge of abortion procedure and the numerous hotel tags on his luggage—as grounds for a speculation that the man is an irresponsible playboy. One might say that he takes the character as a specific individual rather than as an allegorical male. A different teacher might praise this response for its circumstantial observations rather than criticize the student's judgmental attitude toward the character. Indeed, if the underlying structure of "classical" fiction pits a protagonist against an antagonist, this student might be thought of as going about his reading in just the right interactive way—looking for the writer's clues about whose side he's to take. A different teacher might agree that the depiction of the male character is highly critical and be pleased that the student recognizes this in a story by a writer often thought to be a prototypical man's man.

Consistent with the teacher's emphasis on reading as equivalent to deciphering meaning and figuring out the right interpretation, Flynn put all responses that acknowledged difficulties with reading the stories in the category of "resisting." And it is only men who said that they find the stories hard to read. To the teacher this means that the women are better readers than the men. But since, in fact, all three stories *are* difficult when compared to the kind of fiction that the non-major undergraduate student is likely to know, one might counter that the men are more honest readers than the women—or, more precisely, that they are more honest responders.

Here is one male student's response to "Hills like White Elephants": "My impression of the story was that it wasn't a story at all. It was just a short conversation between two people. The story consisted of just a couple of pages filled with quotes. . . . The story just starts right up and doesn't tell anything about who the people are or about what is going on. I had to read through the story a couple of times just to figure out what they were talking about. Nothing was said right out in the open about getting an abortion" (277).

To this teacher, the student "rejected the story because he could not understand it. The text, for him, was 'just a couple of pages filled with quotes' " (277–78). Actually the student doesn't say that this is what the story "was," but rather what it "consisted of," and one could maintain that he is correct. He has approached the story as a construct as well as a transparent medium for the conveying of meanings, has noted its unconventional brevity and its virtually exclusive reliance on dialogue. Though lacking a technical vocabulary, he points toward the absence of the omniscient narrator, the omission of a description of the setting, the lack of capsule biographies for the characters, the reliance on dialogue, and the use of dialogue that is particularly unrevealing. In other words, he senses that "Hills like White Elephants" omits almost all the aid that a traditional narrator gives a reader. One could argue that a response to this story that recognizes its formally innovative features is interactive with it. Or, one could argue that the reader response to a writer who omits traditional reader aids *should* be resistant. The avant-garde artist wants to distress the bourgeois; Hemingway is, or was, an avant-garde writer.

Now, what is it that makes the women students ignore (or at least fail to write about) the experimental craft of "Hills like White Elephants" and focus on relationships? As in this example: "typically, in the end, the male's dominant views have come through. She agrees to have the abortion and says that there is nothing wrong. Unfortunately this relationship will probably end because conflicts are not resolved. To have a meaningful relationship, they must be more open" (281).[23] It could be that the women are more experienced readers than the men, so that Hemingway's formal innovations no longer presented difficulty to them and have therefore become invisible. If so, the difference discovered might be linked to gender, although not by virtue of the different character traits that Flynn attributes to women and men. Women might be better readers than men—if, indeed, theirs *is* a better reading—because they read more. Then the question would be: why do women read more? Again, though, the women might have been more hesitant to admit difficulties because they are more concerned with the teacher's good opinion than the men. Perhaps the women readers, even in their discursive volubility, have been silenced.

Do I have an easy solution, or even a difficult one, to the dilemmas I describe here? No voluntary disempowerment of the teacher, per se, will be of much use. Yet, to teach a wide range of works in a variety of ways, to rethink the dominance of interpretive activity in the classroom, to understand that all interpretations are contingent and none are correct, may allow a teacher to tap into the possibilities that feminism suggests. Above all, perhaps, the teacher needs to encourage her women students to say what she does not expect them to say and perhaps would rather not hear. Otherwise, the only real reader in the class will be the teacher, whether she is a feminist or not.

NOTES

1. See Linda Gordon, "What's New in Women's History," *Feminist Studies/Critical Studies*, ed. Teresa de Lauretis (Bloomington: Indiana UP, 1986) 20–30.

2. I use feminine pronouns because there are very few male feminists and because, after all, feminism is about women. It is the difficulties of women teachers who are feminists as we try to bring about feminist goals in the literature classroom that concern me. As the title of my essay means to suggest, the incarnation of the teacher in a woman feminist creates part of her problem.

3. See Peggy Kamuf, "Writing like a Woman," in *Women and Language in Literature and Society*, ed. Sally McConnell-Ginet, Ruth Borker, and Nelly Furman (New York: Praeger, 1980) 284–99.

4. The questions of what a specifically female writing might look like, whether it has yet to come into existence, and whether it is in fact confined to the productions of biological females, are central in the deliberations of academic feminist literary theory, which has become inextricably involved with what is called—on this side of the Atlantic—French feminism and accordingly with principles of Lacanian psychoanalysis. See Toril Moi, *Sexual/Textual Politics: Feminist Literary Theory* (New York: Methuen, 1985), and Alice Jardine, *Gynesis: Configurations of Women and Modernity* (Ithaca: Cornell UP, 1985). Jardine's study, which follows Julia Kristeva's lead, makes such male modernists as James Joyce into paradigmatic authors of "écriture feminine."

5. See Nina Baym, "Melodramas of Beset Manhood: How Theories of American Literature Exclude Women Authors," in *The New Feminist Criticism*, ed. Elaine Showalter (New York: Pantheon, 1985) 63–80; and Paul Lauter, "Race and Gender in the Shaping of the American Literature Canon: A Case Study from the Twenties," *Feminist Studies* 9 (1983): 453–65.

6. J. Hillis Miller, "Presidential Address 1986: The Triumph of Theory, the

Resistance to Reading, and the Question of the Material Base," *PMLA* 102 (1987): 285.

7. See Gerald Graff, *Professing Literature* (Chicago: U of Chicago P, 1987).

8. E.g., Elaine Showalter, "Critical Cross-Dressing: Male Feminists and the Woman of the Year," in *Men in Feminism*, ed. Alice Jardine and Paul Smith (New York: Methuen, 1987) 116–32; and Jonathan Culler, *On Deconstruction* (Ithaca: Cornell UP, 1982) 43–64.

9. The most important statement of this position is Laura Mulvey, "Visual Pleasure and Narrative Cinema," *Screen* 16 (1975): 6–18.

10. See Tania Modleski, *Loving with a Vengence: Mass-Produced Fantasies for Women* (Hamden: Archon, 1982); Janice A. Radway, *Reading the Romance: Women, Patriarchy, and Popular Literature* (Chapel Hill: U of North Carolina P, 1984); Madonna Miner, *Insatiable Appetites: Twentieth-Century American Women's Bestsellers* (Westport: Greenwood P, 1984); Kay Mussell, *Fantasy and Reconciliation: Contemporary Formulas of Women's Romance Fiction* (Westport: Greenwood P, 1984); Leslie W. Rabine, "Romance in the Age of Electronics: Harlequin Enterprises," *Feminist Studies* 11 (1985): 39–60. Since works designed for female mass consumption are constructed from evidence of what women like to read, they can be thought of as having in some sense been written by their women readers. But the cited studies exemplify the difficulty of understanding why women like these books. Of the group, only Radway has worked with "real" reader responses—that is, with responses provided by women who read these books for pleasure rather than by the critic herself, who has read them in pursuit of a thesis. But finally, like the other authors, she turns to some version of psychoanalytic theory for explanation. Such theory, by its very nature, presumes that women cannot really say why they like these books and also that there is within the culturally constructed women a "real" (i.e., noncultural) self tapped into during the reading process.

A different approach can be seen in Elizabeth Long, "Women, Reading, and Cultural Authority: Some Implications of the Audience Perspective in Cultural Studies," *American Quarterly* 38 (1986): 591–612.

Perhaps, however, the question that literary critics can answer is not why people read, but how they read.

11. See Elaine Marks and Isabelle de Courtivron, eds., *New French Feminisms* (Amherst: U of Massachusetts P, 1980). The idea that pleasure for a male consists of mastery and consumption of the object, while for a female it consists in oceanic submission to the power of the same object, represents another dualism in which the female is devalued. The dichotomy derives from crude distinctions between male and female sexual pleasure. Not only does this model assume that sexual pleasure is the only kind of pleasure that there is; it presents a caricature of human sexualities.

12. See Ann Douglas, *The Feminization of American Culture* (New York: Knopf, 1977); and Andreas Huyssen, "Mass Culture as Woman: Modernism's Other," in *Studies in Entertainment: Critical Approaches to Mass Culture*, ed. Tania Modleski (Bloomington: Indiana UP, 1986) 188–207.

13. I owe a great deal to Susan Sontag's classic essay, "Against Interpretation," although she did not identify her approach as feminist (New York: Dell, 1966).

14. A good description of this goal is Constance Penley's "Teaching in Your Sleep," *Theory in the Classroom*, ed. Cary Nelson (Urbana: U of Illinois P, 1986) 129–48.

15. The original and still best formulation of this concept is to be found in Judith Fetterley, *The Resisting Reader: A Feminist Approach to American Fiction* (Bloomington: Indiana UP, 1978).

16. See Vladimir Propp, *The Morphology of the Folktale*, 2nd ed. (Austin: U of Texas P, 1968).

17. See Nina Baym, *Novels, Readers and Reviewers: Responses to Fiction in Antebellum America* (Ithaca: Cornell UP, 1984).

18. Robert Scholes, "Reading like a Man," in *Men in Feminism*, ed. Jardine and Smith, 206.

19. Elizabeth A. Flynn, "Gender and Reading," in *Gender and Reading*, ed. Elizabeth A. Flynn and Patrocinio P. Schweickart (Baltimore: Johns Hopkins UP, 1986) 267–88. Since I quote only some of Flynn's examples, I urge the reader of this essay to think of "Flynn" in my text as a personage constructed *by* my text.

20. Ibid., 286. Two theoretical books on which academic literary feminists have depended for accounts of gender difference are Nancy Chodorow, *The Reproduction of Mothering* (Berkeley: U of California P, 1987), and Carol Gilligan, *In a Different Voice: Psychological Theory and Women's Development* (Cambridge: Harvard UP, 1982). An opposing view can be found in Anne Fausto-Sterling, *Myths of Gender: Biological Theories about Women and Men* (New York: Basic Books, 1985). The burden of several essays in Catharine A. MacKinnon's *Feminism Unmodified* (Cambridge: Harvard UP, 1987) is that "a concept like difference is a conceptual tool of gender inequality" (9).

21. At the end of the spring semester 1989 I solicited anonymous evaluations from students in a large lecture course, an Introduction to American Literature. The hundred or so critiques I received ranged in length from a sentence to a long paragraph, and in no case (except where one respondent mentioned that she was a woman) was I able to identify the writer's gender. None of the assessments were framed in putatively feminine rhetoric—but none of them were stereotypically masculine either. More than likely, if I had asked the writers to give information about their gender, I would then have "recognized" the gender in their answers. But: such recognition is as much a construction of gender as a reflection of it.

22. Flynn, "Gender and Reading," 270. The two narrative theorists contrasted here are Wolfgang Iser, *The Act of Reading: A Theory of Aesthetic Response* (Baltimore: Johns Hopkins UP, 1978), and M. M. Bakhtin, *The Dialogic Imagination* (Austin: U of Texas P, 1981).

23. The teacher approves this reading. But one might ask: from what perspective is the ending of this relationship "unfortunate"? how would being "more open" align the antithetical goals of the two participants? what does the student mean by "meaningful relationship"?

PATROCINIO P. SCHWEICKART

Reading, Teaching, and the Ethic of Care

The most rudimentary observations one can make about reading is that it is an activity involving a subject and an object; a human reader reads a text; the text is written in language; the activity of reading is concerned with meaning. But is meaning located in the text, *there* to be discovered or apprehended by the reader, or is it something that is produced by the reader? Does meaning refer to textual characteristics or to the experience and reactions of the reader? Whether one favors an objectivist (text-dominant) model, a subjectivist (reader-dominant) model, or some kind of "bi-active," "trans-active," or "inter-active" construction within this bi-polar conception, the principal theoretical problem appears to be one of determining the proper distribution of authority and activity between the objective characteristics of the text and the subjective interests and activity of the reader.

Recent developments dispute the adequacy of individualistic bi-polar models and promise to take the discussion beyond the objectivism/subjectivism impasse. David Bleich argues that the picture of reading as a one-to-one encounter between a reader and a text does not match what happens in reality. Certainly, there is individual private reading, but whatever attains the status of meaning and knowledge proceeds from what is shared with others. Citing research from a variety of disciplines ranging from philosophy of science to women's studies, Bleich argues that cognition is essentially intersubjective. "The pre-existence of intersubjectivity makes possible *both* the dialectic of object cognition and the dialogue that governs object cognition. Intersubjectivity is the framework that will explain the intermingling of the cognitive and the affective, and it signals the appearance of an epistemology that is far more suitable for the study of language than those [bi-polar individualistic models] that led to abstract formalisms, language games, paradox, and mystery."[1]

In a sense, the emphasis on intersubjectivity, which is promoted also by Stanley Fish's argument about the authority of interpretive communities and by Richard Rorty's neo-pragmatism, is a "natural" development once the recognition of subjectivity has rendered the idea of objective knowledge problematical, for while it assumes that relativity is the organizing problematic of life, it does not entail the epistemological paralysis of "anything goes" relativism. Given an intersubjective framework, communication becomes central, for it is the way through which individual ideas, feelings, perceptions, and opinions "pass muster" as knowledge.[2]

Now, if knowledge and meaning are social constructs and as such are functions of their concrete social context, it becomes important to observe that the theoretical tradition described above is dominated by (white) male voices. This means that the theories of reading and discourse produced in this tradition are gendered constructs, stemming from masculine subjectivities and from masculine perspectives on sociality. The crucial question becomes: what has been the effect of the exclusion of women on theories of reading? what difference would it make if women's distinctive subjectivites and social interests were fully incorporated in such theories?

While the shift from the individualistic model of traditional epistemology to the idea of knowledge as a social construct is certainly most welcome to feminists, I think it is important not to make the move too quickly. The conversion from an individualistic to an intersubjective and social model is in itself too abstract to clarify the significance of gender. But more important, androcentric perspectives and thought styles embodied in individualistic models pass easily into intersubjective models. Here I wish to reconsider the subject-object picture of reading in the hope of restoring concerns that have been set aside at the earliest stages of this theoretical construction. However, I have no interest in redeeming individualistic models; my discussion proceeds from the understanding that both text and reader are social entities and that the encounter between them is always conditioned by the social context in which it occurs.

The literent determines the story. If I choose to read *Romeo and Juliet* as a spiritualist tragedy . . . you or any jury of literary critics may ridicule me, but the *text* cannot stop me, if for no other reason than that words do not exert physical force, but I do. . . . I can choose to follow approved procedures for doing so, or I can be as wacky as I please. . . .

A story does not "cause" or even "limit" the responses to it. . . . The literent sets up a feedback loop. . . . I bring text schemata from previous literary experiences, from my historical or critical knowledge, my sense of human nature, my values, my preferences in language, my politics, my metabolism—I bring all these things to bear on the text, and the text feeds back to me what I bring to it either positively or not at all. It rewards my hypotheses or, so to speak, ignores them. That is all the text does, for always it is I who am in control. It is I who ask questions of the text and I who hear and interpret its answers. The text may change the payoffs on various fantasies, defenses, themes or expectations I bring to it, but that is all it does (and even then I decide what is good payoff and what is not).[4]

The dispute between objectivist and subjectivist theories turns on two normative issues, the issue of validity (or truth) and the issue of power. Although both camps phrase their arguments in terms of claims about what reading *is*, neither relies entirely on the force of factual evidence. Objectivists do not deny that, if the author of the above remarks, Norman Holland, is determined to be wacky, the text cannot stop him. What they claim is that the text authorizes certain readings and establishes criteria according to which some readings can legitimately be ruled out as wacky. The objectivist position does not hinge on what readers actually do but on what they ought to do: if we wish to read properly, then we must devote ourselves to apprehending the meaning authorized by the text. If we deny that there is a core "verbal meaning" objectively latent in the text, then, according to the objectivist argument, the notion of validity becomes meaningless. There would be no way of distinguishing appropriate from erroneous readings, competent readings from incompetent ones. And if one reading is good as another, then how are we to justify what we teach students? How are we to evaluate their interpretations of texts? Denying the existence of a meaning authorized by the text leads to relativism, which in turn undermines the status of literary studies as a discipline.

Subjectivists, in a sense, have the facts on their side. Readers do vary in the way they read the same text. Nonetheless, the appeal of the subjectivist position is also based in large measure on a normative argument. The advocacy of subjectivism generally goes hand in hand with a defense of the right of readers to read according to their own interests and perspectives. The subjectivist position confers value on reader response as a legitimate source of meaning and as a focus for critical inquiry.

One of the focal points of the subjectivist critique is the issue of power. Power, according to this argument, is behind the invocation of the authority of the text: to claim that the text supports this or that meaning and refutes others is only "moralistically [to] claim . . . that one's own objectification is more authoritative than someone else's."[5] The definition of validity in terms of textual criteria often masks authoritarian practices, and the subjectivist position appears by contrast to be more democratic, for it validates the freedom of individual readers and affirms the value of appreciating diverse points of views.

Feminists generally find the subjectivist position appealing—that is, they share the subjectivist critique of objectivism. But many feminists, myself among them, have reservations about the subjectivist position itself.[6] I do not think it adequately represents the way I and, I believe, other women relate to texts. Ludwig Fleck argues that a "thought collective" is characterized by a certain "thought style" and by a certain "mood," and these in turn condition the process by which the collective discriminates between what is valid and what is invalid.[7] Borrowing Fleck's terms, I would say that, in spite of its initial appeal, subjectivism is at odds with the characteristic thought style and mood of feminist theory.

So where does this leave me? I think objectivism is untenable, but I have serious misgivings about subjectivism. Simply adopting a middle ground will not do. As Jonathan Culler has pointed out, the various bi-active, trans-active, and inter-active models that have been offered within the current theoretical framework tend to collapse into either a monism of the text or a monism of the reader.[8] The theoretical framework is itself problematical. Eventually, gender will emerge as a key issue. However, in order to clarify some of the difficulties associated with the subjectivist position, it is useful at this point to take a detour through another area of concern, namely the pedagogical situation.

In the literature classroom, the reader-text relationship can be concretized as follows: the reader is a student, the text is literary, and the interaction is overseen by the professor. Let us take Holland's transactive model as exemplary of the subjectivist position.[9] According to this theory, a student will assimilate the text into her[10] "identity theme":

> We perceive a literary work in terms of the *expectations* we bring to this particular text (our notions of Dickens, for example . . .), [and in terms of] our characteristic expectations toward any other entity (our degree of trust in others, for example). As we admit the text to our mental processes, we shape and filter it through our characteristic patterns of *defense* and adaptation (projection, repression, identification, and the like). As part of those mental processes, we imbue the story with our characteristic clusters of wishes—our *fantasies*. As another part of those mental processes, we *transform* the text and the fantasy with which we endowed it into an experience of moral, intellectual, social, or aesthetic coherence. In short, we DEFT the text, recreating our identities through our own characteristic patterns of *d*efense, *e*xpectation, *f*antasy, and *t*ransformation (14).

Last semester a student in my "Science and Literature" class (a born-again Christian) read *all* the assigned texts (e.g., Shelley's *Frankenstein*, Wells's *The Time Machine*, Hersey's *Hiroshima*, Carson's *The Silent*

Spring, Orwell's *1984*, Piercy's *Woman on the Edge of Time*) in terms of the question of the existence of God and of our proper relation to "Him." This example (I'm sure others have encountered similar situations) corroborates Holland's theory that one reads "so as to achieve a new variation on [his] identity theme" (14). If I were persuaded by Holland's theory, I would not be so quick to dismiss the "god" interpretation of, say, *1984* as invalid or inadequate, and I would be uneasy about using my authority and my critical and rhetorical expertise to overpower my student into adopting my version of the meaning authorized by the text. According to Holland, the student has the right to use literature as an occasion to re-create his identity theme. In principle I have no right to impose on him the reading that I take to be valid (which in the end is only my re-creation of my identity theme). Indeed, Holland's theory (like other subjectivist theories) makes the position of the teacher problematical. Even so, I like the idea of reading literature as an occasion for self-re-creation and expression, and as part of the process of cultivating, nurturing, and elaborating one's identity. I am inclined to favor a theory that values the freedom of expression of students, even if this implies the need to rethink the discipline.

But suppose we vary the situation. Consider the case of a teacher reading a student paper. According to Holland, I will *necessarily* read my student's paper in terms of my own characteristic DEFT pattern, and I will use the paper as an occasion for the re-creation of my own identity theme. The theory says nothing about my responsibility regarding what my student was trying to do in his paper. Holland's assertions—"I can choose to follow approved procedures or I can be as wacky as I please"; "The text cannot stop me"; "It is I who am in control"—now sound ominous rather than beneficent. The authoritarian potential of a subjectivist theory of reading becomes apparent in the situation of a professor reading a student paper. If the student's paper does not "pay off" on the fantasies, defenses, expectations, and themes that the professor brings to it, then the professor has an adverse response to the paper, and according to the model, the student has no recourse. Since there is no way in principle to rule on the validity of a reader's response to a text, there is no way to rule on the validity of a professor's response to a student paper.[11]

But the problem is not just that Holland's model leaves a student defenseless against arbitrary grading (although this is troubling enough). A more serious problem, I think, is that it appears to make the role of a teacher impossible. A teacher is supposed to help the student to develop and to learn to express herself, or in Holland's terms, to appreciate, cultivate, and elaborate her own identity theme. But how can a teacher do this if she is deaf to any identity theme that is different from her own? The same concern for the student that made the self-centeredness of Holland's model so appealing when we were thinking of a student reading a literary text makes it problematical when applied to the situation of a teacher reading student papers. Moreover, on reflection we see other questionable normative implications. Subjectivist theories of reading silence the text. Do we really want to promote such a picture of reading among our students? Do we want them to develop into readers who can read and appreciate only texts that resonate with their own fantasies and expectations?

As we have seen, a literature class contains two reading situations. In the first, the readers are the members of the class (the students and the professor) and the text is a literary text. The text is an object, a book, one of innumerable mechanical reproductions bought and sold in the marketplace comparable, say, to a tube of toothpaste. At the same time, especially when it is a classic, a literary text has cultural prestige. It has the authority of tradition conferred upon it by the cultural institutions that form the context for the reading. Thus, the text appears to be both powerless and powerful. As black marks on paper, it is the passive component of the reading process, becoming meaningful only as a result of the subjective action of the reader. However, regarded as a prestigious cultural artifact, it becomes the dominant component: the reader becomes subject to its authority. In objectivist theories, the professor is the privileged reader: he determines which readings conform to the meaning of the text and which do not. Subjectivist theories democratize the situation: the professor becomes only one reader among many; he loses his prerogative (in principle, if not in practice) to enforce the authority of the text.

In the above analysis, the reader-text relation is taken to be a subject-object relation. However, it is important to keep in mind that the text is not a mere object, like a stone, but the objectification of a subject. Perhaps this is not so evident when we are dealing with something like *Romeo and Juliet*, for here the subjectivity of the author, who has been dead for centuries, is overwhelmed by the objectivity of the book. Moreover, it is not clear why Shakespeare's project should take precedence over that of the reader—in this case the student in a literature class. As subject, Shakespeare is truly absent. His interests can no longer be served or harmed by the reading process. But the student is present: his needs and his interests are at stake in his encounter with literature.

The status of the text as objectified subjectivity is more evident in the second reading situation that occurs in the literature classroom—namely, that of the professor reading a student paper. Here the text is not one of many mass-produced identical objects. The subjective presence of the student author overrides the objectivity of the text, and given the educational context, her needs are supposed to be a salient concern. The paper is not supposed to be an occasion for the re-creation of the identity of the professor, but part of a process whose goal is the development of the student's capacity to express herself. The professor's role is to foster the student's project.

Another feature that becomes evident in both pedagogical situations is the asymmetry of text and reader. In particular, there is an asymmetrical distribution of power and vulnerability. In the case of the student reading literature, the reader is vulnerable to the cultural authority of the text (that is, to the authority of the institution of literature). In the case of the professor reading a student paper, the text is vulnerable to the subjective power of the reader. In the first case, Holland's model is appealing because it mitigates the vulnerability of the student reader. In the second, it is questionable, because the implication that the professor-reader has the prerogative to take advantage of the vulnerability of the student text is at odds with the educational context.

The basic paradigm for theories of reading is that of a reader reading a literary (or similarly authoritative) text. Thus, when theories of reading are applied to the classroom, they generally address the first reading situation. I have never seen them applied to the second. While I do not think that the second reading situation is more basic than the first, I do think it odd that the situation of the professor reading a student paper should be beneath the notice of theories of reading. After all, such activity constitutes a sizeable portion of the professional reading that we (teachers of language and literature) do. I suspect that the elision of the (mundane) activity of reading and grading student papers is related to the obliviousness of theories of reading to their gendered origins.

Now suppose we perform the by now familiar operation of displacing our attention from the traditional center to the margins. Suppose we take the situation of the professor reading a student paper to be the paradigmatic reading situation. What theory of reading might we come up with? The immediacy of the subjectivity of the student author suggests an analogy with a speech situation: the (student) author speaks, the (professor) reader listens. Although this model is problematical, it is by no means implausible. I will use it, first, because it represents the reader-text relation as an intersubjective relation, and second, because it represents reading as involving two modalities of subjectivity—speaking and listening. These features match the two characteristics of the reading situation that we noted earlier: the status of the text as the objectification of a subject, and the asymmetrical relation between the reader and the text.[12]

Having set up the analogy between a reading and a speech situation, it seems that the next step should be to look at discourse theories to see how they might shed light on reading. However, when we look at current theories of discourse, we observe that they are based on the assumption that only *one* mode of subjectivity counts theoretically—that of speaking. A speech situation is generally defined as the interaction between speakers, and much of discourse theory is devoted to argument. Because argument has long been regarded as the principal mode of rational inquiry and critical decision-making, studies of argumentation are thought to be "fertile resources for understanding rationality, reasonableness, and how ideas pass muster as knowledge."[13] Some theorists go even further. According to Scott Jacobs and Sally Jackson: "A cursory inspection of the contents of ordinary conversation will quickly reveal the pervasiveness of argument. . . . [The possibility and use of argument] provide a basic condition of all conversational exchanges as we know them . . . whether manifest as an event or latent as an unexercised possibility, [argument] leaves its mark on whatever goes on in conversation."[14]

Jürgen Habermas is typical in assuming that argumentation is the paradigmatic form of rational discourse and the principal means of testing the validity of statements. He holds a consensus theory of truth: "In order to distinguish true from false statements I make reference to the judgment of others. . . . The condition of the truth of statements is the potential agreement of all others."[15] Habermas carefully distinguishes between *truth*, or *validity*, and *belief*. *Belief* is a subjective "certainty-experience," but a *validity* or *truth claim* is something that is meant to be tested intersubjectively. I *have* beliefs, prejudices, or presuppositions; but I *make* validity claims.

I vindicate my validity claims by persuading others to agree with me—that is, by winning arguments. Obviously, mere de facto consensus is not an acceptable warrant for truth. It must be stipulated further that agreement cannot be obtained through coercion, intimidation, deception, or suppression of contrary points of view. To be a warrant for truth, agreement must be freely given; the winning argument must emerge in a fair contest. Or to put it in Habermas's terms, the warrant for truth is agreement attained in an ideal speech situation where the outcome of the discussion is determined only by "the unforced force of the better argument." Essentially, an ideal speech situation is domination-free discourse. It satisfies the "universal symmetry requirement": the opportunity to select and employ speech acts must be uniformly distributed among the discourse participants, and there must not be any internal or external structures that impose nonreciprocal obligations on participants or allow some to dominate others. Habermas's theory of ideal discourse reflects the deeply held (Western) belief that free speech is essential for preserving truth.

For Habermas, as for other theorists of discourse, the norm is communicative interaction between two or more symmetrically positioned speakers. Membership in the discourse community entitles an individual equal access to the floor and commits him to respect the right of others to speak without interference. Of course, it is assumed that when one is not speaking, one is listening, and some theorists go so far as to identify rationality and reasonableness with the willingness to listen to others.[16] Nevertheless, listening is on the whole regarded as unproblematical and theoretically insignificant.

At this point, let me raise the issue of gender. Since the theories described above come from a tradition that is predominantly (white) male, they embody intuitions about discourse that arise out of masculine subjectivity and the intersubjectivity of man-to-man relations. According to Carol Gilligan, men think of morality and human relations in terms of an "ethic of rights."[17] Commenting on Gilligan's work, Annette Baier characterizes the masculine idea of morality as "finding workable traffic rules for self-assertors, so that they do not needlessly frustrate one another, and so that they could, if they choose, cooperate in more positive ways to mutual advantage."[18] A similar sensibility is discernible in the tendency in current discourse theories to view subjective action almost exclusively in terms of speech (the obvious form of self-assertion) and in the preoccupation with codifying (traffic) rules for argumentation.

Since this essay is about reading, not spoken discourse, it might be objected that the discussion above proves that we should not think of reading on the model of a speech situation. Because the reader (a subject) and the text (an object) are incommensurable, the relation between them is necessarily asymmetrical, and this is compromised by the usual picture of spoken discourse as a relationship between speaking subjects. In response, I would point out that current theories of reading, no less than theories of discourse, are imbued with the sensibility of an ethic of rights. This is evident in the preoccupation with the issues of partition (how do we distinguish what belongs objectively to the text and what has been produced by the reader?) and control (should the authority of the text take precedence over the subjective interests of the reader, or vice versa?). Stress on asymmetry in these theories works against the maintenance of genuine bi-polarity. This is the reason for the instability of dualistic theories and their tendency (noted by Culler) to collapse into a monism of the text or a monism of the reader. Emphasis on subjectivity, whether of the reader or the author, eclipses the textuality of the text, and concern with textuality eclipses the subjectivity of both reader and author.

If concern with asymmetry is likely to undermine the duality of text and reader, the converse is likewise true: bi-polarity is maintained at the expense of asymmetry. One sees this most clearly in theories that refer the meaning of the text to the intention of the author. Here, the text becomes the site of the crossing of two subjectivities, and theory has to devise ways of regulating traffic between them. A good example is Hirsch's distinction between "verbal meaning" and "significance": the intention of the author has the right of way on the plane of verbal meaning, the interest and experience of the reader on the plane of significance.[19]

The discussion above underscores the advantage offered by the analogy of reading and listening. It keeps before us the task of articulating a theory of asymmetrical intersubjectivity and impresses upon us the theoretical significance of listening/reading as a subjective modality different from speaking/writing.

The highest stage of the development of a morality of rights involves a commitment to justice, defined as a principled commitment to reciprocity and the symmetrical distribution of "human rights" to everyone. Habermas's definition of ideal discourse in terms of a universal symmetry requirement is a reflection of this highest stage. The exclusive commitment to an ethic of rights is not conducive to the theoretical elaboration of the role of the listener. For this we must look for a model of intersubjectivity that incorporates the *ethic of care* associated with feminine moral reasoning. The point is not that all women are necessarily good listeners, nor that men don't listen (although this is a familiar feminine complaint), but rather that prevailing theories of discourse (and of reading) overlook the subjective *activity* of listening and that this oversight correlates with the fact that the theoretical discussion has been virtually uninformed by the subjective and intersubjective experience of women.

What difference could an ethic of care make in a theory of discourse? To see how this question could be answered, let us turn to the work of Nel Noddings.[20] A full treatment of her richly suggestive theory is beyond the scope of this essay. All I can do is give a sketch that would indicate how it could be used as a resource for theories of reading and discourse.

In Noddings's view, morality as an "active virtue" is rooted in two sentiments. The "initial, enabling sentiment" comes out of the experience of "natural caring — that relation in which we respond as one caring out of love or natural inclination. The relation of natural caring . . . [is] the human condition that we, consciously or unconsciously, perceive as 'good.'" The second sentiment arises out of the memory of "our best moments of caring and being cared for." It is the longing to maintain, recapture or enhance this "good" that "provides the motivation for us to be moral. We want to be *moral* in order to remain in the caring relation and to enhance the ideal of ourselves as one caring" (5).

The caring relation is essentially an asymmetrical relation between two modalities of subjectivity—between the *one caring* and the one *cared for*. The one caring adopts a "subjective-receptive" attitude characterized by "engrossment" and "motivational displacement." *Engrossment* is Noddings's term for "nonselective attention" toward the other during the interval of caring. To explain why she prefers *engrossment* to the more familiar *empathy*, Noddings cites the *Oxford English Dictionary* definition of empathy as "the power of projecting personality into, and so fully understanding, the object of contemplation." The self-projection associated with this "peculiarly rational, Western masculine way of looking at 'feeling with' " is not in keeping with the emphasis on receptivity that she wishes to stress by the term *engrossment* (30). She invokes the example of a mother responding to an infant's cry: "We say, 'Do you have a pain?' or its equivalent in baby talk. We do not expect, certainly, that the infant will respond verbally, but the question and its tone impel us to attentive quietude. We await an answer of some sort. We watch a knee to be drawn up, the head to be tossed, a fist to be sucked" (31). Noddings stresses that the "outer quietude and inner voices and images," the "absorption and sensory concentration," the "listening, looking, feeling" characteristic of engrossment are essential components of intellectual work.

Although she values emotion and repeatedly points out the affective grounds of both cognition and morality, Noddings insists that caring is not just a feeling. It requires motivational displacement. "My motive energy flows toward the other and perhaps, although not necessarily, toward his ends. . . . I allow my motive energy to be shared; I put it at the service of the other" (33). Aware of the likelihood of misunderstanding, she stresses that the caring attitude is not the same as "romantic love or the sort of pervasive and compulsive 'thinking of the other' that characterizes infatuation" (176). Engrossment and motivational displacement do not imply that the one caring must lose himself in the relation: he receives the cared for (e.g., a teacher receives a student) and "views the world through both sets of eyes. . . . The one-caring assumes a dual perspective and can see things from both his own pole and that of the cared-for" (63).[21]

Certainly, a person need not be fixed either in the role of one caring or of cared for (it would be morally disastrous should this be the case), and there could be relations of genuine mutuality where the parties adopt each role alternately. However, Noddings focuses most of her analysis on necessarily "unequal meetings," such as those between parent and child, patient and therapist, and teacher and student, where the position of the cared for is defined by need and vulnerability and the position of the one caring by the authorization to help or instruct and the power to give or withhold care. But even in cases where there is genuine mutuality, Noddings insists that each particular caring moment is characterized by asymmetry: the roles of one caring and cared for may be exchanged, but they are necessarily incommensurable.

The completion of the caring relation requires reciprocity, but the cared for need not respond as one caring. The reciprocity of an ethic of care (unlike the reciprocity required by an ethic of rights) is not defined in terms of the "identity of gifts given and received." He (the one caring) meets her (the cared for) "as subject—not as an object to be manipulated nor as a data source." He shifts his motive energy toward her projects and offers the "vital gift" of the dual perspective that allows him to form and convey a vision of the "cared-for as [she] is and as [she] might be." Through his commitment, she is "confirmed" and "set free to pursue her legitimate projects" (177). For her part, the cared for gives the gift of "responsiveness," which Noddings defines as pursuing her own projects freely and vigorously and sharing accounts of them spontaneously. "The sharing enables [him] to care more easily. With a fuller knowledge of what [she] is striving for, of what pleases and delights [her], [he] can readily contribute [his] support to [her] efforts. The motivational displacement of caring occurs naturally, supported by the buoyant responsiveness of the cared for. The one-caring for a fully participating cared for is sustained and invigorated, and [his] caring is unlikely to deteriorate to "cares and burdens" (72).

Returning now to the case of a professor reading/listening to a student paper, we can see how easily the listener-speaker relation maps onto the caring relation: listener $\rightarrow$ one caring, and speaker $\rightarrow$ cared for. In this model, the receptive subjectivity of the one caring—defined by engrossment, motivational displacement and duality of perspective—defines the role of the listener. To listen with care is to treat the text not merely in its textuality but as the expression of a subject. During the interval of care (which may be brief or extended), the speaker as subject "fills the firmament." "The teacher receives and accepts the student's feeling toward the subject matter; [he] looks at it and listens to it through [her] eyes and ears. How else can [he] interpret the subject matter for [her]? As [he] exercises this inclusion, [he] accepts [*her*] motives, reaches toward what [*she*] intends, so long as these motives and intentions do not force an abandonment of [his] own ethic" (177).

As one caring, the listener will respect the fragility of the other's

speech. Rather than expecting fully formed utterances, he will be attentive not only to what is written but also to what is yet to be written. He
will try to discern and to bring out what the author is trying to express.
"The one-caring [listener] sees the best self [text] in the cared-for [speech
of the other] and works with [her] to actualize that self [text]" (64). For
her part, the student/speaker will be "confirmed." She will "grow" and
"glow" under the caring attitude of the teacher/listener. She will not only
understand the failings of the text she has written but also attain a
vision of the truly worthwhile paper she could write. She will respond by
showing her delight, and by devoting herself vigorously to revising her
paper, and later to writing others. The buoyant responsiveness of the
student invigorates the teacher and allows him to fulfill his role more
easily. "A teacher is captivated by the student who thinks aloud and uses
what [her] teacher has presented in [her] own way and for [her] own
purposes." This is the "major intrinsic reward of teaching," the lack of
which often results in "teacher burnout" (73).

It is instructive to compare the model of reading/discourse derived
from Noddings's theory with those proposed by Holland and Habermas.
The contrast with Holland cannot be more pronounced. For Holland,
reading involves only one subject—the reader, whose subjectivity is
unequivocally identified with the impulse toward self-interest and self-
assertion. The reader projects himself into what he reads. His engrossment and his motive energy are directed entirely toward his own ends. He
is capable of adopting only one perspective, his own.

It should be clear that I am disturbed by the normative implications of
Holland's representation of reading. In spite of these misgivings, it is
important not to discount the reality of the model. We do read for
self-gratification and self-enhancement. Reading is a way of working and
re-working our drives, anxieties, fantasies, and patterns of encountering
the world, a way of elaborating and reinforcing identity. There is no need
to proscribe self-interested reading and the pleasures associated with it.
As Noddings points out, caring can be reflexive. The problem comes with
the unequivocal definition of reading as *always* and *only* the re-creation of
the reader's identity theme. Of course, one can say that a caring reading is
the re-creation of the identity theme of a reader who needs to see herself
as one caring, but this logical play trivializes the situation and forecloses
the elaboration of the themes and issues entailed by an ethic of care.

Holland's theory is real in another way: it heightens our awareness of
the problem of the uneven distribution of power. Any ethic of care has to
address the issue of power, and Noddings does so specifically with regard
to the teacher-student relation.

The one-caring as teacher is not necessarily permissive. [He] does not abstain . . . from leading the student, or persuading [her], or coaxing [her] toward an examination of school subjects. But [he] recognizes that, in the long run, [she] will learn what [she] pleases. . . . This recognition does not reduce the power of the teacher or [his] responsibility. . . . the teacher may indeed coerce the student into choosing against [her]self. [She] may be led to diminish [her] ethical ideal in the pursuit of achievement goals. The teacher's power is, thus, awesome. It is [he] who presents the "effective world" . . . [from which the student, as ethical agent, will select his projects]. (176–77)

In other words, although power is distributed in favor of the one caring, it is exercised in the service of the cared for. While this solution works adequately for the case of the professor reading a student paper, the asymmetrical distribution of power and vulnerability remains a live issue in general theories. (It is also an unresolved ethical issue, since for at least one important case, that of women and men in adult relationships, the role of one caring, which is traditionally given to women, generally coincides with greater vulnerability and less power.)

Habermas resolves the issue of power negatively, by putting forth the (admittedly counterfactual) notion of domination-free discourse as the constitutive ideal presupposed by speech that is directed toward the vindication of cognitive and normative validity claims. The key assumption of this ideal is the full equality and reciprocity of free individuals who have set aside all concerns except the commitment to truth, which is to say, the commitment to forego all force except the "force of the better argument." The model works on the principle of collaboration by competition: you put forth your strongest case, I'll do the same, and we will see which is strongest. What is lacking, clearly, is any concession to the fact that the ability to argue, and even the capacity for articulate speech, is not uniformly distributed in the population and that this model of ideal discourse effectively rules out those who, for whatever reason, lack the capacity or inclination for competitive argumentation. Moreover, even in discourse (written or oral) among equals, speech is often fragile and not fully formed when uttered, and meanings of utterances are more likely to be opaque than transparent even to those who have uttered them. We need to encourage and facilitate each other's speech, not merely to abstain from undue interference. Truth, to the extent that it depends on speech, is likewise fragile and elusive and must be coaxed out and cultivated. It is unlikely to emerge undistorted in uncaring argumentation. My point is not that Habermas is uncaring, but rather that his theory of communicative action suffers from the exclusion of the morality and sense of sociality that is rooted in the experience of the caring relation.

Clearly, the asymmetrical reciprocity of an ethic of care is an apt model for the professor reading a student paper. Moreover, this combination of model and basic paradigm case sets the stage for a critique that shows the inadequacies of the prevailing models of discourse and reading. But, one might ask, is the caring model generalizable to other reading situations? In particular, does it apply when we have a literary text whose author is absent? I can only suggest the beginning of an answer here.

The problem stems from the fact that, in the case of a person reading literature, the subject-object relation is (usually) not mitigated by direct contact with the author, and the subjective interests of the author are (generally) not at issue. Thus, there is no genuine cared for: the text as object is not really in need of help or instruction, and it is not capable of the responsiveness that is required to complete the circle of care.

In another essay, I used Adrienne Rich's reading of Emily Dickinson to illustrate a dialogic model of reading derived from (some) feminist readings of female texts.[22] In this model, the dialectic of control (implicit in traditional theories) is supplanted by a dialectic of communication consisting of three moments. In the first moment reading induces a doubling of the reader's subjectivity, so that one can be put in the service of the text while the other remains with the reader. Rich is not content to revel in the textuality of Dickinson's poems and letters. She reads so as to hear the "voice" of the other, to make present the "personal dimensions" of the "woman of genius" who authored the texts. The second moment is marked by the realization that, in fact, there is only one subject, the reader. The subjectivity roused to life by reading is not a separate subjectivity but only a projection of the subjectivity of the reader. This second moment affirms the truth of Holland's DEFT model of reading. Rich recognizes that her reading of Dickinson is necessarily imbued by her own "identity theme"—her drives and fantasies, her personal and social history, her identity "as a woman poet finding my own methods." However, even if reading is necessarily subjective, the third moment of the dialectic shows that it need not be wholly so. Rich struggles to maintain a duality of perspective. To avoid imposing an alien point of view on Dickinson, she informs her reading with knowledge of Dickinson's "premises," the conditions under which she lived and worked. At the same time, she maintains a keen awareness of the context of her reading. In the third moment of the dialectic, the duality of subjects is referred to the duality of contexts.

Toward the end of my earlier discussion of the dialogic model sketched above, I suggested that it embodies the ethic of care that has been the focus of some recent feminist research. Noddings's work allows a more explicit structuring of the basic caring relation which is evident in Rich's reading of Dickinson. Rich performs the characteristic engrossment and motivational displacement of the one caring so that she can attain the duality of perspective that will allow her to meet the text as subject. "Dickinson"—the "figure of powerful will" that is brought to life by the reading, rather than the text—"fills the firmament." Rich deploys her subjective powers—intuition, imagination, sensitivity, rhetorical skill—so that she can cultivate, entertain, play host to—in her own metaphor, "visit with"—another subjectivity within herself. The alternation between active analysis and intuitive receptivity, between self-assertion and engrossment with the "object turned subject" that Noddings describes in her brief discussion of caring for ideas, matches the process of reading represented by Rich's essay on Dickinson (161–69). As in Holland's model, reading brings the reader pleasure and self-enhancement. However, the "payoff" in the dialogic model is the experience of connecting with another no less than the re-creation of self-identity. Noddings puts it this way: "joy" is the "basic effect" that accompanies the realization of relatedness. "It is the relation, our recognition of the relation [whether with persons, other living beings, or ideas] that induces the affect we call joy" (132). "The occurrence of joy is a manifestation of receptive consciousness—a sign that we live in a world of relation as well as in one of instrumentality" (147).

Although the ethic of care and the intersubjectivity of caring relation have their roots in women's experience, I do not mean to imply that all women conform to the ideal it projects. Individuals don't always live up to their sense of morality. Furthermore, I do not think that the ethic of care is applicable and accessible only to women. To the extent that it is an authentic ethic, the ethic of care is an appropriate standpoint upon which to understand and to evaluate all human actions. It certainly represents a perspective for critical reflection on the masculine ethic of rights.[23] Similarly, it is not true that theories of discourse and of reading that are based on the caring relation apply only to women. For one thing, I believe that the intersubjective competence of actual men incorporates an ethic of care to a greater degree than is apparent in traditional theories so that, in fact, one can argue that traditional theories reflect a hypermasculine perspective.

Finally, I must say that the idea of a theory of reading and discourse incorporating an ethic of care remains very much a promissory note. Many issues need to be clarified, among them the vexing issue of power. In theories of reading, there is in particular the issue of the cultural power of canonical (almost always) androcentric texts over female and male readers. What I have tried to argue in this essay is that theories of meaning need to be concerned with three rather than two issues—with the issue of care no less than the issues of truth and power.

NOTES

1. David Bleich, "Intersubjective Reading," *New Literary History* 17 (1986): 418.

2. Charles Arthur Willard, *Argumentation and the Social Grounds of Knowledge* (Tuscaloosa: U Alabama P, 1983), especially 7–24.

3. David Bleich's recent work is a notable exception in that it is informed in a significant way by perspectives and concerns arising from recent feminist theory. See "Intersubjective Reading" and *The Double Perspective: Language, Literacy and Social Relations* (Oxford: Oxford UP, 1988).

4. Norman Holland, "Reading Readers Reading," *Researching Responses to Literature and the Teaching of Literature: Points of Departure*, ed. Charles R. Cooper (Norwood: Ablex, 1985) 6–7. Further references will be indicated in the text by page numbers in parentheses.

5. Bleich, *Subjective Criticism* (Baltimore: Johns Hopkins UP, 1978) 112.

6. For a clear and concise account of the feminist critique of objectivity see Elizabeth Fee, "Women's Nature and Scientific Objectivity," *Woman's Nature: Rationalizations of Inequality*, ed. Marian Lowe and Ruth Hubbard (New York: Pergamon, 1981).

7. Ludwig Fleck, *The Genesis and Development of a Scientific Fact*, ed. and trans. Thaddeus Trenn, Robert K. Merton, and Fred Bradley (Chicago: U of Chicago P, 1979).

8. Jonathan Culler, *On Deconstruction: Theory and Criticism after Structuralism* (Ithaca: Cornell UP, 1982) 75.

9. I am aware that Holland may object to being classed with the subjectivists. Although his theory has undergone some modification, his basic DEFT model has remained essentially intact, and I think it is exemplary of the subjectivist position and of the theoretical problems it entails. For a recent version of Holland's position, see "The Miller's Wife and the Professors: Questions about the Transactive Theory of Reading," *New Literary History* 17 (1986): 423–45.

10. In this essay, the generic third-person singular will be indicated either by a masculine or a feminine pronoun. The selection will be made randomly, without regard to consistency.

11. For another argument regarding the authoritarian potential of the subjectivist position, see my "Engendering Critical Discourse," in *The Current in Criticism*, ed. Victor Lokke and Clayton Koelb (West Lafayette, IN: Purdue UP, 1988).

12. It is possible that listening and reading involve very different physiological and mental operations, but I do not think these differences matter here. The distinction proposed by Derrida, however, is relevant. Briefly, Derrida argues that the (age-old) identification of language with speech (phonocentricism) has fostered the illusion of the presence of meaning in linguistic utterances (logocentricism) as well as the presence of a subject in a text. Thinking of language as writing leads to the more correct (except Derrida would not use the word *correct*) view that language is *absence*. Meaning is a "différance," a difference forever deferred. Similarly, the text does not express an originary subjectivity but stands witness to the *absence* of the subject. Although Derrida begins by distinguishing speech and writing, in the end there is no difference between the two. His analysis reveals the

textuality even of spoken utterances. All language is writing, bespeaking absence rather than presence. See, for example, *Of Grammatology*, trans. Gayatri Chakravorty Spivak (Baltimore: Johns Hopkins UP, 1974).

My analogy between listening and reading reverses Derrida's argument, but not necessarily back to the initial position of logocentrism. What is at stake for me is less the presence of meaning in the text than the recovery of the relation of linguistic utterances—spoken or written—to human projects. Against deconstruction I would argue that the issue of the signified and the issue of the subject are not necessarily the same.

13. J. Robert Cox and Charles Arthur Willard, eds., *Advances in Argumentation Theory and Research* (Carbondale: Southern Illinois UP, 1982) xiii.

14. Scott Jacobs and Sally Jackson, "Conversational Argument: A Discourse Analytic Approach," ibid., 205–6.

15. Jürgen Habermas, "Wahrheitstheorien," in *Wirklichkeit und Reflexion: Walter Schulz zum 60 Geburstag* (Pfullingen: Nesge, 1973) 219. The translation is Alan Soble's (unpublished).

16. See Ray. E. McKerrow, "Rationality and Reasonableness in a Theory of Argument," in Cox and Willard, *Advances in Argumentation Theory*, 105–22.

17. Carol Gilligan, *In a Different Voice* (Cambridge: Harvard UP, 1982).

18. Annette C. Baier, "What Do Women Want in a Moral Theory?" *Nous* 19 (1985): 62.

19. E. D. Hirsch, *Validity in Interpretation* (New Haven: Yale UP, 1967) 8–9.

20. Nel Noddings, *Caring: A Feminine Approach to Ethics and Moral Education* (Berkeley: U of California P, 1984). Further references will be indicated parenthetically in the text.

21. Noddings consistently uses the feminine pronoun for the one caring, the masculine for the cared for. The choice of the generic feminine for the one caring is consistent with the project of building an ethic of general validity on a paradigm derived from female experience. Noddings explains that she decided to use the masculine pronoun for the cared for for the sake of "balance." I have decided in upcoming quotations to reverse Noddings's choice for the sake of the alternative possibilities associated with the counter-stereotypical usage.

22. Patrocinio Schweickart, "Reading Ourselves: Toward a Feminist Theory of Reading," *Gender and Reading: Essays on Readers, Texts, and Contexts*, ed. Elizabeth Flynn and Patrocinio Schweickart (Baltimore: Johns Hopkins UP, 1986) 31–62. Adrienne Rich's reading of Emily Dickinson is "Vesuvius at Home: The Power of Emily Dickinson," *On Lies, Secrets and Silence: Selected Prose, 1966–1978* (New York: Norton, 1979).

23. My article has been shaped in large measure by my ongoing conversation with Barbara Houston about the problematics of a distinctive morality of care. For an excellent discussion of the theoretical and political implications of the works of Gilligan and Noddings, see her "Gilligan and the Politics of a Distinctive Women's Morality," in *Feminist Perspectives: Philosophical Essays on Methods and Morals*, ed. Lorraine Code, Sheila Mullet, and Christine Overall (Toronto: U of Toronto P, 1989), and her "Rescuing Womanly Virtues: Some Dangers of Moral Reclamation," in *Science, Morality, and Feminist Theory*, ed. Kai Nielsen and Marsha Hanen (Calgary: U of Calgary P, 1987).

ROBERT CON DAVIS

Woman as Oppositional Reader: Cixous on Discourse

> I began by dismissing God, whose uselessness was only too apparent, and replaced him with my father. Then I abolished the distinction between man and woman, which seemed to me to be an excuse for every kind of sloth. Finally I pushed aside the limit of life on both sides of the present: the past was just a story, I would tell myself another past instead of the one my mother had not preserved; then I would invite someone to join in it.
>
> —Hélène Cixous, *Inside*

> As history proves, to be a worldly success in anything, especially revolution, you have to wear blinders like a horse and see only straight in front of you. You have to see, too, that this is all black, and that is all white.
>
> —Eugene O'Neill, *The Iceman Cometh*

Hélène Cixous is generally known in America as the avant-garde feminist author of "The Laugh of the Medusa" and *The Newly Born Woman*, works in which she is the theorist of *écriture féminine*—the visionary guide to reading and writing like a woman.[1] I want to discuss her here, though, in her role as "oppositional critic," one who self-consciously chooses a style of confrontation with dominant cultural practices in order to understand and change the prevailing order. The designation of "oppositional critic" should not surprise anyone who has read Edward W. Said, Michel Foucault, Monique Wittig, Jean Baudrillard, or Fredric Jameson—other contemporary critics who take up positions calculated to tear the fabric of a controlling discourse and disrupt reigning ideologies. Like these critics, Cixous reads the discourses of contemporary culture to expose crucial oppositions, key binarities—such as man/woman, active/passive, nature/culture, superior/inferior—that govern the exercise of power. Like other such critics, she has tried, in effect, to maneuver herself into strategic conflicts with oppressive cultural practices, as was evident when she emerged from the student/worker uprisings of May 1968 in France as a radical academic in a "revolutionary" university (in Vincennes), a feminist theorist writing for the Women's Press, and an avant-garde fiction writer. She did all of this in the "oppositional" style of one working from within an institution—in this case as teacher and writer—to challenge prevailing authority and to engineer contrary, alternative modes of reading and writing.

One of Cixous's primary strategies has been to alter the effect of gender relations in the way people read. She has attempted to do this in her classroom, criticism, and fiction—at least into the middle 1980s—through her own innovative reading and writing of cultural texts; her goal has been to expose, and even to begin to dismantle, patriarchal authority in the academy and in the institution of cultural criticism and theory. She strives to create for her students and readers, in short, a revolutionary cultural frame which legitimizes a feminine dimension of textuality and, therein, shifts the cultural relations of power between male and female. Thus, her work has been avant-garde in a pedagogic, literary, and political sense.

Ann Rosalind Jones, Monique Wittig, and various other feminist critics describe Cixous's teaching and writing in this way, too, but they also worry that the intensity of her oppositional reading of culture may have the hidden weakness of, at the same time, imprisoning her work within "the very ideological system [of "oppositional" thinking] feminists want to destroy."[2] The fact is that in the late 1980s Cixous and her strategies for instituting and understanding "feminine discourse"—a theoretical approach to "feminine" reading and writing—are far less appealing to those thinking and writing about women's issues, whether in literary or in cultural studies. Many critics currently committed to *"theories of writing and reading,"* as Alice Jardine reports, actually "posit themselves and their work as hostile to, or 'beyond,' feminism" such as Cixous's,[3] there being a strong commitment in the late 1980s, as Jones says, "to move outside that male-centered, binary logic [identified with Cixous's oppositionalism] altogether" (369). With this decline of Cixous's version of "feminine writing," Cixous becomes a case in point for assessing the prospects, the difficulties in particular, of an oppositional reading of culture. Cixous's decline becomes a case for determining what is required to read, critique, and rewrite the texts of the dominant discourse as a step toward changing the culture producing those texts.

Cixous's case raises these questions, in particular, because as the powerful academic, feminist theorist, writer, and political activist that she is, she has been an unusually strong agent for initiating change. That is, given the extent of her intervention in literary and cultural studies, and the uncommon strength and appeal of her work, she in many ways has been an ideal initiator of cultural change from within. If she cannot initiate change, we must wonder, who can? Thus, Jones's and others' judgments of Cixous's apparent "failure" to inform and influence women's studies in the 1980s raises disturbing questions about the very nature of oppositional critical strategies in contemporary culture—about the potential to subvert and change culture from within, the goal common to Western intellectuals in the late 1960s through the middle 1970s (most prominently with Noam Chomsky). What are the limits of critical/ oppositional practices such as Cixous's, Said's, Jameson's, and Baudrillard's? When are such strategies successful and when not? While Cixous's case cannot settle these questions, it can clarify the difficulty and suggest the limits of the oppositional strategy in reading the texts of contemporary culture.

Let's start with Cixous's idea of *écriture feminine*—"feminine writing." Since the middle 1970s Cixous, Luce Irigaray, Julia Kristeva, Michele Montrelay, and Catherine Clément, among others, have developed theories about reading women's texts in the particular contexts of women's experience. The general strategy of this thought reflects Virginia Woolf's notion of a feminine writing that does not rely on a biological conception of the sexes—a "given" essence of male and female characteristics—but on culturally determined features, such as "openness" in feminine texts and a tendency to retain a sense of the indeterminant and the random. "Openness," a lack of repressive patterning in discourse, would be a designation as much applicable to a man as a woman—to the reading of Marcel Proust as well as Virginia Woolf. These theorists of feminine reading and writing have tried to expose the mechanism by which Western texts (literary and otherwise) have been written to advance the prestige of patriarchal culture; to understand how women's writing has been effaced and suppressed by male discourse; and finally to recover, or reinvent, a way of reading feminine writing (particularly writing *by* women) that does not duplicate and advance the institution of patriarchy. Such theorizing, pursued in the atmosphere of post-May 1968 France and deconstruction, has predictably asked questions about the relations of writing, politics, pedagogy, and gender—what "writing" is, how texts deploy power, how to read and teach a feminine (nonpatriarchal) text, and what the "feminine" is.

Common among these critics, whose ideas are otherwise divergent, is that feminine writing—both escaping from and situated within a patriarchal economy—is best understood in metaphors related to "orgasm" (*jouissance*) or, in Cixous's case, *sortie*, which means "excess" (again suggestive of jouissance) and the "way out," "exit," or a "leaving."[4] Taken together, these metaphors suggest the common aim, through an underlying metaphor, of finding a "beyond" or "way out" from patriarchal discourse and the analytical double binds it fosters. Cixous, for example, calls for "leaving" behind "the signs of sexual opposition" altogether, that is, simply abandoning the binarity of gender as a way of defeating the Western tendency to elevate men and efface women.[5] Cixous cites oppositions such as man/woman, active/passive, great/small, nature/culture, transformation/inertia, white/black in which the second term in each case is effaced or made peripheral. Patriarchal (Western) culture, Cixous argues, is generated out of these oppositions based ultimately on what she calls "the power relation between a fantasized obligatory virility meant to invade, and colonize, and the consequential phantasm of woman as a 'dark continent' to penetrate and to 'pacify.'"[6] Cixous focuses on these oppositions, which all "come back to the man/woman opposition," as requiring fundamental adjustments in language and "discourse," changes in the linguistic and social context of language use ("Castration" 44).

"The Laugh of the Medusa" and "Castration or Decapitation?" present Cixous's views on reading feminine writing. In "Laugh," for example, she presents the scenario of writing as structured by a "sexual opposition" favoring men, one that "has always worked for man's profit to the point of reducing writing . . . to his laws" (313). She argues that writing is constituted in a "discourse" of social, political, and linguistic relations— and that these relations can be characterized in a masculine or feminine "economy." According to Cixous, the masculine, traditionally dominant in the West, is a system of militant exclusion wherein patterns of linearity and patriarchal "logic" overemphasize the hierarchical features of (sexual) difference in discourse and give a "grossly exaggerated" view of the "sexual opposition" actually inherent in language (311). Cixous does not say this to denigrate a masculine economy. If seen outside the exaggerations of patriarchy, the masculine economy is naturally a part of writing and reading, Cixous argues. "Castration," she says—the symbolic rule of discourse conceived on the male model—"is fundamental [to writing]."[7] "Isn't it evident," she asks, "that the penis gets around in my texts, that I give it a place and appeal?" ("Laugh" 319). The exclusion symbolized by castration is necessary, she goes on, because it would be "humanly impossible to have an absolute economy without a minimum of [masculine] mastery" (Conley 139), a rule of exclusion to organize the dynamics of writing. The problem is, of course, that the male economy has gone beyond the functional need for "repression" in writing to impose very restrictive rules on the deployment of power—rules which always favor men.

Whereas Cixous sees the masculine economy as superimposed linearity and tyranny, she sees the feminine as the "overflow" of "luminous torrents"

("Laugh" 309), a margin of "excess" eroticism and free play not governed by the fixed hierarchies of masculinity. In the feminine economy there are not the strict rules of dismissal but the play of writing as an "openness" containing "that element which never stops resonating," writing as an undecidable inscription of "white ink" on white paper that writes itself apart from masculine rules of decidable order and (hierarchical) contrast ("Laugh" 312). The "openness" of such writing is evident in Cixous's own style, as when she writes that "we the precocious, we the repressed of culture, our lovely mouths gagged with pollen, our wind knocked out of us, we the labyrinths, the ladders, the trampled spaces, the bevies—we are black and we are beautiful" ("Laugh" 310). In such writing Cixous forces expository sense into the economy of poetic association and controls the "excess" of imagery through repetition and nonlinear (non-male) accretions. Woolf also speaks of such writing in contrast to "male" ("shadowed," or violently imposed) writing—the writing always linear and reasonable. This is Kristeva's conception, too, of *jouissance*, the poetic discourse "beyond" the masculine text of reason and order. And for all three critics, there is the further assumption that the feminine economy of excess does not need re-creation so much as rediscovery because it has always persisted, and continues to persist, in the margins and gaps (as the repressed) of male-dominated culture. It follows, therefore, that women, and in theory, even men, can find the *sortie* from, the "beyond" of, patriarchal culture precisely by looking for and acknowledging the feminine economy that already exists within, alongside, and around the margins of male discourse—hence the importance of the *sortie* ("excess" and "exit") as the controlling metaphor of Cixous's discourse.

Cixous goes on in "The Laugh of the Medusa" and "Castration or Decapitation?" (also in "Sorties" in *The Newly Born Woman*) to explore the oppositional logic relating the masculine economy to the "overflow" of erotic "excess." In "Castration or Decapitation?" she emphasizes the extent to which the man/woman opposition "cut endlessly across all the oppositions that order culture" (44). "Everything . . . that's spoken," she goes on, "everything that's organized as discourse, art, religion, the family, language, everything that seizes us, everything that acts on us—it is all ordered around hierarchical oppositions that come back to the man/woman opposition . . . " (44). This primary opposition, she concludes, "makes it all work." Therefore, "it's on the [concept of the] couple that we have to work if we are to deconstruct and transform culture" (44). Cixous in this way argues for the primacy of a sexual logic, the "couple" (man/woman) as an orienting polarity of texts. In this concentration, repeated throughout her work—prominent in these essays but equally so in "Sorties"—she shows the extent to which she assumes a basic oppositional matrix as formative for culture. She commits herself to the implications of this approach as she posits a strategy for reading the feminine and making "opposition"—for good or ill—the primary tool of her critique.

Cixous, of course, does not intend to confine her discourse on feminine writing within the bounds of the linear, patriarchal economy. Cixous, the joyous and oracular reader of cultural texts, rather, chides women and hopes to lure them to follow her to "excess" beyond the patriarchy. In "The Laugh of the Medusa," for example, as if composing a feminine "Song of Myself," she challenges women to rise and become more than they have been: "And why don't you write? Write! Writing is for you, you are for you; your body is yours, take it. I know why you haven't written. (And why I didn't write before the age of twenty-seven.) Because writing is at once too high, too great for you, it's reserved for the great—that is for 'great men'; and it's 'silly'" (310). She implores the untutored woman to rise and live fully in the open space of ecstatic discourse and "laughter." Likewise, in "Castration or Decapitation?" she invites women to "laughter that breaks out, overflows, a humour that no one would expect to find in women" (55). Thus intending to transcend narrow male economies, Cixous fashions the "newly born woman" (as in *La Jeune Née—The Newly Born Woman*) as a reader/writer who will be intent on "leaping," who "crosses limits: she is neither outside nor in, whereas the masculine would try to 'bring the outside in, if possible'" ("Castration" 54). The new woman and the female discourse that Cixous calls for, in other words, will follow the reprise of a female Dionysian experience, the "way out" of the patriarchy and the living of joyful lives at the margins of excess. Finally, just as Cixous calls for reading literature "beyond" the traditional assumptions about realistic (Cartesian) models of character, her new woman will live "beyond" the "character" assigned to her by the patriarchy.[8]

This exuberant discourse, however, regardless of its claims, has come under relentless attack from other feminists for its inadvertent collaboration with the patriarchy. Ann Rosalind Jones, for example, documents a list of objections to Cixous's work (relying on Wittig) in "Toward an Understanding of *l'écriture feminine*." Jones notes principally Cixous's conception of femininity as "feminine economy," a notion not applicable exclusively to women (as Cixous makes clear) but "natural" and intrinsic to them all the same. Underpinning Cixous's feminine economy, regardless of her sophistication in articulating it, is the assumption of an "essential" femininity in some texts, the identifiable quality that allows feminine discourse to be named as such, the quality of openness that allows a text to resist external control and the imposition of (patriarchal) patterns. Ironically, essentialism—or "meaning" as unproblematic, discrete, and non-relational—is one of the myths, of course, that Cixous's deconstructive project intends to critique. In any other context, Cixous-the-deconstructor would set about to dismantle the authority of such absolute essences. Likewise, because Cixous's feminine discourse is based on a theory of an essential "femininity," it is problematic. Jones also points up, understandably, that in positing such idealized femininity, "French feminists [such as Cixous] make of the female body too unproblematically pleasurable and totalized an entity" (368). The female body, in this view, actually houses the erotic "essence" supposedly distributed throughout a feminine discourse. Thus, Jones argues, persuasively and probably decisively, that Cixous's version of *femininity* —based as it is on an essentialist conception of gender—is not viable in theory or practice.

Also problematic for a feminist theorist is the extent of Cixous's reliance on utopian thought. In "Castration or Decapitation?" for example, Cixous asks the reader to learn to read feminine writing—a space of inscription in which "all this [patriarchal discourse] functioned otherwise" (50). She then goes on to formulate feminine writing as follows: "Let's imagine that all this [patriarchal discourse and the suppression of the feminine] functioned otherwise. . . . We'd first have to imagine resistance to masculine desire conducted by woman as hysteric, as distracted. We'd first have to imagine her ceasing to support with her body what I call the realm of the proper" (50). Her speculation about reading the feminine includes revalorizing traits the patriarchy casts as negative and offers a call to "imagine resistance to masculine desire," a "resistance" effected with the counter authority of "her body," the female body whose corporeality will oppose the hegemony of an abstract male "desire." Cixous intentionally evokes a level of idealism—where the liberated female body challenges the male—but cannot characterize the conflict beyond its ideal projection, saying that it will, or could, take place.

In such gestures Cixous exemplifies the resistance to male "desire" with her own writing—that is, by opposing the "body" and materiality (the style) of her own writing to masculine writing practices. In effect, Cixous wagers the "body" of her eroticized writing against the repressions of masculine textuality. But, judging from the testimony of other feminists, the overall success of this performance—in light of the difficulty of actually altering cultural discourse—is questionable. Sandra M. Gilbert judges Cixous's "imaginative journeys across the frontier of prohibition" to be pure utopian "voyages out into a no place that must be a no man's and no woman's land" (*Newly Born Woman* xvi)—a provocative performance but not sufficiently grounded in cultural practice to have a significant impact.

Jones's major objection to Cixous is that Cixous's ultimate appeal is to oppositional thinking. This is a problem for Cixous as cultural critic, Jones argues, because any term conceived in binarity necessarily inscribes, and even legitimizes, the oppositional network—the differential system—it is articulated in. Thus, if Cixous strategically advances feminine writing in opposition to masculine discourse—as Jones says—Cixous merely succeeds in reversing "the values assigned to each side of the polarity, but . . . still leaves man as the determining referent, not departing from the male-female opposition, but participating in it" (369). Jones's point is that the opposition to men will have the effect of making men (the patriarchy) stronger. This is the predicament of the Foucauldean intellectual, as Jim Merod comments, who "is inscribed within the dominant culture and within the operations of power which he wants to contest. He is [therefore], in some undismissible sense, an agent of that power."[9] Cixous's discourse, then—actually an agent of what it opposes—inadvertently returns to and reinforces the masculine discourse it was supposed to go beyond and subvert. Cixous-as-oppositional-reader, as Jones summarizes, misunderstood the inherent dangers of oppositional criticism and, accordingly, was lured by the appearance of analytical clarity into the trap of accepting a patriarchal ethos. Cixous's oppositional reading is confined and neutralized in effectiveness, therefore, by the patriarchal frame—the male form of reading—she chose to employ.

This difficulty is another version of the impasse often faced by contemporary "engaged" theorists. The problem is that intellectuals, like Cixous, who wish to think *and* act, or at least to theorize the impact of their reading and writing, have great trouble finding avenues to action uncompromised by internal contradictions. Worse, they cannot even theorize a mode of action that does not subvert what they set out to achieve. This paradox is particularly disturbing because, especially in Cixous's case, it so vividly challenges the prospect of deliberate and rational intervention, of any political action.[10] In short, the "failure" of Cixous's project, given her reliance on oppositional reading, does not bode well for the possibility of any effective cultural opposition—for change from within. If opposition automatically cancels itself by restoring legitimacy to the dominant discourse, the spectre of paralysis and quietism, of no response to cultural and political oppression, is raised. This danger does not plague only the self-identified "oppositional" critic, the radical cultural theorist (like Foucault), or the political strategist of the Left (like Baudrillard); the "failure" of Cixous's oppositional project, in important ways, puts the possibility of intervention itself into question. Is this the lesson to be learned from Cixous—that a cultural discourse cannot be opposed from within and that all such calculated action is defeated in advance?

I want it to be clear that I admire Cixous and her project—the evident appeal of her aims, the bold execution in her texts, and the exuberance of her style as a Dionysian reader of culture. These characteristics foreground the honesty of her dilemma—her consistent willingness to advance her cultural readings forthrightly to fare as they will. I also want it to be clear that Cixous does not literally endorse oppositional criticism. As far as I can tell, she *intends* to reject oppositionalism and believes that she has already gone beyond it. Verena Conley, for one, places Cixous close to Gilles Deleuze in believing that "there is no [inherent] logic of meaning" in discourse—in other words, no structure of relations like opposition implied by discourse (Conley 15). As I have shown, though (and could show further), Cixous's work finds and advances itself within the logic of oppositional analysis and within a fundamentally oppositional view of culture. A number of other theorists see her work in this light as well.

The oppositional tradition I associate with Cixous—traceable to the Pre-Socratics and Aristotle and moving through Hegel, Marx, Antonio Gramsci, Jean Baudrillard, Robert Blanche, A. J. Greimas, Edward Said, and Fredric Jameson—formulates specific strategies for thinking about what it means for one idea to oppose another, what is required to effect change in cultural relations, and at what point opposition can become neutralized and then appropriated by its "opposition."[11] This tradition, in short, speculates on the workings of cultural conflict and how to understand it according to certain rules in specific historical settings.

The oppositional critics that Cixous follows, moreover, tend to assume a common foundation for language and politics. Like Aristotle before them, they assume the existence of four transformations that govern the possibilities for opposition in any cultural practice. Aristotle's own practice is elaborated in *On Interpretation*,[12] and it is the prototype of A. J. Greimas's "semiotic square" and the model behind Jameson's oppositional critique in *The Political Unconscious*.[13] Aristotle's attempt to theorize opposition shows why interpretive possibilities move along particular lines and not others. If this were not so, oppositional critics believe, political change could not "be accounted for" or, at least, it could not be marked or indicated within the cultural text.[14] That is, without the control of the oppositional metaphor, differences would be lost in the iteration of heterogeneity and chance and would have no intelligible significance. "There can be no knowledge," as Aristotle warns in the *Posterior Analytics*, "of that which [exists or comes to be] by chance. . . ."[15] Aristotle sees the concept of opposition, as Baudrillard and Greimas affirm after him, as embodying the very possibility of rational analysis and of what could be termed "intelligibility" in reading the world text.

Cixous's discourse and her manner of reading belong in this tradition. In the classical oppositional square, there are always two levels of cultural opposition to any discourse.[16] The first is a coupling of two propositions that form a "contrary" relationship, as in Cixous's opposition of Man/Woman. These two terms must relate to each other as arbitrary poles that mark a range of difference. By "arbitrary" I mean that they cannot be, for example, logical opposites like "yes" and "no." The coupling of these terms, even though their relationship is fundamentally arbitrary, establishes a range of cultural references, that is, a spectrum of possible significations—as in the possibilities of courtship, marriage, incest, homosexuality, etc.—that can be related to the coordinates of Man and Woman.

On a second level is a third term that indicates the specific hierarchy, ultimately the ideology, by which meanings are being organized within the range of reference established on the first level. The third term, in effect, "interprets" the first level and precisely "describes the 'nature' of the category upon which the [first-level] binary opposition is inscribed. . . ."[17] In Cixous's Man/Woman opposition the third term is patriarchalism—the "Father" as the designation of power in the Man/Woman opposition, the signal that Man will be the controlling term. The Father as indicator of ideology in this oppositional square, therefore, "understands" the first level of reference, interprets and limits it, by identifying the (patriarchal) hierarchy that organizes it. The third term, thus, inscribes "ideology" as a set of values positioned as a particular pattern in the square's hierarchy.

The fourth term completes this ideological reading with "Mother"—female sexuality and power. At this furthest reach of the square, "Mother" repeats and alters the category of "Woman," stands in opposition to "Father," and gives final expression to (even while it challenges) the patriarchal values this discourse is generated from. This fourth term, in effect, goes "beyond" (as if to "escape" or as if "exceeding") the other oppositional relations. Whereas the first-level relationship signals the coexistence of "contrary" possibilities and the third articulates the values inherent in the square, the fourth term is a potential resituating of this discourse—what Jacques Lacan calls, in a similar context, a resituated "subjectivity," a new "moi." The fourth term, therein, foregrounds an "other" potentiality, an "other" within discourse, made possible by the play of difference between the initial terms (Man/Woman) on the first level. In this way, the fourth term marks a new authority emanating from, but at the same time alien to, this discourse. The economy of Cixous's Man/Woman opposition can be projected as follows:

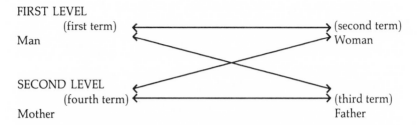

FIRST LEVEL
    (first term) ⟷ (second term)
Man   Woman

SECOND LEVEL
    (fourth term) ⟷ (third term)
Mother   Father

These cultural relationships are all established by an oppositional tie, of one kind or another, to the first term—except in the case of the fourth term, which "closes" the square by articulating a possibility effaced, or repressed, in the articulation of the first three terms. In so doing, the fourth term goes "beyond" the square by recognizing female power. "Mother" comes into the square, that is, as the instance of what was suppressed all along through the insistence in the discourse of various formal oppositions. The square, then, implicitly recognizes the fourth term as the completion but also as the potential destruction—the oppositional "other"—of its own logic.

As a historical phenomenon the oppositional square shows "Mother" to be a specific proposition emerging as a rupture in the historical fabric, a "rupture" that has left its trace but is not yet representable as a specific textual practice. This is precisely Kristeva's conception, too, of "Motherhood." It is at this historical moment within the articulations of the dominant patriarchal discourse, "without a discourse" and, at the same time, on the verge of "reawakening," of being retextualized, that there is an emergent but not yet "readable" discourse of women.[18] Thus, "Mother" is a historical event that the logic of patriarchal ideology inscribes within itself *and* suppresses, and her power persists in patriarchal logic specifically as an effacement—hence the disruptive nature of Motherhood as an agency of power. The representation of this double writing, of Mother's simultaneous inscription and suppression, is at the heart of the square's ideological discourse.

It is in this way that Cixous's reading of the Man/Woman opposition demonstrates the economies of relationship engendered by binarity, especially the economy of ideological reading. This happens as each term of the square further defines a hierarchy of values and maps the boundaries of a cultural text. This system of ideological reading—the progressive articulation of oppositional "systems," as John Peter Anton says—has the effect of rendering cultural discourses readable by submitting "all the differences to . . . the principle of contrariety, which in turn becomes the pivot-point for relating, organizing, and systematizing differences" (86). The result for Cixous is a gendered hierarchy of values inscribed by the square's four terms—themselves rising from and thus "escaping" the unintelligibility of "mere" differences, unorganized and non-politicized heterogeneity. It follows that reading the pattern of these values, articulated according to a rule made evident in the square's operation, constitutes an ideological critique.

What we are viewing in Cixous's method, as with that of Jameson, Said, Greimas, and the oppositional critics generally, is an ideological approach to the problematic of decipherment, of reading. Ideology, in this view, is not an immutable system of belief but an "effect" of discourse produced within a system of cultural differences that are continually subject to transformation within that system. One cannot arrest the cycle of semiosis on the square because its momentum is tied to history. One must, therefore, view the eruption of Mother in feminine discourse as a disruptive cultural event. That is, the fourth term—equivalent to "female sexuality" or "feminine political power"—is not on the order of a mere logical projection or fantasy. As a cultural phenomenon it is a manifestation of "history"—the diachronic emergence of the unthought and the initially unreadable.

Cixous does not follow Aristotelian protocols in any literal fashion to generate the oppositions of her cultural reading. She has perceived, however, as Aristotle, Greimas, and Jameson also believe, that the relations of opposition map a logic of resistance within the world text and that this "logic" is what we call ideology. To the extent that Cixous casts the oppositions she examines in terms of gender, she, in fact, is moving around the square's positions and playing out the possibilities of an ideological critique and of the "explosion" (eruption) of something unrepresentable and new. It is in this specific sense—regarding the potential of ideological analysis—that Cixous's reading of the Man/Woman discourse is oppositional.

Cixous's oppositional reading—as I said at the outset—raises questions about current directions in cultural and political theory. According to Cixous's own logic of dissent, she as an oppositional critic does not (cannot) change culture directly, cannot directly shape history, but she can contribute to the historical conditions that, in turn, will register changes, although often unanticipated ones, in the dominant discourse. Somewhat skeptical of the logic inherent to this scenario, the theorist Laurie Finke puts "feminine writing" in its oppositional frame to say that she agrees with Jones, Wittig, and others about the limits of oppositionalism as productive feminist theory. "We cannot simply oppose woman and feminism," Finke warns, "to man and patriarchy; we must investigate internal conflicts, the tensions within the 'dialogics of culture' problematically represented by contemporary feminist discourse."[19] The point is that the true difficulty of feminist theory in the aftermath of post-structuralism, as Finke observes, must be precisely the question of "whether or not it is possible to have feminist literary theory at all—that is, whether we can construct a theory or theories that are not simply exercises of power . . . that are open to real women and their historical situations" (266). More pointedly, Finke even asks whether "theory" as we know it is possible at all in an age that has deconstructed the foundations for logic, objectivity, goodness, and proportion—the age-old instruments of "truth" and metacommentary. Such concepts in contemporary culture have been appropriated by "discourses" that have enormous and far-reaching political implications and yet are situated (especially as Michel Foucault describes them) as inherently transpersonal—beyond the reach of any person's action or intervention.

The difficulty of Cixous's position, thus, is inherent to the enterprise of the oppositional critic—is not resolvable and cannot be "managed." Simply put, much contemporary theory, especially as influenced by Foucault, understands change as belonging to grand historical discourses not situated at the level of individual human action. However, since actual people act at the level of their lives, at the level of personal intervention and response, in this contemporary scenario historical activity and human action are connected only distantly and ironically. This is one of the dilemmas that haunt modernist and postmodern thought, and it is one that a generation of French intellectuals after World War II—Jacques Lacan, Derrida, Foucault, and Jean-François Lyotard among them—have responded to in their institutional, anti-Hegelian, anti-totality critiques. This is the same dilemma, as Heidegger and Paul de Man exemplify for many on the political left, that opposes (fragmentary) action and (totalized) knowledge and, in so doing, promotes political solipsism and quietism, even a kind of "collaboration."

Cixous's oppositionalism, however, is an object lesson on how a *person* does resist and, therein, can interact with the dominant discourse. Cixous's situation, even in view of the "failure" I spoke of earlier, points up the importance of oppositional reading, whatever its local effect, to cultural criticism. That is, Cixous's own ideological critique shows that change occurs in an economy of resistance in which the oppositional critic may fulfil a circumscribed but significant function. Cixous's project for reading *écriture féminine* —carried out in her classroom, in her criticism, and in her fiction—is itself an activity, an instance of intervention and resistance in the larger ideological economy of resistance. There are certainly limits on what Cixous can accomplish *personally*, but this is not at all an argument for political isolation or quietism. Cixous's case, in fact, is a contemporary demonstration of how cultural discourse works, the manner in which the interaction of "literary," political, and ideological forces interact to constitute possibilities realized in, or in the spaces not completely filled by, the dominant discourse.

In this analysis of Cixous and oppositional reading, I intend to suggest that the personal intervention of critics and theorists in culture is limited but also enfranchised in specific ways. Critics such as Cixous at times may seem to be merely doing the police in different voices and contributing not at all to the resistance that is the activity of ideological formation. But they—in their role *as critics*, even if they do not author those analyses (as Cixous's case shows)—do act at micro-levels, as Foucault says, of intervention. They do not cause change, but they participate in the ideological economy that does. I grant, however, that this scenario, in turn, could force a politically engaged critic like Cixous to think about cultural criticism somewhat schizophrenically, at times to be forced to read the personal separately from the historical and to have to act in the first while seeing the possible futility of action in the second. Contemporary political response to this postmodern condition, which Cixous exemplifies, is what Deleuze and Guattari in *Anti-Oedipus* have called "schizo-analysis," the strategic separation of the personal and the historical— not a view of "reality," not a solution to a problem, not an epistemology, but a strategy for survival and for the avoidance of paralysis in the postmodern age.[20]

We can envision Cixous at a particular moment in France, in the U.S., or in Oran, Algeria, where she was born, as she chose to learn to read *écriture feminine* —to attempt an oppositional reading of cultural texts that potentially could liberate her students and, more broadly, her female (and male) readers. She set out to read one thing and, in fact, read another—several others. There is clearly a theme of "failure" here. We need to think very carefully, though, about this "failure" because in every way that should matter to us it is not Cixous's—not a person's—"failure" I am describing. Cixous's "failure" to read the feminine demonstrates an emergent and important aspect of contemporary discourse, what could be called the "rhetoric of oppositionality"—the example of Cixous being an important staging and a signal event of contemporary culture. Her "failure" and—as Foucault would have it—oppositionalism's "failure" indicate, I would think, not the dead end of oppositionalism at all. On the contrary, in "The Laugh of the Medusa" Cixous began an ideological critique of the patriarchy as applied to contemporary reading and writing. The uses made of her oppositional reading, even the discussions of her "failure," are still having effects that Cixous could not foresee. The limitation of the oppositional stance, as I have been trying to suggest all along and as Cixous's case demonstrates especially well, is not an argument against oppositional criticism in the understanding of ideology but precisely an argument for it—a cultural mode of "reading" ideologically that we are only beginning to situate as a historical practice, a kind of "reading" that, in fact, as Cixous hoped, would move us out of linear and oppressive masculine patterns.[21]

NOTES

1. For an overview of Cixous's work in relation to other theorists, see Toril Moi, *Sexual/Textual Politics: Feminist Literary Theory* (London: Methuen, 1985).

2. Ann Rosalind Jones, "Writing the Body: Toward an Understanding of *l'écriture féminine,*" *The New Feminist Criticism: Essays on Women, Literature, and Theory,* ed. Elaine Showalter (New York: Pantheon, 1985).

3. Alice Jardine, *Gynesis: Configurations of Woman and Modernity* (Ithaca, NY: Cornell UP, 1985) 20.

4. Hélène Cixous and Catherine Clément, *The Newly Born Woman,* trans. Betsy Wing (Minneapolis: U of Minnesota P, 1986).

5. Hélène Cixous, "The Laugh of the Medusa," trans. Keith Cohen and Paula Cohen, *Critical Theory Since 1965,* ed. Hazard Adams and Leroy Searle (Tallahassee: Florida State UP, 1986) 309–20.

6. Hélène Cixous, "Castration or Decapitation?" trans. Annette Kuhn, *Signs* 7 (1981): 41–55.

7. Verena A. Conley, *Hélène Cixous: Writing the Feminine* (Lincoln: U of Nebraska P, 1984) 156.

8. Hélène Cixous, "The Character of 'Character,' " trans. Keith Cohen, *New Literary History* 5 (1974): 384–402.

9. Jim Merod, *The Political Responsibility of the Critic* (Ithaca, NY: Cornell UP, 1987) 158.

10. See Robert Con Davis, "Theorizing Opposition: Aristotle, Greimas, Jameson, and Said," *L'Esprit Createur* 27.2 (1987): 5–18; and Catherine Gallagher, "Politics, the Profession, and the Critic," *Diacritics* 15.2 (1986): 37–43.

11. For a discussion of this mechanism, see Davis, "Theorizing Opposition."

12. Aristotle, *"Categories" and "De Interpretatione,"* trans. J. L. Ackrill (Oxford: Clarendon, 1963).

13. Fredric Jameson, *The Political Unconscious: Narrative as a Socially Symbolic Act* (Ithaca, NY: Cornell UP, 1981).

14. John Peter Anton, *Aristotle's Theory of Contrariety* (London: Routledge & Kegan Paul, 1857).

15. Aristotle, *Posterior Analytics,* trans. Hippocrates G. Apostle (Grinnell, IA: Peripatetic P, 1981) 42.

16. See Aristotle's *On Interpretation.* Also A. J. Greimas and F. Rastier, "The Interaction of Semiotic Constraints," *Yale French Studies* 41 (1968): 86–105.

17. Ronald Schleifer, *A. J. Greimas and the Nature of Meaning: Linguistics, Semiotics, and Discourse Theory* (Lincoln: U of Nebraska P, 1987) 54.

18. Julia Kristeva, "Stabat Mater," *Tales of Love,* trans. Leon S. Roudiez (New York: Columbia UP, 1987) 234–63.

19. Laurie Finke, "The Rhetoric of Marginality: Why I Do Feminist Theory," *Tulsa Studies in Women's Literature* 5 (1986): 251–72.

20. *The Anti-Oedipus,* trans. Robert Hurley, Mark Seem, and Helen R. Lane (New York: Viking, 1977).

21. Several friends read and helped me to improve an earlier draft of this essay: James Comas, Laurie Finke, Patrick McGee, Valerie Moore, Thaïs Morgan, Gita Rajan, Ronald Schleifer, and Isaiah Smithson.

ELIZABETH A. FLYNN

Composing as a
Woman

It is not easy to think like a woman in a man's world, in the world
of the professions; yet the capacity to do that is a strength which we
can try to help our students develop. To think like a woman in a man's
world means thinking critically, refusing to accept the givens, making
connections between facts and ideas which men have left unconnected.
It means remembering that every mind resides in a body; remaining
accountable to the female bodies in which we live; constantly retesting
given hypotheses against lived experience. It means a constant critique
of language, for as Wittgenstein (no feminist) observed, "The limits of
my language are the limits of my world." And it means that most
difficult thing of all: listening and watching in art and literature, in the
social sciences, in all the descriptions we are given of the world, for
silences, the absences, the nameless, the unspoken, the encoded—for
there we will find the true knowledge of women. And in breaking
those silences, naming ourselves, uncovering the hidden, making ourselves present, we begin to define a reality which resonates to *us*,
which affirms *our* being, which allows the woman teacher and the
woman student alike to take ourselves, and each other, seriously:
meaning, to begin taking charge of our lives.

—Adrienne Rich,
"Taking Women Students Seriously"

The emerging field of composition studies could be described as a feminization of our previous conceptions of how writers write and how writing
should be taught. In exploring the nature of the writing process, composition specialists expose the limitations of previous product-oriented
approaches by demystifying the product and in so doing empowering
developing writers and readers. Rather than enshrining the text in its final
form, they demonstrate that the works produced by established authors
are often the result of an extended, frequently enormously frustrating
process and that creativity is an activity that results from experience and
hard work rather than a mysterious gift reserved for a select few. In a

sense, composition specialists replace the figure of the authoritative father with an image of a nurturing mother. Powerfully present in the work of composition researchers and theorists is the ideal of a committed teacher concerned about the growth and maturity of her students who provides feedback on ungraded drafts, reads journals, and attempts to tease out meaning from the seeming incoherence of student language. The field's foremothers come to mind—Janet Emig, Mina Shaughnessy, Ann Berthoff, Win Horner, Maxine Hairston, Shirley Heath, Nancy Martin, Linda Flower, Andrea Lunsford, Sondra Perl, Nancy Sommers, Marion Crowhurst, Lisa Ede. I'll admit the term *foremother* seems inappropriate as some of these women are still in their thirties and forties—we are speaking here of a very young field. Still, invoking their names suggests that we are also dealing with a field that, from the beginning, has welcomed contributions from women—indeed, has been shaped by women.

The work of male composition researchers and theorists has also contributed significantly to the process of feminization described above. James Britton, for instance, reverses traditional hierarchies by privileging private expression over public transaction, process over product. In arguing that writing for the self is the matrix out of which all forms of writing develop, he valorizes an activity and a mode of expression that have previously been undervalued or invisible, much as feminist literary critics have argued that women's letters and diaries are legitimate literary forms and should be studied and taught alongside more traditional genres. His work has had an enormous impact on the way writing is taught on the elementary and high school levels and in the university, not only in English courses but throughout the curriculum.[1] Writing-across-the-curriculum programs aim to transform pedagogical practices in all disciplines, even those where patriarchal attitudes toward authority are most deeply rooted.

Feminist Studies and Composition Studies

Feminist inquiry and composition studies have much in common. After all, feminist researchers and scholars and composition specialists are usually in the same department and sometimes teach the same courses. Not surprisingly, there have been wonderful moments when feminists have expressed their commitment to the teaching of writing. Florence Howe's essay, "Identity and Expression: A Writing Course for Women," for example, describes her use of journals in a writing course designed to empower women.[2] Adrienne Rich's essay, " 'When We Dead Awaken': Writing as Re-Vision," politicizes and expands our conception of revision, emphasizing that taking another look at the texts we have generated necessitates revising our cultural assumptions as well.[3]

There have also been wonderful moments when composition specialists have recognized that the marginality of the field of composition studies is linked in important ways to the political marginality of its constituents, many of whom are women who teach part-time. Maxine Hairston, in "Breaking Our Bonds and Reaffirming Our Connections," a slightly revised version of her Chair's address at the 1985 convention of the Conference on College Composition and Communication, draws an analogy between the plight of composition specialists and the plight of many women. For both, their worst problems begin at home and hence are immediate and daily. Both, too, often have complex psychological bonds to the people who frequently are their adversaries.[4]

For the most part, though, the fields of feminist studies and composition studies have not engaged each other in a serious or systematic way. The major journals in the field of composition studies do not often include articles addressing feminist issues, and panels on feminism are infrequent at the Conference on College Composition and Communication.[5] As a result, the parallels between feminist studies and composition studies have not been delineated, and the feminist critique that has enriched such diverse fields as linguistics, reading, literary criticism, psychology, sociology, anthropology, religion, and science has had little impact on our models of the composing process or on our understanding of how written language abilities are acquired. We have not examined our research methods or research samples to see if they are androcentric. Nor have we attempted to determine just what it means to compose as a woman.

Feminist research and theory emphasize that males and females differ in their developmental processes and in their interactions with others. They emphasize, as well, that these differences are a result of an imbalance in the social order, of the dominance of men over women. They argue that men have chronicled our historical narratives and defined our fields of inquiry. Women's perspectives have been suppressed, silenced, marginalized, written out of what counts as authoritative knowledge. Difference is erased in a desire to universalize. Men become the standard against which women are judged.

A feminist approach to composition studies would focus on questions of difference and dominance in written language. Do males and females compose differently? Do they acquire language in different ways? Do research methods and research samples in composition studies reflect a male bias? I do not intend to tackle all of these issues. My approach here is a relatively modest one. I will survey recent feminist research on gender differences in social and psychological development, and I will show how this research and theory may be used in examining student writing, thus suggesting directions that a feminist investigation of composition might take.

Gender Differences in Social and Psychological Development

Especially relevant to a feminist consideration of student writing are Nancy Chodorow's *The Reproduction of Mothering*, Carol Gilligan's *In a Different Voice*, and Mary Belenky, Blythe Clinchy, Nancy Goldberger, and Jill Tarule's *Women's Ways of Knowing*.[6] All three books suggest that women and men have different conceptions of self and different modes of interaction with others as a result of their different experiences, especially their early relationship with their primary parent, their mother.

Chodorow's book, published in 1978, is an important examination of what she calls the "psychoanalysis and the sociology of gender," which in turn influenced Gilligan in *In a Different Voice* and Belenky et al. in *Women's Ways of Knowing*. Chodorow tells us in her preface that her book originated when a feminist group she was affiliated with "wondered what it meant that women parented women." She argues that girls and boys develop different relational capacities and senses of self as a result of growing up in a family in which women mother. Because all children identify first with their mother, a girl's gender and gender role identification processes are continuous with her earliest identifications whereas a boy's are not. The boy gives up, in addition to his Oedipal and pre-Oedipal attachment to his mother, his primary identification with her. The more general identification processes for both males and females also follow this pattern. Chodorow says:

> Girls' identification processes, then, are more continuously embedded in and mediated by their ongoing relationship with their mother. They develop through and stress particularistic and affective relationships to others. A boy's identification processes are not likely to be so embedded in or mediated by a real affective relation to his father. At the same time, he tends to deny identification with and relationship to his mother and reject what he takes to be the feminine world; masculinity is defined as much negatively as positively. Masculine identification processes stress differentiation from others, the denial of affective relation, and categorical universalistic components of the masculine role. Feminine identification processes are relational, whereas masculine identification processes tend to deny relationship (176).

Carol Gilligan's *In a Different Voice*, published in 1982, builds on Chodorow's findings, focusing especially, though, on differences in the ways in which males and females speak about moral problems. According to Gilligan, women tend to define morality in terms of conflicting responsibilities rather than competing rights, requiring for their resolution a mode of thinking that is contextual and narrative rather than formal and abstract (19). Men, in contrast, equate morality and fairness and tie moral development to the understanding of rights and rules (19). Gilligan uses the metaphors of the web and the ladder to illustrate these distinctions. The web suggests interconnectedness as well as entrapment; the ladder suggests an achievement orientation as well as individualistic and hierarchical thinking. Gilligan's study aims to correct the inadequacies of Lawrence Kohlberg's delineation of the stages of moral development. Kohlberg's study included only male subjects, and his categories reflect his decidedly male orientation. For him, the highest stages of moral development derive from a reflective understanding of human rights (19).

Belenky, Clinchy, Goldberger, and Tarule, in *Women's Ways of Knowing*, acknowledge their debt to Gilligan, though their main concern is intellectual, rather than moral, development. Like Gilligan, they recognize that male experience has served as the model in defining processes of intellectual maturation. The mental processes that are involved in considering the abstract and the impersonal have been labeled "thinking" and are attributed primarily to men, while those that deal with the personal and interpersonal fall under the rubric of "emotions" and are largely relegated to women. The particular study they chose to examine and revise is William Perry's *Forms of Intellectual and Ethical Development in the College Years.*[7] While Perry did include some women subjects in his study, only the interviews with men were used in illustrating and validating his scheme of intellectual and ethical development. When Perry assessed women's development on the basis of the categories he developed, the women were found to conform to the patterns he had observed in the male data. Thus, his work reveals what women have in common with men but was poorly designed to uncover those themes that might be more prominent among women. *Women's Ways of Knowing* focuses on "what else women might have to say about the development of their minds and on alternative routes that are sketchy or missing in Perry's version" (9).

Belenky et al. examined the transcripts of interviews with 135 women from a variety of backgrounds and of different ages and generated categories that are suited for describing the stages of women's intellectual development. They found that the quest for self and voice plays a central role in transformations of women's ways of knowing. Silent women have little awareness of their intellectual capacities. They live—selfless and voiceless—at the behest of those around them. External authorities know the truth and are all-powerful. At the positions of received knowledge and procedural knowledge, other voices and external truths prevail.

Sense of self is embedded either in external definitions and roles or in identifications with institutions, disciplines, and methods. A sense of authority arises primarily through identification with the power of a group and its agreed-upon ways for knowing. Women at this stage of development have no sense of an authentic or unique voice, little awareness of a centered self. At the position of subjective knowledge, women turn away from others and any external authority. They have not yet acquired a public voice or public authority, though. Finally, women at the phase of constructed knowledge begin an effort to reclaim the self by attempting to integrate knowledge they feel intuitively with knowledge they have learned from others.

Student Writing

If women and men differ in their relational capacities and in their moral and intellectual development, we would expect to find manifestations of these differences in the student papers we encounter in our first-year composition courses. The student essays I will describe here are narrative descriptions of learning experiences produced in the first of a two-course sequence required of first-year students at Michigan Tech. I've selected the four because they invite commentary from the perspective of the material discussed above. The narratives of the female students are stories of interaction, of connection, or of frustrated connection. The narratives of the male students are stories of achievement, of separation, or of frustrated achievement.

Kim's essay describes a dreamlike experience in which she and her high school girlfriends connected with each other and with nature as a result of a balloon ride they decided to take one summer Sunday afternoon as a way of relieving boredom. From the start, Kim emphasizes communion and tranquility: "It was one of those Sunday afternoons when the sun shines brightly and a soft warm breeze blows gently. A perfect day for a long drive on a country road with my favorite friends." This mood is intensified as they ascend in the balloon: "Higher and higher we went, until the view was overpowering. What once was a warm breeze turned quickly into a cool crisp wind. A feeling of freedom and serenity overtook us as we drifted along slowly." The group felt as if they were "just suspended there on a string, with time non-existent." The experience made them contemplative, and as they drove quietly home, "each one of us collected our thoughts, and to this day we still reminisce about that Sunday afternoon." The experience solidified relationships and led to the formation of a close bond that was renewed every time the day was recollected.

The essay suggests what Chodorow calls relational identification processes. The members of the group are described as being in harmony with themselves and with the environment. There is no reference to competition or discord. The narrative also suggests a variation on what Belenky et al. call "connected knowing," a form of procedural knowledge that makes possible the most desirable form of knowing, constructed knowledge. Connected knowing is rooted in empathy for others and is intensely personal. Women who are connected knowers are able to detach themselves from the relationships and institutions to which they have been subordinated and begin to trust their own intuitions. The women in the narrative were connected doers rather than connected knowers. They went off on their own, left their families and teachers behind (it was summer vacation, after all), and gave themselves over to a powerful shared experience. The adventure was, for the most part, a silent one but did lead to satisfying talk.

Kathy also describes an adventure away from home, but hers was far less satisfying, no doubt because it involved considerably more risk. In her narrative she makes the point that "foreign countries can be frightening" by focusing on a situation in which she and three classmates, two females and a male, found themselves at a train station in Germany separated from the others because they had gotten off to get some refreshments and the train had left without them. She says:

> This left the four of us stranded in an unfamiliar station. Ed was the only person in our group that could speak German fluently, but he still didn't know what to do. Sue got hysterical and Laura tried to calm her down. I stood there stunned. We didn't know what to do.

What they did was turn to Ed, whom Kathy describes as "the smartest one in our group." He told them to get on a train that was on the same track as the original. Kathy realized, though, after talking to some passengers, that they were on the wrong train and urged her classmates to get off. She says:

> I almost panicked. When I convinced the other three we were on the wrong train we opened the doors. As we were getting off, one of the conductors started yelling at us in German. It didn't bother me too much because I couldn't understand what he was saying. One thing about trains in Europe is that they are always on schedule. I think we delayed that train about a minute or two.

In deciding which train to board after getting off the wrong one, they deferred to Ed's judgment once again, but this time they got on the right train. Kathy concludes, "When we got off the train everyone was waiting.

It turned out we arrived thirty minutes later than our original train. I was very relieved to see everyone. It was a very frightening experience and I will never forget it."

In focusing on her fears of separation, Kathy reveals her strong need for connection, for affiliation. Her story, like Kim's, emphasizes the importance of relationships, though in a different way. She reveals that she had a strong need to feel part of a group and no desire to rebel, to prove her independence, to differentiate herself from others. This conception of self was a liability as well as a strength in the sense that she became overly dependent on the male authority figure in the group, whom she saw as smarter and more competent than herself. In Belenky et al.'s terms, Kathy acted as if other voices and external truths were more powerful than her own. She did finally speak and act, though, taking it on herself to find out if they were on the right train and ushering the others off when she discovered they were not. She was clearly moving toward the development of an authentic voice and a way of knowing that integrates intuition with authoritative knowledge. After all, she was the real hero of the incident.

The men's narratives stress individuation rather than connection. They are stories of individual achievement or frustrated achievement and conclude by emphasizing separation rather than integration or reintegration into a community. Jim wrote about his "Final Flight," the last cross-country flight required for his pilot's license. That day, everything seemed to go wrong. First, his flight plan had a mistake in it that took an hour and a half to correct. As a result, he left his hometown two hours behind schedule. Then the weather deteriorated, forcing him to fly as low as a person can safely fly, with the result that visibility was very poor. He landed safely at his first destination but flew past the second because he was enjoying the view too much. He says:

> Then I was off again south bound for Benton Harbor. On the way south along the coast of Lake Michigan the scenery was a beautiful sight. This relieved some of the pressures and made me look forward to the rest of the flight. It was really nice to see the ice flows break away from the shore. While enjoying the view of a power plant on the shore of Lake Michigan I discovered I had flown past the airport.

He finally landed and took off again, but shortly thereafter had to confront darkness, a result of his being behind schedule. He says,

> The sky turned totally black by the time I was half-way home. This meant flying in the dark which I had only done once before. Flying in the dark was also illegal for me to do at this time. One thing that made flying at night nice was that you could see lights that were over ninety miles away.

Jim does not emphasize his fear, despite the fact that his situation was more threatening than the one Kathy described, and his reference to his enjoyment of the scenery suggests that his anxiety was not paralyzing or debilitating. At times, his solitary flight was clearly as satisfying as Kim's communal one. When he focuses on the difficulties he encountered, he speaks only of his "problems" and "worries" and concludes that the day turned out to be "long and trying." He sums up his experience as follows: "That day I will long remember for both its significance in my goal in getting my pilot's license and all the problems or worries that it caused me during the long and problem-ridden flight." He emerges the somewhat shaken hero of his adventure; he has achieved his goal in the face of adversity. Significantly, he celebrates his return home by having a bite to eat at McDonald's by himself. His adventure does not end with a union or reunion with others.

Jim's story invites interpretation in the context of Chodorow's claims about male interactional patterns. Chodorow says that the male, in order to feel himself adequately masculine, must distinguish and differentiate himself from others. Jim's adventure was an entirely solitary one. It was also goal-directed; he wanted to obtain his pilot's license and, presumably, prove his competence to himself and others. His narrative calls into question, though, easy equations of abstract reasoning and impersonality with male modes of learning, since Jim was clearly as capable as Kim of experiencing moments of exultation, of communion with nature.

Joe's narrative of achievement is actually a story of frustrated achievement, of conflicting attitudes toward an ethic of hard work and sacrifice to achieve a goal. When he was in high school, his father drove him twenty miles to swim practice and twenty miles home every Tuesday through Friday night between October and March so he could practice for the swim team. He hated this routine and hated the Saturday morning swim meets even more but continued because he thought his parents, especially his father, wanted him to. He said, "I guess it was all for them, the cold workouts, the evening practices, the weekend meets. I had to keep going for them even though I hated it." Once he realized he was going through his agony for his parents rather than for himself, though, he decided to quit and was surprised to find that his parents supported him. Ultimately, though, he regretted his decision. He says,

> As it turns out now, I wish I had stuck with it. I really had a chance to go somewhere with my talent. I see kids my age who stuck with something for a long time and I envy them for their determination. I wish I had met up to the challenge of sticking with my swimming, because I could have been very good if I would have had their determination.

Joe is motivated to pursue swimming because he thinks his father will be disappointed if he gives it up. His father's presumed hold on him is clearly tenuous, however, because once Joe realizes that he is doing it for him rather than for himself, he quits. Finally, though, it is his gender role identification, his socialization into a male role and a male value system, that allows him to look back on his decision with regret. In college, he has become a competitor, an achiever. He now sees value in the long and painful practices, in a single-minded determination to succeed. The narrative reminds us of Chodorow's point that masculine identification is predominantly a gender role identification rather than identification with a particular parent.

I am hardly claiming that the four narratives are neat illustrations of the feminist positions discussed above. For one thing, those positions are rich in contradiction and complexity and defy easy illustration. For another, the narratives themselves are as often characterized by inconsistency and contradiction as by a univocality of theme and tone. Kathy is at once dependent and assertive; Joe can't quite decide if he should have been rebellious or disciplined. Nor am I claiming that what I have found here are characteristic patterns of male and female student writing. I would need a considerably larger and more representative sample to make such a claim hold. I might note, though, that I had little difficulty identifying essays that revealed patterns of difference among the twenty-four papers I had to choose from, and I could easily have selected others. Sharon, for instance, described her class trip to Chicago, focusing especially on the relationship she and her classmates were able to establish with her advisor. Diane described "An Unwanted Job" that she seemed unable to quit despite unpleasant working conditions. Mike, like Diane, was dissatisfied with his job, but he expressed his dissatisfaction and was fired. The frightening experience Russ described resulted from his failed attempt to give his car a tune-up; the radiator hose burst, and he found himself in the hospital recovering from third-degree burns. These are stories of relatedness or entanglement; of separation or frustrated achievement.

The description of the student essays is not meant to demonstrate the validity of feminist scholarship but to suggest, instead, that questions raised by feminist researchers and theorists do have a bearing on composition studies and should be pursued. We ought not assume that males and female use language in identical ways or represent the world in a similar fashion. And if their writing strategies and patterns of representation do differ, then ignoring those differences almost certainly means a suppression of women's separate ways of thinking and writing. Our models of the composing process are quite possibly better suited to describing men's ways of composing than to describing women's.[8]

Pedagogical Strategies

The classroom provides an opportunity for exploring questions about gender differences in language use. Students, I have found, are avid inquirers into their own language processes. An approach I have had success with is to make the question of gender difference in behavior and language use the subject to be investigated in class. In one honors section of first-year English, for instance, course reading included selections from Mary Anne Ferguson's *Images of Women in Literature*, Gilligan's *In a Different Voice*, Alice Walker's *Meridian*, and James Joyce's *A Portrait of the Artist as a Young Man*. Students were also required to keep a reading journal and to submit two formal papers. The first was a description of people they know in order to arrive at generalizations about gender differences in behavior, the second a comparison of some aspect of the Walker and Joyce novels in the light of our class discussions.

During class meetings we shared journal entries, discussed the assigned literature, and self-consciously explored our own reading, writing, and speaking behaviors. In one session, for instance, we shared retellings of Irwin Shaw's "The Girls in Their Summer Dresses," an especially appropriate story since it describes the interaction of a husband and wife as they attempt to deal with the husband's apparently chronic habit of girl-watching. Most of the women were sympathetic to the female protagonist, and several males clearly identified strongly with the male protagonist.

The students reacted favorably to the course. They found Gilligan's book to be challenging, and they enjoyed the heated class discussions. The final journal entry of one of the strongest students in the class, Dorothy, suggests the nature of her development over the ten-week period:

> As this is sort of the wrap-up of what I've learned or how I feel about the class, I'll try to relate this entry to my first one on gender differences.
>
> I'm not so sure that men and women are so similar anymore, as I said in the first entry. The reactions in class especially make me think this. The men were so hostile toward Gilligan's book! I took no offense at it, but then again I'm not a man. I must've even overlooked the parts where she offended the men!
>
> Another thing really bothered me. One day after class, I heard two of the men talking in the hall about how you just have to be really careful about what you say in HU 101H about women, etc. *Why* do they have to be careful?! What did these two *really* want to say? That was pretty disturbing.
>
> However, I do still believe that MTU (or most any college actually) does

bring out more similarities than differences. But the differences are still there—I know that.

Dorothy has begun to suspect that males and females read differently, and she has begun to suspect that they talk among themselves differently than they do in mixed company. The reading, writing, and discussing in the course have clearly alerted her to the possibility that gender affects the way in which readers, writers, and speakers use language.

This approach works especially well with honors students. I use somewhat different reading and writing assignments with non-honors students. In one class, for instance, I replaced the Gilligan book with an essay by Dale Spender on conversational patterns in high school classrooms. Students wrote a paper defending or refuting the Spender piece on the basis of their experiences in their own high schools. I have also devised ways of addressing feminist issues in composition courses in which the focus is not explicitly on gender differences. In a course designed to introduce students to fundamentals of research, for instance, students read Marge Piercy's *Woman on the Edge of Time* and did research on questions stimulated by it. They then shared their findings with the entire class in oral presentations. The approach led to wonderful papers on and discussions of the treatment of women in mental institutions, discrimination against minority women, and the ways in which technology can liberate women from oppressive roles.

Gender Differences and Power

I return now to my title and to the epigraph that introduces my essay. First, what does it mean to "compose as a woman"? Although the title invokes Jonathan Culler's "Reading as a Woman," a chapter in *On Deconstruction*, I do not mean to suggest by it that I am committed fully to Culler's deconstructive position.[9] Culler maintains that "to read as a woman is to avoid reading as a man, to identify the specific defenses and distortions of male readings and provide correctives" (54). He concludes: "For a woman to read as a woman is not to repeat an identity or an experience that is given but to play a role she constructs with reference to her identity as a woman, which is also a construct, so that the series can continue: a woman reading as a woman reading as a woman. The noncoincidence reveals an interval, a division within woman or within any reading subject and the 'experience' of that subject" (64).

Culler is certainly correct that women often read as men and that they have to be encouraged to defend against this form of alienation. The strategy he suggests is almost entirely reactive, though. To read as a woman is to avoid reading as a man, to be alerted to the pitfalls of men's ways of reading.[10] Rich, too, warns of the dangers of immasculation, of identifying against oneself and learning to think like a man, and she, too, emphasizes the importance of critical activity on the part of the woman student—refusing to accept the givens of our culture, making connections between facts and ideas which men have left unconnected.[11] She is well aware that thinking as a woman involves active construction, the re-creation of one's identity. But she also sees value in recovering women's lived experience. In fact, she suggests that women maintain a critical posture in order to get in touch with that experience—to name it, to uncover that which is hidden, to make present that which has been absent. Her approach is active rather than reactive. Women's experience is not entirely a distorted version of male reality, it is not entirely elusive, and it is worthy of recuperation. We must alert our women students to the dangers of immasculation and provide them with a critical perspective. But we must also encourage them to become self-consciously aware of what their experience in the world has been and how this experience is related to the politics of gender. For ultimately questions of difference are questions of power, questions of whose interpretation of reality will prevail and of whose decisions will construct that reality. A recognition that women are different in important ways from men is a necessary first step in a recognition that power has been distributed inequitably throughout history and in every culture. As writing teachers, we have an opportunity— indeed, an obligation—to attempt to rectify those inequities by placing women's texts at the center of our curricula and by encouraging our women students to write from the power of their experience.[12]

NOTES

1. James Britton et al., *The Development of Writing Abilities (11–18)* (London: Macmillan Education, 1975).

2. Florence Howe, "Identity and Expression: A Writing Course for Women," *College English* 32 (May 1971): 863–71, rpt. Howe, *Myths of Coeducation: Selected Essays, 1964–1983* (Bloomington: Indiana UP, 1984) 28–37.

3. Adrienne Rich, " 'When We Dead Awaken': Writing as Re-Vision," *On Lies, Secrets, and Silence: Selected Prose, 1966–1978* (New York: W. W. Norton, 1979) 33–49.

4. Maxine Hairston, "Breaking Our Bonds and Reaffirming Our Connections," *College Composition and Communication* 36 (October 1985): 272–82.

5. The 1988 Conference on College Composition and Communication was a notable exception. It had a record number of panels on feminist or gender-related issues and a number of sessions devoted to political concerns. I should add, too, that an exception to the generalization that feminist studies and compo-

sition studies have not confronted each other is Cynthia Caywood and Gillian Overing's very useful anthology, *Teaching Writing: Pedagogy, Gender, and Equity* (Albany: State U of New York P, 1987). In their Introduction to the book, Caywood and Overing note the striking parallels between writing theory and feminist theory. They conclude, "the process model, insofar as it facilitates and legitimizes the fullest expression of the individual voice, is compatible with the feminist re-visioning of hierarchy, if not essential to it" (xiv). The essays in the volume contribute significant insights. Pamela Annas, in "Silences: Feminist Language Research and the Teaching of Writing," describes a course she teaches at the University of Massachusetts at Boston entitled "Writing as Women." In the course, she focuses on the question of silence: "What kinds of silence there are; the voices inside you that tell you to be quiet, the voices outside you that drown you out or politely dismiss what you say or do not understand you, the silence inside you that avoids saying anything important even to yourself, internal and external forms of censorship, and the stress that it produces" (3–4). Carol A. Stanger, in "The Sexual Politics of the One-to-One Tutorial Approach and Collaborative Learning," argues that the one-to-one tutorial is essentially hierarchical and hence a male mode of teaching, whereas collaborative learning is female and relational rather than hierarchical. She uses Gilligan's images of the ladder and the web to illustrate her point (31–44). Elisabeth Däumer and Sandra Runzo suggest that the teaching of writing is comparable to the activity of mothering in that it is a form of "women's work." Mothers socialize young children to insure that they become acceptable citizens, and teachers' work, like the work of mothers, is usually devalued (45–46).

6. Nancy Chodorow, *The Reproduction of Mothering: Psychoanalysis and the Sociology of Gender* (Berkeley: U of California P, 1978); Carol Gilligan, *In a Different Voice: Psychological Theory and Women's Development* (Cambridge: Harvard UP, 1982); Mary Field Belenky et al., *Women's Ways of Knowing: The Development of Self, Voice, and Mind* (New York: Basic Books, 1986).

7. William G. Perry, *Forms of Intellectual and Ethical Development in the College Years* (New York: Holt, Rinehart & Winston, 1970).

8. It should be clear by now that my optimistic claim at the outset of the essay that the field of composition studies has feminized our conception of written communication needs qualification. I have already mentioned that the field has developed, for the most part, independent of feminist studies and as a result has not explored written communication in the context of women's special needs and problems. Also, feminist inquiry is beginning to reveal that work in cognate fields that have influenced the development of composition studies is androcentric. For an exploration of the androcentrism of theories of reading see Patrocinio P. Schweickart, "Reading Ourselves: Toward a Feminist Theory of Reading," *Gender and Reading: Essays on Readers, Texts, and Contexts,* ed. Elizabeth A. Flynn and Patrocinio P. Schweickart (Baltimore: Johns Hopkins UP, 1986) 31–62.

9. Jonathan Culler, *On Deconstruction: Theory and Criticism after Structuralism* (Ithaca: Cornell UP, 1982).

10. Elaine Showalter, in "Reading as a Woman: Jonathan Culler and the

Deconstruction of Feminist Criticism," argues that "Culler's deconstructionist priorities lead him to overstate the essentialist dilemma of defining the *woman* reader, when in most cases what is intended and implied is a *feminist* reader" (in *Men and Feminism*, ed. Alice Jardine and Paul Smith [New York: Methuen, 1987] 126).

11. Adrienne Rich, "Taking Women Students Seriously," *On Lies, Secrets, and Silence* 237–45. Judith Fetterley first used the term *immasculation* in *The Resisting Reader: A Feminist Approach to American Fiction* (Bloomington: Indiana UP, 1977). In speaking of canonical male texts, she says, "in such fictions the female reader is co-opted into participation in an experience from which she is explicitly excluded; she is asked to identify with a selfhood that defines itself in opposition to her; she is required to identify against herself" (xii).

12. I received invaluable feedback on drafts of this essay from Carol Berkenkotter, Art Young, Marilyn Cooper, John Willinsky, Diane Shoos, John Flynn, Richard Gebhardt, and three anonymous reviewers for *College Composition and Communication*.

SUSAN L. GABRIEL

Gender, Reading, and Writing: Assignments, Expectations, and Responses

As composition instructors, we often rely on reading to serve as the foundation for our courses; we routinely select readings from which we create assignments that ask students to write critical analyses, interpretations, and argumentative essays. Yet, if we are not aware of the complex factors which can affect our students' responses to a specific reading task, we cannot make informed choices as to what we are asking our students to read; we cannot design appropriate writing assignments; and we cannot evaluate fairly the responses elicited by our assignments.

Reading is by its very nature covert; on the way to creating meaning, the mind of the reader transforms markings on a page into words and sentences. Although the reader begins with what is on the page, he or she fills in the gaps with memories, experiences, and perceptions. The phrase "the dark and abandoned house" may conjure up a vague image from a movie for one reader, while another reader might imagine a real house that was next door during childhood; the image may or may not have frightening connotations, depending on the past, personality, and attitudes of the person. The memories and experiences of each reader shade and define the ways in which the text takes on meaning. It has become increasingly evident that one factor influencing the perceptions an individual brings to a reading task is gender.

The effects of gender on reading have only recently come to be considered, although understanding the nature of reading has long fascinated scholars in a variety of fields, including education, psychology, and literary criticism. In a study published in 1952, Anne Selley McKillop, an educational psychologist, suggests that "reading may be considered a complex response made by the whole organism. What the response will be in a particular situation is determined by a variety of complex interwoven factors, some related to the nature of the reading material, others to the nature of the reader."[1] McKillop goes on to postulate three factors which can influence and determine a reader's response.

> One group of factors . . . centers around the reader's ability to perceive and recognize printed symbols and to understand the meaning of these symbols in relation to each other. . . . Other factors which may determine the reader's response to any reading include the reader's past experiences and his [sic] general information. A third group of factors may interact with the first two in determining the specific response to any reading situation. This group of factors involves attitudes, values, interest, and appreciations (3).

She uses "frame of reference" to refer to the latter two groups of factors and concludes that a student's "frame of reference" comes into effect when he or she is asked to write responses that are value judgments, rather than objective determinations. McKillop does not specifically mention gender as a factor affecting reading, but gender does play a role in one's past experiences, attitudes, values, and interests.

A more recent article by psychologists Mary Crawford and Roger Chaffin discusses reading and gender while summarizing cognitive research on gender and comprehension.[2] Crawford and Chaffin use the term *schema*, which is similar to McKillop's "frame of reference." Schema theory, as developed by several theorists, suggests that the background experience of an individual provides "an organizing structure called a schema, which provides the framework necessary to understand" what is being read (4). Crawford and Chaffin go on to speculate about the role of gender in the schemata of an individual. "Differences in background between women and men in our society should, by themselves, lead to differences in the way women and men understand a wide variety of texts. The primacy and centrality of the gender schema should ensure differential encoding of experiences by men and women" (23–24). But what is the difference between female and male schemata?

A significant difference is explained by the theories of behavioral psychologists such as Jean Baker Miller, Nancy Chodorow, and Carol Gilligan.[3] Miller points out that "the ego and the super-ego develop in relation to reality (that is reality as is defined by one's culture) and the demands it places upon the individual" (72). Culturally, males and females receive different messages which teach them the "proper" roles for men and women in each society. As Chodorow explains, "Women and men grow up with differently constructed and experienced inner object worlds, and are preoccupied with different relational issues" (169). She delineates these different relational issues by showing that "feminine identification processes are relational, whereas masculine identification processes tend to deny relationship" (176). Chodorow concludes, "Masculine personality, then, comes to be defined more in terms of denial of relations and connections (and denial of femininity), whereas feminine personality comes to include a fundamental definition of self in relationship" (169). Gilligan, drawing on the work of Chodorow and others, posits that these distinct patterns of differentiation in males and females are linked to the fact that most early child care is done by women. She concludes that "female identity formation takes place in a context of ongoing relationship . . . girls, identifying themselves as female, experience themselves as like their mothers . . . " (7–8). For males the process is much different. "Boys, in defining themselves as masculine, separate their mothers from themselves . . . male development entails a 'more emphatic individuation . . . ' " (8). With respect to relationality, the frame of reference, or schema, developed by females and males is markedly different.

The role of gender schema in the act of reading became an issue with the advent of feminist literary criticism. Feminist theorists began to examine the role gender plays in the interpretation of a literary text by addressing questions such as the one posed by Jonathan Culler: "If the meaning of a work is the experience of a reader, what difference does it make if the reader is a woman?"[4] Culler and others draw upon theories put forth by reader-response critics such as Wolfgang Iser and Stanley Fish, who have speculated about the role of the reader in determining literary meaning.[5] These theorists, although differing in approach and critical stance, have served to destroy "the traditional separation between reader and text" and to make "the response of the reader rather than the contents of the work the focus of critical attention."[6] Reader-response theorists are responsible for focusing attention on the reader; feminist critics are responsible for adjusting this focus to include gender.

One area of concern for many feminist critics is the choice of readings assigned to students and the resultant sense of powerlessness that the interaction with these readings may cause female students. These critics suggest that women are not validated, empowered, by the traditional literary curriculum. As Patrocinio Schweickart says, "The literary canon is androcentric, and this has a profoundly damaging effect on women readers."[7] As early as 1971, Elaine Showalter suggests that a female college freshman is being taught to "think like a man."[8] Taking this idea further, Judith Fetterley suggests that the traditional canon is "immasculating" women.[9] "As readers and teachers and scholars, women are taught to think as men, to identify with a male point of view, and to accept as normal and legitimate a male system of values, one of whose central principles is misogyny" (xx). What Showalter, Fetterley, and others are suggesting is that the choice of readings assigned in college classrooms glorifies and emphasizes the male cultural experience (breaking away, autonomy, etc.) while deemphasizing and negating the female experience (relationships, nurturing, etc.). Huck's journey down the river, Captain Ahab's confrontation at sea, and Tom Wingfield's leaving his mother and Laura are but three examples from classics that revolve around masculine themes. Thus, a male student, with his masculine schema, receives affirmation from what he is assigned to read; a female student, with her feminine schema, realizes no such empowerment from these assigned reading experiences. In order to respond effectively to such readings, a female student must learn to identify with the male frame of reference. A similar adjustment is not required of a male student.

Changes have come about in the curriculum with the addition of more female authors and female texts in anthologies, yet many instructors still do not consider gender differences in reader response when creating or evaluating writing assignments. One problem has been the absence of data to corroborate such theories as "immasculation" of women and gender schema. To this end I determined to design a study which I hoped would provide some much-needed data in the study of gender, reading, and writing. The premise for my study was a simple one; agreeing with Showalter and Fetterley, I reasoned that since the traditional literary canon emphasizes the male experience, female students are continually being asked to identify with feelings and experiences which are not consistent with their experiences as women. Therefore, female readers, who are trained within this literary curriculum, evidently learn to identify equally well with either male or female characters. Conversely, since males in our schools are seldom required to read about female experiences, they should be able easily to identify with male fictional characters but should exhibit some difficulty in relating to female characters or feminine experiences.

Although determining whether and how a reader identifies with a character is an elusive task, I decided that one way to judge reader identification would be to have readers write journal entries while pretending to be a fictional character in a story they had read. Following completion of this task, the readers would then be asked to comment on the relative ease or difficulty with which they had written the journal entry. To test my assumptions about gender and identification, I designed a study requiring first-quarter freshman composition students to read two short stories, one focusing on a male character and one dealing with a female character; to write journal entries for those two characters; and to write a reaction to the task of creating the fictitious journal entries. My expectation was that the female participants would be able to complete the required journal writing easily, whether identifying with either a male or female character, but that male participants would be less able to complete the journal writing tasks successfully when asked to identify closely with a female character.

I was aware that several variables needed to be taken into account in the planning of this study. Because the student participants were going to be asked to perform both reading and writing tasks, some variations in response were likely to occur based solely on the reading and/or writing ability of each student. Obviously, these differences could not be attributed to gender. I determined that a reading-level test score, if available, should be noted for each participant. Since all students in these composition classes were required to pass a stringent department-wide writing diagnostic test on the first day of class, I was able to assume a standard level of writing competency. Also, I was aware that I would need to concentrate on what was being said in the journal entries, rather on than the way in which it was written. Some students, regardless of gender, would be more expressive than others.

Having developed the premise and considered the variables around which I would design my project, I needed to choose the readings; I had several criteria to satisfy. I wanted to use no more than one class session (two hours) on this project; therefore, the stories needed to be short, requiring only ten to fifteen minutes to read. Also, because I assumed many of my students had average or lower-level reading skills, the stories needed to be simple to comprehend and easy to relate to. In addition, to make my comparison of student responses possible, the stories had to encompass the same subject matter; specifically, they both needed to describe a human experience that is common for both males and females. Finally, the texts needed a clear female or male orientation—that is, one of the stories would have to relate the experience from a male point of view, while the other would have to describe the incident from a female standpoint. I had intended to choose one story by a female author and one by a male writer. However, I was not able to find two stories that would meet all the requirements. I had to settle on two stories that met all of the criteria except both were written by men: Sherwood Anderson's "Nobody Knows," to represent the male experience, and "Up in Michigan" by Ernest Hemingway, to represent the female perspective.[10] (Although Hemingway usually draws female characters poorly, "Up in Michigan" presents a sensitive treatment of a female character. As Kenneth S. Lynn points out in his biography, *Hemingway*, "Up in Michigan" is a story which "refutes charges that Hemingway can't identify with women in his fiction. . . . "[11] The plot of each story centers around a young and naive character, one male and one female, who in the course of the narrative experiences a "first time" sexual encounter. For each of them, the loss of innocence takes place with a partner for whom the sexual encounter is casual and purely physical, thus rendering the entire episode meaningless for the young character.[12]

"Nobody Knows" is told through the point of view of George Willard, a youthful, inquisitive newspaper reporter in the small midwestern town of Winesburg, Ohio. While at work one day, he receives a note from a woman named Louise Trunnion; the note reads, "I'm yours if you want me" (60). Louise is a woman who is the subject of much town gossip because of her loose reputation. George debates all day as to whether he should arrange to meet Louise, but finally he summons his courage and arranges a rendezvous. There is a break in the story as George and Louise walk into a vacant field and sit down on a pile of boards; when we next see George, he is walking back through town. "George Willard felt satisfied. He had wanted more than anything else to talk to some man" (61).

Hemingway's story centers around a woman named Liz Coates, who works in a boarding house located in a small northern Michigan town. One of the men who takes his meals at the house where Liz works is a blacksmith named Jim Gilmore. Liz has secretly admired Jim for a long time, spending much of her time thinking about him. The feelings are not mutual. Jim "liked her face because it was so jolly but he never thought about her" (81). One evening, following his return from a deer-hunting trip, Jim drinks a great deal of whiskey and begins to take notice of Liz. She is thrilled finally to receive some attention from him. When everyone else has gone to bed, he approaches her in the kitchen, kissing and caressing her. At his suggestion they go out for a walk and end up on a deserted dock. Jim's advances become more insistent, and Liz is unable to stop him. Having achieved a climax, Jim falls into a drunken sleep; Liz pushes him off, covers him with her coat, and leaves him there. "She was cold and miserable and everything felt gone" (85).

During the class period set aside to carry out this study, I informed my students that I was working on a project and needed their responses for my data. I also stressed that their participation was purely voluntary and that at any time during the class period they could choose to discontinue.[13] They were told that their responses were only going to be used as part of my study and that at no time would their identities be revealed. The students were given copies of "Nobody Knows," without the name of the author; when all the students had finished reading the story, I passed out a sheet on which they were to record their social security number (in order to obtain reading test scores), age, and sex. In addition to asking the students to record these data, the assignment sheet also instructed the students to perform two tasks, both to be completed on separate paper attached to the assignment sheet. The first prompt read, "Imagine that George was keeping a journal. Write a journal entry which he might have written following his sexual encounter with Louise." Next were the following instructions: "Now that you have written George's journal entry, write a paragraph in which you react to the assigned task. Consider if it was difficult or easy for you to produce the imaginary journal entry. Explain why."

When the students had completed the journal writing and commentary, we took a short break before I handed out the Hemingway story. The sequence was the same for the second story. The students completed the same personal data as before; they wrote another imaginary journal entry, this time writing as Liz; and they expressed their reaction to writing the entry. Three of my colleagues agreed to test their students in order to obtain a larger sample. Each of the instructors who had agreed to help me administered the same series of tasks in the same order outlined above, assuring students of their anonymity.

A total of 129 students participated in the study—85 females and 44 males. (Since the females outnumbered the males nearly 2 to 1, rather than randomly choosing 44 females to match the number of males, I decided to use all the responses I collected but to record the results in percentages.) All 129 students were members of 7 beginning composition classes, offered during the fall quarter of 1986. With the exception of 4 women aged 24, 25, 29, and 43 and 4 men aged 22, 23, 25, and 30, the student participants were in the 18- to 20-year-old range. The lowest reading level of the students was ninth grade, with the majority of the students reading at or just below the college level. Because the stories were written with simple vocabulary, the reading scores did not become a factor in any of my results; even students with low reading scores were able to comprehend the stories.

I began compiling my data by reading the reactions of the students to the journal writing task, recording what had been written, and keeping track of how many males and how many females were reporting a sense of ease and/or difficulty in executing the assignment. Turning first to the male responses to "Nobody Knows," which required the students to write as George, 64 percent wrote that they found writing this journal entry to be a fairly simple task. Thirty-six percent of the men reported that they had had some difficulty with the writing. Their reasons for this difficulty included: "I didn't really get to know George well enough." "The encounter was described too generally." "The author could have put in more details." Several students commented on the comprehension difficulty created by the lack of details. Their problems seemed to stem more from Anderson's writing style than from an inability to identify with the character.

As for the male reactions to writing Liz's journal entry ("Up in

Michigan"), the task was considered difficult by 66 percent of them, while 34 percent felt that the task was not a problem. Those for whom the journal entry was troublesome wrote, "It's hard for me to know what a woman is thinking or feeling." "It's hard to think like a girl." "I can only imagine how she felt, but I can't really feel what she went through." Given my original hypothesis, none of these reactions was unexpected. Comments from the few males who felt that the writing was not difficult included, "I have been in Jim's place, and I know that the woman gets really disappointed." "I know how girls are. They're much more sensitive than guys when it comes to sex." "This story had more details; therefore it [the assignment] was easier." These responses reflect little identification with Liz; rather, they are expressions of men who think that they under-stand Liz because of their own experiences with women or because of generalizations they have heard about women.

Turning to the responses written by the women students, writing a journal entry for Liz was no problem for 84 percent of them; only 16 percent felt that the assigned task was difficult. Two comments written by women in the latter group were, "Journal entries are too personal to write for someone else," and "I would have reacted in a totally different manner if I had been subjected to such force by a man." These reactions do not reflect a lack of identification with Liz, but, in the first case, a wish to respect Liz's, and probably the student's, privacy, and in the second case, a disagreement with the way Liz chose to react to her situation. Both of these comments may have been written by women who had been in similar circumstances and were uncomfortable with the feelings that the assignment was arousing in them. (Fear of forcing a female student to relive a painful experience was one reason I had insisted all students were free to quit at any time, or not participate at all.)

When I began to examine the responses of the females to writing as a man (George), my figures showed a clear deviation from my original hypothesis. I had anticipated that the majority of the women would not have a problem identifying with this male character; however, 71 percent of the women wrote that they had trouble writing George's journal entry, and only 29 percent responded that the assigned task was easy to complete. A sample of some of the responses from women experiencing difficulty indicates that they were, indeed, having a difficult time identify-ing with George. "Since I am a woman, how am I supposed to know everything that is going through a man's mind after having sex?" "I couldn't feel how he felt for sure." "It is usually difficult for me to understand men anyway." Other comments from this group suggested, as did some of the male responses to this story, that the author had given the reader too little detail to work with. "I didn't know exactly what went on," and "The story didn't allow the reader to get to know George," were two responses that illustrated the frustration of these women regarding Anderson's economy of words. For the few female students who found the assignment easy, the responses seem indicative of an ability to understand and identify with George. A typical response echoed by more than one of the women in this group was, "Although I disagree with how George acts, I can understand what he feels." Even considering these comments, which show strong female identification with a male character, my figures show no significant difference between males and females in ability to switch gender roles. Females have as much trouble empathizing with characters of the opposite sex as males do. Thus, my results cannot prove that females are more readily able to identify with characters of either sex simply because of their past reading experiences and training.

Although my statistics did not illustrate the differences I had expected, they did reveal other patterns. After reading each entry, I made a short summary of the content, sometimes by quoting exact sections but generally looking for a key phrase or two from each entry to convey its essence. Then I kept a tally of the number of times responses were repeated within the sample. It did not take long or require the reading of too many journal entries before some definite patterns began to emerge. As I looked carefully at the journal entries, I discovered that the students were exhibiting surprising differences in their responses—differences that reflected their cultural gender expectations and that drew a firm line between the females and the males. Although this study does not prove or disprove the "immasculation" theory, it does offer some evidence in support of the gender schema theory as discussed by Crawford and Chaffin.

Within the journal entries written as George ("Nobody Knows"), some males and females wrote similar entries. Some students of both sexes wrote about feeling nervous and yet anxious to embark on a real adventure. One female wrote, "What finally made me decide to go through with it was the fact that it was an adventure." The text supports these interpretations. "The young man was nervous. All day he had gone about his work like one dazed by a blow. . . . George Willard had set forth upon an adventure" (58).

Among males, the response which was repeated most often was, "Now I have become a man." Some of the men wrote of suddenly becoming confident and taking control of the situation; they interpreted George's experience as stepping into the world reserved for mature adult males. For example, "Today I, George Willard, have been transformed from a nervous young man to a bold, aggressive male." Again, the text supports this reading. "Sylvester West's Drug Store was still open and he went in and brought a cigar. . . . He had wanted more than anything to talk to some man" (61). The fact that this response was the one most often repeated in the journal entries produced by men points to a frame of reference which the male participants brought to the reading of this story, allowing them to see what is clearly in the text. This schema bears the stamp of our cultural stance that when a young boy has his first sexual experience, he is truly a "man."

Only two of the women wrote entries for George which contained the idea that he had achieved manhood. Instead, what was most often repeated in the women's journal entries was a hope, and in some cases a certainty, that this night was to be the beginning of a relationship with Louise. As one female put it, "I feel I love her, but I am not sure that her feelings are the same for me. I only hope that our relationship will work out someway." There is nothing in the text to support such a reading; we learn little about Louise during the story, and she does not appear at the end. In fact, George is apprehensive that she might tell someone whom she had been with and what they had been doing. He reassures himself by thinking, "She hasn't got anything on me. Nobody knows" (62). Are the females simply misreading, or is the schema that they as women have brought to this story influencing their interpretation? This need to find a relationship, even where clearly none exists, is consistent with the theories of Miller, Chodorow, and Gilligan. None of the men's journal entries contained a suggestion that there would be some emotional commitment following this sexual encounter. Thus, responses to Anderson's brief story divide readers according to gender schema; males most often read the story as a "coming of age," while most females looked in vain for some type of relationship between these two people.

"Up in Michigan" illustrated even more telling gender differences. As in the first story, some females and males wrote similar responses in their journal entries written as Liz. The most notable of these shared responses was a feeling of disappointment; having looked forward to having such an encounter with Jim, the results were much less than she (Liz) expected. For female students only, the response repeated most often was one of being overpowered by Jim. One woman wrote, "Even though I [Liz] asked him to stop, he wouldn't." Another said, "He really hurt me—I felt like a piece of meat." For the women who wrote this type of entry, a strong imagery of rape was evident; feelings of fear, pain, panic, and powerlessness were expressed in these entries. The journal entry from one of the females included the following: "He was very forceful. I couldn't make him stop. He hurt me, and it didn't seem to matter to him." The Hemingway text supports the interpretation of this woman and the others who wrote similar entries. "She was frightened. . . . Then the hand that felt so big in her lap went away and was on her leg and started to move up it. 'Don't Jim,' Liz said. Jim slid the hand further up. 'You mustn't Jim. You mustn't.' Neither Jim nor Jim's big hand paid any attention to her" (85).

Surprisingly, none of the forty-four males wrote journal entries which in any way conveyed this sense of being overpowered or raped; all of the men ignored (read over) the "No" which was clearly being expressed by Liz. The reaction most often repeated in the male entries written as Liz was, "I didn't like it, but I asked for it." One of the males wrote, "Being with Jim was a frightening experience, but above all of my resistance, I wanted it much more than ever." Responses such as this one do not represent a misreading because the text supports this interpretation as well. "The boards were hard. Jim had her dress up and was trying to do something to her. She was frightened but she wanted it. She had to have it but it frightened her" (85). The sharp contrast between the most often repeated female response and the most often repeated male response is a clear indication of yet another culturally developed gender schema. Males in our society are given so many confusing and mixed messages about female sexual response. Young men are told that most girls will probably say "No," but what they really mean is "Yes." Equally damaging is the idea that women really like sex when it is rough. When males find themselves in sexual situations, they often will respond based on the misinformation they have received from their society. The women with their gender schema read of a violent assault and a sense of powerlessness, while the men with their gender schema do not acknowledge the "No" or often translate it to a "Yes."

Although my study does not offer any suggestion that female readers can identify with male characters more readily than male readers can identify with female characters, my study does suggest that some males and females are indeed reading the same text differently and in accordance with a gender-based schema they have brought to the reading of the text.[14] Studies such as mine point to the need for more research projects which will test the nature of reader identification, the role of gender in the act of reading, and the theory of female "immasculation." Similar studies could be designed using sets of stories with a variety of themes to see if the gender-based differences I found are apparent in other contexts.

If more studies confirm what my study suggests, that female and male students are reading texts differently, this information cannot be ignored by any composition instructor who bases any part of his or her course on assigned readings. Writing assignments will have to be designed to address the gender-based schema of males and females and to acknowledge the power of the cultural expectations that define male and female behavior.

Since proper evaluation of student responses to writing assignments will have to take into account the gender of the student, the "ideal" answer will have to be reevaluated and more room will have to be allowed for divergent readings and responses. Also, class time will have to be allocated to allow students to discuss and analyze their gendered readings.[15] Finally, we as male and female teachers will have to acknowledge that we are bringing our own influential "frames of reference" to our reading of literature, as well as to our reading of student papers; this subject, too, needs further study and consideration. Our students, both male and female, deserve to be affirmed and empowered by their education. Only as we continue to research the effects of gender on reading and writing will we be able to offer this affirmation and empowerment.

NOTES

1. Anne Selley McKillop, *The Relationship between the Reader's Attitude and Certain Types of Reading Response* (New York: Columbia UP, 1952) 2.

2. Mary Crawford and Roger Chaffin, "The Reader's Construction of Meaning: Cognitive Research on Gender and Comprehension," *Gender and Reading: Essays on Readers, Texts, and Contexts,* ed. Patrocinio P. Schweickart and Elizabeth A. Flynn (Baltimore: Johns Hopkins UP, 1986) 3–30.

3. Jean Baker Miller, *Toward a New Psychology of Women* (Boston: Beacon, 1976); Nancy Chodorow, *The Reproduction of Mothering: Psychoanalysis and the Sociology of Gender* (Berkeley: U of California P, 1978); and Carol Gilligan, *In a Different Voice: Psychological Theory and the Theory of Women's Development* (Cambridge: Harvard UP, 1982).

4. Jonathan Culler, "Reading as a Woman," *On Deconstruction: Theory and Criticism after Structuralism* (Ithaca: Cornell UP, 1982) 43.

5. See Stanley Fish, *Is There a Text in This Class?: The Authority of Interpretive Communities* (Cambridge: Harvard UP, 1980), and Wolfgang Iser, *The Implied Reader* (Baltimore: Johns Hopkins UP, 1984).

6. Jane P. Tompkins, "An Introduction to Reader Response Criticism," *Reader Response Criticism from Formalism to Post-Structuralism,* ed. Jane P. Tompkins (Baltimore: Johns Hopkins UP, 1980) xvii.

7. Patrocinio P. Schweickart, "Reading Ourselves: Toward a Feminist Theory of Reading," *Gender and Reading,* ed. Schweickart and Flynn, 40.

8. Elaine Showalter, "Women and the Literary Curriculum," *College English* 32 (1971): 855.

9. Judith Fetterley, *The Resisting Reader: A Feminist Approach to American Fiction* (Bloomington: Indiana UP, 1978). For another good discussion of "immasculation," see Schweickart, "Reading Ourselves."

10. Sherwood Anderson, *Winesburg, Ohio* (New York: Viking, 1958) 58–62; Ernest Hemingway, *The Short Stories of Ernest Hemingway* (New York: Scribners, 1966) 81–86. All page references will be cited parenthetically in the text.

11. Diane Johnson, rev. of *Hemingway*, by Kenneth S. Lynn, *New York Times Book Review* 19 July 1987: 3, 25.

12. I was somewhat hesitant to use this particular subject because I teach in a conservative midwestern university, and I was concerned about how my students would feel writing about sexual experiences. I decided that it would be important to stress to the students that if they became uncomfortable with the project, they could simply quit. Two of my colleagues refused to allow their classes to be part of my study because of the subject matter. I realized from their reactions that my reservations had been justified.

13. My primary concern was that some of the women students may have been rape victims, and the assignment would cause them to relive some painful and frightening memories. Interestingly, of the 129 students, only two (both males) refused to finish the assignments. They both balked at writing the journal as the woman character, Liz; their reasons for refusing to continue were not clear.

14. For two other studies investigating differences in the reading of males and females, see David Bleich, "Gender Interests in Reading and Language," and Elizabeth Flynn, "Gender and Reading," both in *Gender and Reading*, ed. Schweickart and Flynn, 234–66 and 267–88, respectively.

15. My study presents a strong case against the theory of developing a standardized list of readings to achieve basic literacy, as suggested by E. D. Hirsch's *Cultural Literacy* (Boston: Houghton Mifflin, 1987). The possibility of differing responses by males and females to a text will preclude any standardization of readings. Hirsch has already received much criticism from the academic community regarding his call for a standardized body of knowledge and its elitist implications. See for example, Patricia Bizzell, "Arguing about Literacy," *College English* 50 (1988): 141–53; K. Edgington, "The Cloning of the American Mind," *On Our Minds*, newsletter of the Women's Studies Program, Towson State University, 2.1 (1988): 6–7; and John Warnock, "Cultural Literacy: A Worm in the Bud?" *ADE Bulletin* 82 (Winter 1985): 1–7.

LINDA LAUBE BARNES

Gender Bias in
Teachers' Written Comments

Barely fifteen years ago, researchers began to examine issues in gender
and the English language. As one line of inquiry, researchers attempted to
gather evidence to either support or refute the standard claims that had
come from Otto Jespersen's argument for a biological basis regarding
gender differences in language. He claimed that it was "natural" that
women prefer refined (even hyper-correct), euphemistic, and hyperbolic
language.[1] The collective findings of investigators like Robin Lakoff and
Mary Ritchie Key established a set of characteristics that seemed to
perpetuate some of Jespersen's description of women's speech: a significant use of tag-questions, "That's not right, *is it?*" and hedges, "Well,
perhaps you are right in *some* ways"; a preference for polite words and
correct (if not hyper-correct) forms, "*Whom* did you say is calling?";
more varied intonation patterns, seen as one of the positive qualities in
women's speech that give them power; and an adherence to "women's"
topics, such as children, clothes, and dieting.[2] However, these investigators suggested that, instead of stemming from any "naturalness," many of
these characteristics clearly reflect women's relatively powerless, second-
class position in a male-dominated society.

Many linguists were dissatisfied with the questionable research methods
and findings from this line of inquiry. During the second decade of
gender and language study, linguists have sought sound empirical evidence of gender differences and examined closely the contexts in which
men and women talk. From this recent research, a different understanding of gender and spoken language is forming. The most important
conclusions illustrate the interactive roles of gender, context and participants: (1) most of the features previously marked as "female" also
occur in males' speech; (2) the sociolinguistic context is a greater determi-
nant of which features speakers use than is gender; (3) perceived gender
differences in language are often the result of listeners' stereotypes about

(or belief in) such differences rather than the result of the existence of any real differences.[3]

As with oral language, women's written language, especially fiction, has been traditionally devalued because of the allegedly narrow topics women choose to write about. The underlying assumption is that men write about more universal topics. Women's writing is also said to be more "hysterical," more emotional, and more indirect and indecisive. These stereotypes echo those established by Jespersen regarding women's oral language.[4] Even though empirical evidence to dispute some of these stereotypes has accumulated, the stereotypes about women's written language persist as tenaciously as those about their oral language and inhibit women and girls from exercising and developing authentic voices which bear power and authority when they write. In an early study, Mary Hiatt examined men's and women's fiction and nonfiction in order to study the commonly held stylistic stereotypes about men's and women's writing. She analyzed 100 fictional and nonfictional books, 50 by men and 50 by women.[5] Although Hiatt sometimes drew conclusions not supported by the data, her study is valuable because it challenges the stereotypes, showing that men and women do write differently but not in stereotypic ways.

Hiatt's sentence length analysis reveals that, in contrast to the stereotype, men are wordy and women are terse, especially in their nonfiction (22). Women write more sentences under twenty words in length than do men. Contrary to stereotyped beliefs that women's writing is more emotional, Hiatt's investigation reveals that men display more excitability, as evidenced by their higher use of the exclamation mark (44).[6] Hiatt also attacks the stereotype that women's writing is illogical. Counting the occurrences of five types of connectives, Hiatt finds that women use more causatives and additives and that men use more illustratives and adversatives (56–57). She concludes that, in terms of logical development, women offer more reasons and justifications and fewer examples and conclusions in their logical arguments.

Hiatt looks at structural parallelism and repetition in men's and women's writing to determine whose is more orderly and balanced. Investigating six types of parallelism and eight types of repetition devices, she concludes that women employ all types of parallelism and repetition more often and in more varied ways than men do. Hiatt takes this as evidence that female writers are more balanced (64) and more focused and organized, not scatter-brained (77).

A common notion is that women use more -*ly* adverbs than men and are therefore "gushier." Hiatt finds no difference in the number of -*ly* adverbs in the writing analyzed. As for so-called feminine adverbs (hyperbolic adverbs like "simply," "utterly," and "awfully"), Hiatt finds that men use them more often than women. Hiatt also discovers that women use more adverbs of emotion ("bravely," "stiffly," "desperately," "positively") than men do and that men use more adverbs of pace ("abruptly," "gradually") than do women (106). Hiatt shows that women use "really" much more frequently than do men, in what Hiatt calls "an apparent effort to be credible in the face of disbelief" (106).

Finally, Hiatt investigates women's use of "feminine" words and men's use of "masculine" words. While Hiatt finds that women do use some of the feminine adjectives ("cute," "charming," "nice") more often than men do, she finds they also use "masculine" adjectives ("strong," "sturdy," "terrific") more than men do; she finds that men use feminine adjectives rarely. In their pronoun references, Hiatt finds that women's writing encompasses both sexes, while men's is predominantly male directed (116).

Additional inquiry provides more empirical evidence of the qualitative differences that Hiatt illustrates and adds more information. Susan Lynn Peterson analyzes the argumentative compositions of male and female university freshmen. She discovers that women use "I" 50 percent more often than men, indicating a greater emphasis on personal experience. Second, she finds that women use "you" 200 percent more often than men, indicating female emphasis on sharing experience and giving advice. She also finds that women's writing is more anecdotal and "conductive" in its rhetorical reasoning.[7] Paul Hunter et al. offer a study designed to describe how Peterson's sex-preferential patterns affect the writing process and written products of female writers, both basic and freshman writers.[8] The researchers observed ten female basic writers and ten female freshman composition students while they wrote and analyzed three drafts of three papers. The first and last topics were "reflexive" (eliciting personal and private responses); the second topic was an "extensive" version of the first topic (eliciting public and analytic responses). Their study shows both basic and freshman female writers to be dependent on sex-preferential patterns—sharing personal experience, giving advice, and relying more on anecdotes than analysis (6)—though female basic writers exhibit a greater degree of dependence on these patterns. The study also finds that both groups have difficulty revising the reflexive topic into the extensive topic because they cannot find extensive language: although they successfully edit out the "advice language," they return to the first person and become more anecdotal (5–6). The researchers conclude that the female basic writers have difficulty with extensive topics because such topics are rooted in a distinctly male academic/rhetorical tradition and are not related to a female way of knowing that is based on personal experience and relationships with others (8).

The conclusion of Hunter and his colleagues is familiar. Female writers seem less comfortable writing from positions which assume power and the right to influence. Joan Bolker argues that her best female writers' papers are tentative, lacking personality and ownership, because women attend to the needs of the audience rather than to their needs as writers.[9] Johanna Drucker argues that female writers must make compensations and compromises in their writing to mask their femaleness.[10] Carol Gilligan argues that women are socialized to value relationships and, thus, present their arguments personally and with concerns for feelings; she argues that males are socialized to value personal rights and abstract truths and, thus, argue their positions on more universal grounds.[11] Elisabeth Däumer and Sandra Runzo suggest that Gilligan's characterization can be extended to what is called "good" writing in textbooks and argue that the preferred male mode of thought suppresses female writers' voices.[12] Thomas Farrell argues that the features considered "good" writing in composition classrooms—directness, logicalness, formality, and objectivity—are features of writing which stem from a male rhetorical tradition.[13] Teachers, men and women alike, are trained to teach these features and look for them in their students' writing. Indeed, these features have become the basis for the "standards" for assessment being set by boards of education and English departments across the nation.

These studies' findings raise many questions about what happens in classrooms, especially in writing classrooms. Recent research in gender and education has shown a preference for males in teacher's expectations, patterns of interaction, and classroom rewards. Overwhelmingly, the research shows that male efforts are valued over female efforts. In their ongoing study of sex equity in the classroom, Myra and David Sadker have discovered that teachers subconsciously give qualitatively different evaluation and feedback to males and females.[14] Teachers have been shown to challenge boys to expend more effort in order to learn more while they encourage girls to be content with less. It is misleading that from elementary school through high school females receive higher grades than boys because they are being evaluated differently. Twenty percent of the praise received by girls focuses on form-based achievements, such as handwriting or format, while 90 percent of the criticism focuses on the intellectual inadequacy of their work ("Sex Equity" 109). In contrast, only 10 percent of the praise received by boys focuses on form-based achievement and only 50 percent of the criticism focuses on the intellectual inadequacy of their work. Thus, in boys' work teachers attend equally to content-based and form-based problems. Sadker and Sadker argue that these patterns imply that "[boys] can do better if [they] try harder" and that girls have already done their best ("Sex Equity" 105). The dominant message throughout women's academic lives, then, is that their achievements depend on care and compliance with formal rules and that their failures result from inadequate intellectual abilities.[15]

The purpose of my study is to examine how these gender-based teacher expectations do or do not manifest themselves when teachers comment on student papers. In a previous study, I asked my colleagues to comment on one essay written by a male and one written by a female.[16] Each essay had been selected because it exhibited the stereotypic linguistic features commonly attributed to its respective gender. My purpose was to see if the gender of the writer determined the linguistic/stylistic characteristics teachers attend to. Because of the small number of participants, the evidence was inconclusive as to whether the issue of gender is a consideration when teachers evaluate a piece of writing. Recognizing the significant power exercised through teachers' responses to students' papers, I conducted the study again with more colleagues responding to the request—thirty-four compared to twelve for my previous study.

As in my previous study, two student essays which exhibited gender-based stereotypic linguistic/stylistic and rhetorical features were selected according to features established by the research as reviewed above. The essays' authors were given the fictitious names of Martha Ambrose and Richard Hardin. The essays and the assignment they are responding to are reproduced in Appendices 1 and 2; though each essay does not match all the criteria, the significant features found in each essay have been coded with the numbers listed to the left of each feature in Table 1.

TABLE 1

Female	Male
1F "female"-appropriate topic	1M "male"-appropriate topic
2F correctness	2M ungrammaticality
3F emotionality	3M logicalness
4F tentativeness	4M forcefulness
5F "nice" words	5M vulgarity and slang
6F verbosity	6M terseness
7F "female" word choice	7M "male" word choice

Martha's essay exhibits several of the stereotypic female features. First, her essay is "female"-appropriate in topic and content. In response to an assignment posing a moral issue involving a daughter, Judy, and her mother, this female writer values the mother-daughter relationship and presents solutions intended to help Judy preserve this relationship. Martha also relates to the situation in a personal and empathetic way. She writes about hurt feelings and even shares what she would do in Judy's place and how she would feel. Her essay is basically mechanically correct, containing full subjunctive forms and complex sentence patterns. However, she is "wordy." She is comparatively more verbose than Richard, writing 550 words (245 more than Richard does). She writes 30 T-units, averaging 18.3 words per T-unit.[17] She chooses several "female" words: "lovely," "nice," "precious," "awfully," "really," and "utterly." Finally, her solutions are offered more tentatively, as evidenced by her use of "probably," "maybe," and "should," and the hypothetical subjunctive.

Richard's essay exhibits the stereotypic male features. He begins his essay on a universal level of parent-child relationships; this topic is slightly different from the mother-daughter connection Martha refers to. His opinion as to what has happened is unequivocal—Judy's mother is wrong. Richard reiterates his point forcefully in his use of "must" and through his short sentences. Although he writes nearly the same number of T-units (29), his essay is comparatively terser than Martha's, containing only 305 words and averaging only 10.5 words per T-unit. His "male"-appropriate argument appeals to the unfairness of the mother's decision. He attempts to remain detached from Judy's situation, moving from generalities about parents and children to Judy and her mother. He interjects "I" only to further his argument and not to relate to Judy as Martha does. He uses some vulgarity and slang, reiterating his position. Finally, his essay contains mechanical errors, including one fragment and one comma splice.

These 2 essays were distributed to 44 colleagues, all of whom are teachers in a freshman writing program at the same institution; some are regular faculty with Ph.D.'s, some are part-time faculty with Ed.D.'s and M.A.'s, and a few are graduate assistants with B.A.'s. Of the 34 who returned the essays, 18 are males and 16 are females. My colleagues had been divided into 2 groups. One group, consisting of 11 males and 9 females, received Martha's and Richard's essays as reproduced in the appendices. The other group, consisting of 7 males and 7 females, received the same essays with the authors' names switched. This was done to see if the supposed gender of the writer influences the quantity and quality of the comments teachers write. At the time of distribution, my colleagues were asked to write comments on the 2 essays as they normally would if they had received them in English 101, a first-quarter freshman writing class. They were not aware that gender was the object of the study; the directions accompanying the essays included the following:

> Please treat them as if they were papers you had received in an English 101 class. Mark or comment on them as you normally would, and assign a grade. Put notes in the margins or at the end if that's how you do it; circle items if that's how you do it; underline and draw arrows if that's how you do it—just do whatever you normally do.
>
> There's no "right" or "wrong" method that we know of. We just want to see the variety of ways teachers approach student papers. You needn't sign them. We don't want to know specifically who said what—we just need a representative sample of essays rated by writing teachers.[18]

To analyze the comments written by my colleagues, I used a scheme I devised for classifying written teacher comments in terms of speech-act theory.[19] Comments can be classified into two speech acts. (See Appendix 3 for examples.) The dominant speech act written by teachers is the direct or indirect "directive" (comments used to tell someone what to do). When direct, their form is the imperative; when indirect, their form can be the interrogative, the declarative, or simply a word or symbol. The composition teacher's directives are divided into two subtypes according to the revision skills being suggested. The first type, named the "editive," is used when the teacher's intent is to have the student make lower-order revisions—mechanical, grammatical, lexical, or syntactic changes. The second type, named the "revisional," is used when the teacher's intent is to have the student make higher-order revisions—informational, organizational, or holistic alterations. The second speech-act type is the "verdictive" (comments used to praise or criticize). By classifying the comments according to this scheme, I hoped to discover whether males and females receive different responses on their writing as they do in oral classroom discourse.

After classifying the comments, I tallied them. The distribution of editives, revisionals, and verdictives is similar for both essays regardless of the gender of the author. Both essays receive a higher average number of editive directives than either revisional directives or verdictives. Verdictives are the least frequent speech act. These general patterns do not substantiate the claims mentioned previously—that responses given to males attend equally to form and content, and that responses given to females attend more to content than to form. Regardless of whether the indicated writer is Martha or Richard, the teachers in this study tend to provide feedback on form (editives) more than on content (revisionals), and sometimes concentrate exclusively on form.

On the surface, this finding seems to indicate that little gender bias exists in written classroom discourse. Both essays receive the same or nearly the same average number of revisionals and verdictives, while "Judy's Problem" receives slightly more editives than does "What Should Judy Do?" The lack of any definite difference, in fact, would seem to indicate that my colleagues do not significantly attend to the gender-based linguistic/stylistic features of each essay or to the indicated gender of the writer. However, a closer examination of the comment distributions reveals the existence of gender differences along two dimensions: by gender of indicated author (illustrated in Table 2 below) and by gender of the teachers (illustrated in Table 3 below). As evidenced in Table 2, some differences in the average number of each kind of speech act emerge depending on the indicated author.

TABLE 2

Essay	Editives	Revisionals	Verdictives
"What Should?"	7.9	2.30	.7
R vs. M	7.7 < 8.08	1.96 < 2.7	.5 < .9
"Judy's"	11.6	2.3	.9
R vs. M	12.7 > 10.5	2.6 > 2.04	.7 < 1.1

R = Richard
M = Martha

"What Should Judy Do?" (the essay containing the linguistic/stylistic features categorized as "female") averages slightly more of each kind of speech act when Martha is the indicated author. "Judy's Problem" averages slightly more editives and revisionals and slightly fewer verdictives when Richard is the indicated writer. These differences are not provocative. However, when comments are examined with the gender of both the writer and the teacher taken into consideration, the patterns are not only complex but indicative of a subtle gender bias on both male and female teachers' parts.

The gender of the teacher plays a significant role in the comment patterns on the papers independent of the gender of the indicated author. Indeed, the data reveal that the comments are more closely linked to the gender-based linguistic/stylistic features of each essay than to the indicated gender of the writer. Table 3 indicates that male and female teachers attend to these gender-based features slightly differently. In general female teachers write more editives, slightly fewer (or equal) revisionals, and fewer verdictives. Because "What Should

Judy Do?" contains the stereotypes of female writing, the patterns of comment distribution suggest that problems at the word and sentence level are not noteworthy. Female teachers tend to write more of each kind of speech act, especially editives and verdictives, regardless of the author. Male teachers write nearly equal numbers of editives and revisionals and offer few verdictives. Note, however, that the stereotyped ungrammaticality of male writing as in "Judy's Problem" draws many more editives, especially from the male teachers. "Judy's Problem" receives more verdictives from the male teachers.

TABLE 3

"What Should Judy Do?"									
Male Teachers					Female Teachers				
Editives		Revisionals	Verdictives		Editives		Revisionals	Verdictives	
word level	sentence level		Prs.	DsP.	word level	sentence level		Prs.	DsP.
3.9	3.1	3.09	.27	.18	5.7	3.7	2.3	1.2	.3 Martha
3.9	2.9	1.90	.60	0.00	7.2	2.7	2.0	.4	0.0 Richard

"Judy's Problem"									
Male Teachers					Female Teachers				
Editives		Revisionals	Verdictives		Editives		Revisionals	Verdictives	
word level	sentence level		Prs.	DsP.	word level	sentence level		Prs.	DsP.
9.2	2.5	2.6	2.5	.36	9.2	4.7	2.7	1.0	.1 Richard
8.3	3.0	2.3	.6	1.00	7.4	4.2	1.7	.6	0.0 Martha

Male teachers offer more verdictives—especially dispraise—on "Judy's Problem" when Martha is the writer, while female teachers offer more verdictives on the essay when Richard is the writer. Regardless of the author, male teachers write the same average number of each kind of speech act on "What Should Judy Do?" Male teachers also average nearly the same number of editives at both the word and sentence level. Female teachers write word-level editives more often on Richard's essay than on Martha's but more sentence-level editives as well as verdictives and revisionals on Martha's essay. Male teachers offer more revisionals on Martha's essay and fewer on Richard's than female teachers do. Likewise, male teachers offer slightly more praise verdictives for Richard's efforts. In contrast, female teachers offer slightly more praise verdictives for Martha's efforts.

Analysis of the way male and female teachers comment on each of the essays demonstrates how the two dimensions—gender of the writer and gender of the teacher—converge to form a complex picture of gender bias in written discourse in the composition classroom. The female linguistic/stylistic features of "What Should Judy Do?" draw more and varied attention from the teachers. Only a few teachers mark the female word choices "awfully" and "nice," usually crossing through them; however, they criticize the writer's use of "probably" for indicating indecision. "Eliminate 'probably'—you should be definite when expressing your opinions," writes one male teacher. Others write similar comments: "Why 'probably'? You need to make up your mind if you are to have a strong claim in this paper." "Is she or isn't she?" Some teachers attend to the female punctuation: "Tends to over use dashes." "The commas and dashes are too distracting." "Excessive p. [punctuation] high schoolish!!!! WOW!!!!" Others simply cross out the punctuation without additional commentary. The wordiness of this writer frequently receives the comment "wordy" written in the margins. One teacher writes, "Don't use *9* words when *3* say what you *mean.*"

Overwhelmingly, the features that receive the most frequent commentary in "What Should Judy Do?" are the writer's coming to her point at the end of the essay and her emotional/sympathetic orientation to the assignment. When Martha is the indicated author, the comments reveal the pressure put on females to write counter to what research suggests is the "female voice." Male teachers directly criticize the female writer for her sympathetic orientation; female teachers are more indirect. One male teacher's verdictive of the writer's strategy asserts, "You really haven't helped much with Judy's problem, except of course to sympathize with her." At paragraph 5, where the writer begins to present her feelings about Judy's situation, several teachers criticize her. "This gets into a separate issue." "This doesn't fit very well—it deals more with your feelings than with the question of what Judy should do." "The question is not what *you* would do but *what should Judy do?*" "The assignment did not ask that you tell us what you'd do—but what you would recommend that she do." "From this point on your essay changes tone, and reads more like a personal letter than an essay."

Female teachers simply ask that the thesis be placed at the beginning of "What Should Judy Do?" "Your thesis statement is in your concluding paragraph. Too late." "Essay needs thesis statement." "You have a perfectly good thesis statement when you say that mother/daughter relations are precious. If you'd started with this, you'd have found your thoughts easy to organize." "I do not see a definite thesis statement." "In this short a paper, I want to see your thesis/opinion statement in the first paragraph." "Thesis comes too late to be adequately supported." Martha-as-writer receives support for her strategy from two *female* teachers only. "I think this works—I was looking for organization from the beginning but you have it at the end." "A sympathetic and thoughtful look at the problem from Judy's point of view."

However, when Richard is the writer of "What Should Judy Do?" only one male and one female teacher criticize the strategy of the writer. "This [paragraph 5] really waffles the issue." "In brief essays such as this, introduce your argument (your thesis) as quickly as possible." Instead, the comments are more positive or more encouraging, contrasting sharply in tone and content with the comments written to Martha. Male teachers offer these comments: "It appears to me that you have written this draft as a way of thinking through the problem. You finally discover what you want to say in the last paragraph. Use that as an outline for another paper." "Good reasoning in final paragraph." "The topic lends itself to 'I think,' 'I believe,' and 'I feel' but for normal expository discourse you should avoid such self-references." "Your discussion of how you would react, and how you feel about that reaction, adds not only an interesting personal dimension, but addresses some of the emotional and ethical subtleties at stake here." The comments from female teachers are similar: "Good reasoning." "The thesis comes at the end, but it's still affective [*sic*]." "You've examined both sides of the issue."

Comments on the male features (outlined in Table 1) in "Judy's Problem" reveal additional evidence that male and female teachers attend differently to marked gender features. The writer's right-vs.-wrong argument is not addressed, providing tacit approval for the interpretation of the assignment; as I have shown in previous research, if a teacher does not mark something in a paper, the student assumes it is all right ("Communicative" 76).[20] The essay's terseness is occasionally alluded to in revisionals asking for more information: "This idea needs more development and support in the essay." "How do you know this?" The problem is also referred to in verdictives: "Good, if somewhat brief, consideration of personal and emotional dimension of the question." "This is a good point but you don't develop it." "As is, this is a *shallow* essay—not much content. Mostly feeling." When Richard is indicated as the author, female teachers make comments requesting information four times more often than do male teachers. The number of requests is equal when Martha is the indicated writer.

As stated previously, "Judy's Problem" receives more editives than any other speech act. These editives usually refer to the male-marked linguistic/stylistic features (from Table 1). Every teacher marks the ungrammatical structures: the fragment in the second paragraph, the comma splice in the third paragraph, and the "of" instead of "have" or 've in the third and fifth paragraphs. Both male and female teachers comment on the vulgarity and slang. The male teachers are neutral in their comments: One teacher recommends that Richard "use quotation marks" around "hell no." Another advises Martha to "use startling expressions sparingly and at telling points in your papers." However, female teachers are more critical of the language. Two say the tone of the vulgarity conflicts with the "over-all tone of the paper." One writes, "Your message will never be clear if you use words like 'jack' someone around. Not everyone shares those lexical choices." The clichés and colloquial idioms draw occasional comments, usually marked by "idiom," "cliché," or "WW," or simply crossed through. Both male and female teachers mark these slightly more often when Richard is the indicated author, accounting for the slightly higher number of editives as reported in Table 3.

Richard's announcement of his plan in the first paragraph draws a variety of responses—all of them underscoring the value of assertive and logical writing (i.e., male rhetoric). The female teachers frequently praise the strategy, as the following sample of comments indicates. "Good—you state an arguable thesis." "OK—*good* advance organizer. You *do* state that there is a problem and suggest the direction of your paper." "Good. You take a stand and defend it." "Clear statement of purpose." The male teachers seem either to ignore or criticize the execution of this strategy. One writes, "Rather than being *in*direct, just assert your thesis." "Just do it—don't announce it." "A little obvious but safe, I guess." "Two topics to be discussed?" When Richard moves to emotion in the fourth paragraph, nearly 50 percent of the male teachers comment: "The paragraph is all emotion and lacks logic." "Don't expect impassioned rhetoric (or vulgarities) to *prove* anything." "Avoid 'I feel'—suggests little or no objective consideration." "You really warmed to your subject, didn't you." Only one female comments at this point, "The topic is such as to suggest that a warm, mushy, emotional response, such as you might write to a friend, is demanded of the writer, and this you provided. But you are in college now, and the rhetoric that is appropriate for personal letters and journals is not appropriate for nine/tenths of the writing demanded of college graduates."

My findings provide a few noteworthy, and curious, conclusions. Male teachers tend to be generally intolerant of emotional writing but even more critical when the author is female. Female teachers tend to be more fastidious about the language and mechanics and more concerned about the form of an essay. They expect the essay to conform to the male rhetorical tradition of stating the thesis up front and supporting it in grammatically acceptable language. These generalizations substantiate other sociolinguistic findings. William Labov has indicated that, because of their insecure social status, women attend to correctness as a way of exercising linguistic authority; men are less constrained.[21] Thus, as a reflection of a similar status in academe, my female colleagues attend to form more as a way of displaying competence and credibility in composition teaching in our male-dominated departments and institutions.

That my colleagues' comments reveal a preference for the male rhetorical tradition may be traceable to a prevailing practice in composition assessment. Our department (like many English departments) is concerned with "standards." To that end, two rating sessions are held each quarter in order to prepare the faculty for rating the Common Final—an essay exit exam given at the end of English 101. The result of these grading sessions is that the criteria for passing and failing essays are being standardized; my colleagues are being trained to read student essays in a similar manner. Two of the participants in this study even used the Common Final numerical ratings to respond to Martha's and Richard's essays. The criteria developed in the rating sessions define "good" writing as writing exhibiting the linguistic/stylistic features typical of the male rhetorical tradition described above. Thus, a partial explanation for the gender bias in the commenting patterns illustrated in this study may be the standardization of these criteria.

My findings reinforce previous research illustrating that male and female students have different academic experiences. Feminist critics have long claimed that women's written voices are not accepted equally with men's written voices. My findings show that a female student "voice" is less tolerated when the writing belongs to a woman. Richard's permission to violate the male rhetorical norm and still be acceptable contrasts sharply with Martha's experience—her empathy and conductive logic draw harsh attention.

Eliminating the gender bias described in this paper requires a two-pronged strategy. On the one hand, male and female teachers need to become aware of the subtleties in their messages and prejudices. We must understand that what we *write* on students' papers is as powerful interactively and academically as what we say. Gender equity workshops must help faculty identify patterns in both forms of language. On the other hand, teachers need to practice gender-neutral reading of and commenting on students' papers. We also need to learn to value female student writers' *author*ity, and thus to empower our female students. Female teachers, who in order to succeed may themselves have repressed, lost, or never found their own female voice, need to encourage their female students to exercise theirs in confidence. Male teachers need to learn that female rhetorical strategies are legitimate, valuable alternatives.[22]

NOTES

1. Otto Jespersen, *Language* (London: Allen & Unwin, 1922) 250.

2. In addition to Robin Lakoff's *Language and Woman's Place* (New York: Harper, 1975) and Mary Ritchie Key's *Male/Female Language* (Metuchen: Scarecrow, 1975), readers are encouraged to consult S. McConnell-Ginet et al., eds., *Women and Language in Literature and Society* (New York: Praeger, 1980), and Aileen Pace Nilsen, *Sexism and Language* (Urbana: NCTE, 1977).

3. These conclusions are drawn from the articles collected in B. Thorne, Cheris Kramarae, and Nancy Henley, eds., *Language, Gender and Society* (Rowley: Newbury, 1983); Donald Lance, "Sex-Marked Language," paper, Missouri Philological Association, Warrensburg, Mo., March 29, 1985; Cheris Kramer, "Folklinguistics," *Psychology Today* 8 (August 1974): 82–85; Berryman and Wilcox, "Attitudes towards Male and Female Speech: Experiments on the Effects of Stereotyped Language," *Western Journal of Speech Communication* 44 (1980): 50–59; Deborah Cameron, *Feminism and Linguistic Theory* (New York: St. Martin's, 1985); Jitendra Thakerar and Howard Giles, "They Are—So They Spoke: Noncontent Speech Stereotypes," *Language and Communication* 1 (1981): 255–61.

4. These observations are discussed elsewhere in this volume as well as in Dale Spender, *Man-Made Language* (London: Routledge & Kegan Paul, 1980), and in different articles found in Cynthia L. Caywood and Gillian R. Overing, eds., *Teaching Writing: Pedagogy, Gender and Equity* (Albany: SUNY, 1987).

5. Mary Hiatt, *The Way Women Write* (New York: Teachers College Press, 1977) v.

6. Punctuation is another area in which strong notions exist that women use the dash and the exclamation mark, as well as other punctuation marks, more often than men do. In her ongoing investigation of punctuation, Greta D. Little and Kimberly G. Johnson have found no supporting evidence that such is the case. "Punctuation in the Twentieth Century," in *The Fourteenth LACUS Forum 1987*, ed. Sheila Embleton (Lake Bluff: LACUS, 1988): 289-98.

7. Susan Lynn Peterson, "Sex-Based Differences in English Argumentative Writing: A Tagmemic Sociolinguistic Approach," diss. U Texas at Arlington, 1986 (Ann Arbor: UMI, 1986, 8621740).

8. Paul Hunter, Nadine Pearce, Sue Lee, Shirley Goldsmith, Patricia Feldman, and Holly Weaver, "Competing Epistemologies and Female Basic Writers," *Journal of Basic Writing* 7 (1988): 73–81.

9. Joan Bolker, "Teaching Griselda to Write," *College English* 40 (1979): 906–8.

10. Johanna Drucker, "Women and Language," *Poetics Journal* 4 (May 1984): 56–67.

11. Carol Gilligan, *In a Different Voice* (Cambridge: Harvard UP, 1982).

12. Elisabeth Däumer and Sandra Runzo, "Transforming the Composition Classroom," *Teaching Writing*, ed. Caywood and Overing, 52–53.

13. Thomas Farrell, "The Female and Male Modes of Rhetoric," *College English* 40 (1979): 909–21.

14. Myra and David Sadker have actively studied sexism in education. Thorough reports are presented in their *Sex Equity Handbook for Schools* (New York: Longman, 1982) and *Between Teacher and Student: Overcoming Sex Bias in Classroom Interaction* (Washington, D.C.: U.S. Dept. of Education, 1980). An accessible summary is their "Sexism in the Schoolroom of the '80's," *Psychology Today* (March 1985): 54–56. See also "Confronting Sexism in the College Classroom" in this volume.

15. Mary de Nys and Leslie R. Wolfe, "Learning Her Place—Sex Bias in the Elementary School Classroom," *Peer Report* 5 (Autumn 1985): 5.

16. Linda Laube Barnes, "An Investigation of Gender-Bias and Written Language," *The Thirteenth LACUS Forum 1986*, ed. Ilah Fleming (Lake Bluff: LACUS, 1987): 457–64.

17. The T-unit has become a standard measure of syntax. Kellogg Hunt, who devised the measure, defines the T-unit (a minimal terminal unit) as one main clause and all appended modifiers, including subordinate clauses. He claims that the measure is more reliable and avoids ambiguities surrounding definitions of a sentence. For further discussion, readers should consult the following works by Hunt: *Differences in Grammatical Structures Written at Three Grade Levels*, Cooperative Research Project no. 1998 (Tallahassee: Florida State U, 1964); "Syntactic Maturity in School Children and Adults," *Monographs of the Society for Research in Child Development* 35. 1 (1970).

18. Three of my colleagues expressed difficulty or a sense of being constrained, since the task presented to them seemed counter to their own goals as teachers. The following quotes from my colleagues illustrate the range of their comments to me: "The assignment, on one hand, is a case study—a technique I highly approve of and wish to incorporate more into my 101 sections. On the other hand, this particular problem leads to the 'I think,' 'I feel,' and 'I believe' expressions that have to be excised from normal exposition." "Not fair to just look at comments on the paper because conferences and discussions and clarifications are part of whole process of evaluation. Can't isolate comments as independent— [comments are] a dependent variable." "The exercise here [writing comments on the students' papers] makes no sense to me."

19. Linda Laube Barnes, "Communicative Competence in the Composition Classroom: A Discourse Analysis," diss. U South Carolina, 1984 (Ann Arbor, MI: UMI, 1984, 8427716) 46–65.

20. In my dissertation, I show how students' revisions can be linked to the kinds of speech acts their teachers write on their papers. Successful students (those who usually earn "C" or better grades) receive very few comments; the higher the grade, the fewer the comments. As a consequence, students form a working hypothesis that if the teacher does not mark something in their paper, it must be okay.

21. William Labov, *Sociolinguistic Patterns* (Philadelphia: U of Pennsylvania P, 1973).

22. I am indebted to Nancy Ruff, of Southern Illinois University at Edwardsville, for her patient and insightful readings of earlier versions of this paper.

Assignment

Judy is twelve years old. Early in August, her mother told her she could go to see a rock group coming to St. Louis later in the month if Judy were able to save enough money. Judy did manage to save $20, mainly through babysitting. However, at the end of the month, her mother told her she would have to spend the money on school clothes. Judy is considering lying to her mother. She is thinking of telling her mother she has saved only $5 and of using the remaining $15 to go to the concert (telling her mother she is staying overnight with a friend). Judy is wondering what she should do?

What *should* Judy do? Why? Please write an essay in which you discuss the problem and explain your opinion as to what Judy should do.

Judy's Problem

Richard Hardin

The relationship between parents and their children is difficult and sometimes mixed up. [2M] How should a parent react to a certain problem and [2M] how should a child act in certain situations is a problem in these modern times. I feel that nine times out of ten the parent or parents are [1M] right, but in this case, the "fault" is not the child's. In this essay [4M] I'm not only going to state that the Mother is [5M] off base but also [4M] I'm going to state *why* she is wrong. I feel that Judy should not lie to her mother, even though it may seem like the [1M] right thing to do.

[3M] First of all, Judy's mother is trying to stress the importance of saving to Judy. The mother agrees to the concert, but only if Judy can save enough money. This is important to a 12 year old child. [2M] Because it teaches the child to set a goal and then try to achieve it. The only way Judy is going to be able to get the money is by working as a babysitter. This forces Judy to take on additional responsibilities, thus showing signs of maturity.

Judy seems to be learning a valuable lesson until her mother decides to change the rules. Parents can do that, but it is still [1M] unfair. Judy's mother decides to take the money she saved and use it for school [2M] cloths [2M], that's great, but what about the concert? If Judy's mother didn't [2M] entend to let her go to the concert, she shouldn't [2M] of [5M] jacked Judy around. In doing this, Judy now feels that she should try to cheat her mother.

Is all this deception really necessary? I say [4M, 5M] hell no! No matter how the parent feels about something, if they agree to it, they [4M] must back it all the way. Maybe the concert isn't a good idea, but Judy's mother agreed to it and [4M] must [5M] stick to her guns.

In conclusion, I feel communication between child and parent is the [3M] most important thing to a healthy relationship. If Judy's mother didn't like the rock concert idea, she should [2M] of told Judy, not let her work for the goal and then be told "forget it." My advice to Judy is to tell her mother her feelings. By doing this [1M] no lying is needed and every one is satisfied.

Assignment

Judy is twelve years old. Early in August, her mother told her she could go to see a rock group coming to St. Louis later in the month if Judy were able to save enough money. Judy did manage to save $20, mainly through babysitting. However, at the end of the month, her mother told her she would have to spend the money on school clothes. Judy is considering lying to her mother. She is thinking of telling her mother she has saved only $5 and of using the remaining $15 to go to the concert (telling her mother she is staying overnight with a friend). Judy is wondering what she should do?

What *should* Judy do? Why? Please write an essay in which you discuss the problem and explain your opinion as to what Judy should do.

What Should Judy Do?

Martha Ambrose

The problem Judy is facing is that her mother told her to save her money in order for her to be able to go to the concert. Now she is told by her mother that she will have to spend the money on new school clothes.

Judy is [1F, 3F] feeling as if she has been cheated, because she saved her money specifically for this concert, and her mother is changing her mind. First her mother told Judy she could go, and now is telling her that she can't go after all. It seems to me that the mother is [4F] probably being [7F] awfully unfair to Judy—after all Judy did save the money. Her mother should have never given Judy false hopes [3F]!

So now Judy is faced with a difficult decision for a twelve-year-old. She has to decide whether to lie to her mother or not—to decide to go to the concert and not tell her mother about going, or just [3F] sadly give up her plan. Another option she has which is not mentioned is that she can try and discuss this problem with her mother, and try to come to some sort of decision or [1F] compromise. New school clothes can be [5F, 7F] lovely to have, but Judy saved her money for a rock concert. She can try to get her mother to understand her side of the story and [4F] maybe change her mind.

Judy is at a very young age, where she can't see reason, or at least that much of it. [1F, 3F] If I were Judy, and at that age, or any age, I would [4F] probably go to the concert and lie to my mother, simply because she had told me to save the money, and I'd be able to go. I think I would have been [7F] utterly devastated if my mother were to have told me to buy my own school clothes with the money I had saved myself for another purpose—a purpose which my mother had previously agreed upon.

I have told you what I would do, if I were Judy, but that doesn't mean I feel that it is right. I don't feel it is right to lie, but I [1F, 3F] personally would [1F, 3F] feel mistreated and/or cheated. [1F] Mother-daughter relationships are [5F] precious. Judy's mother seems to have forgotten that Judy, although she is 12 years old, has some maturity. Her mother, [3F] sad to say, really didn't treat her with respect for her maturity—or her [3F, 1F] feelings.

My opinion as to what Judy should do is she should talk it over with her mother, and tell her how she feels about what has happened. For instance, tell her she was given permission to go to the concert if she were able to save money, that what her mother did really wasn't nice, and she feels she is being punished for something. There could also be a very good reason why her mother asked her to do that, so the best thing would be to talk it over. If Judy were to lie, she runs the risk of being caught, and losing her mother's trust, and not having any privileges whatsoever. I believe Judy doesn't want that to happen. In the long run, I think talking it over would save a lot of hurt feelings that could happen.

Speech Acts in Written Comments

I. Directives: speech acts intended to get the student to do something.
  A. Editives: so named for their focus on lower-order revision skills like proofreading, lexical substitutions, syntactic changes. These speech acts occur most frequently when the teacher marks the text itself.

  Examples:

  Direct: ha$\hat{s}$e   or ↖⃝

  Indirect: *Do these pronouns say the same thing?*

  B. Revisionals: so named for their focus on higher-order revisions like organizational, informational, or different holistic alterations. These speech acts appear both in the text, especially in the margins, and in the end comments.

  Examples:

  Direct: *Give an example.*   *Take out.*

  Indirect: *Why not bring this down to a more personal level?*

II. Verdictives: speech acts that usually appear at the end of a paper. Their goal is to provide an evaluation of something or the whole paper.
  A. Praise: Tend to be written only on successful papers. Basic writers rarely receive these.

  Example:

  Good work.

  B. Dispraise: Tend to be used to point out the general flaw. Sometimes used in the margins when something is ineffective.

  Examples:

  This is brief.   *You have no thesis.*

  C. Grade: Perhaps the most powerful of the three verdictives. The teacher and student work to accomplish the power of this act.

PENNY L. BURGE & STEVEN M. CULVER

Sexism, Legislative Power, and Vocational Education

Like all other areas of education, vocational education reflects the gender inequities arising from our society. Jean Stockard has noted the sex-typed nature of education in our country: "Women and men hold different jobs within schools. When students start making choices, girls and boys are encouraged to enroll in different subject areas."[1] Rosemary Deem concludes that schools are a critical link in the social processes leading to the existing gender division of labor: "Education does not create the sexual division of labour, nor the kinds of work available in the labour market, nor the class relationships of society, but it rarely does anything to undermine them."[2] However, the links between gender, school, and the workplace are particularly salient in the area of vocational education because, historically, vocational education has consisted of practical instruction aimed at matching students to work positions in industry and commerce.[3] Most of the areas of vocational education are heavily sex-typed and, therefore, nontraditional for one sex or the other; only marketing education is not. Among vocational programs, cosmetology, business, health occupations, and home economics have traditionally been the domain of women; auto mechanics, industrial arts, and agriculture have been perceived as belonging to men.[4]

Vocational education helps youths and adults acquire entry-level work skills; teaches them basic skills such as reading, writing, and mathematics through occupational training programs; and prepares workers for movement within the workplace, either horizontally, across occupations, or vertically, up or down a career ladder structure.[5] These purposes are met through a curriculum which draws much from the workplace: workers and managers play a part in determining not only what should be taught in these classes but also who should be taught. Consequently, student enrollment in vocational education necessarily reflects the sex-segregated nature of the work force. In 1980, females nationally represented 91 percent of students training as nursing assistants, 87 percent of those training for community health workers, and 92 percent of students in cosmetology and secretarial sciences. Similarly, 95 percent of students enrolled in electrical technology, 90 percent in electronics, 94 percent in appliance repair, 96 percent in carpentry, 95 percent in welding, and 96 percent in small engine repair were males.[6] In 1985, females represented only 4 percent of those enrolled in occupational preparation courses or in apprenticeship programs in construction trades and mechanics and machine repair.[7]

In spite of the gender stereotyping inherent in traditional vocational education, notable improvements in breaking down barriers have occurred during the last several years. Because vocational education is closely tied to the nation's work, it is also closely overseen by federal legislation. The 1976 Educational Amendments and the 1984 Carl D. Perkins Vocational Education Act have supported progress in gender equity by providing regulations and funds. Feminist thought is also affecting gender equity in vocational education. Vocational education has always had a commitment to the less powerful members of society, whether they be women, the poor, or skilled laborers. Feminist theory, with its similar commitment to women as one segment of the powerless within society, has provided both a new vocabulary for articulating these concerns and some new methods for acting on them. Currently, vocational education is combining the power of federal mandates, a feminist perspective, and its own traditional mission of training people for the workplace in order to improve gender equity and, at the same time, empower its students.

The Influence of Federal Legislation

Because of its unique position as a direct link from school to work, vocational education, like other educational areas, has had to respond to legislation related to equity issues. While the content of vocational courses has been greatly determined by the needs of the workplace, the field has also been significantly affected by federal guidelines related not only to schooling but also to work and employment procedures. Hence, improving gender equity in vocational education is closely tied to the power of the federal government. And as Richard Adams points out, "political pressures and laws and regulations have been, and continue to be, a potent force in removing barriers" in society as well as in education.[8]

The federal government's policy of support and its definition of vocational education at the postsecondary level was initiated with the first Morrill Act of 1862. This act facilitated education which "promoted liberal and practical education of the industrial classes in the several pursuits and professions of life."[9] With the signing of the Smith-Hughes Act in 1917, federal direction of certain types of vocational education was solidified. Smith-Hughes provided the first federal funding for public school programs in agricultural, trade and industrial, and home economics education. Reflecting sex role norms of the times, the first two programs were specifically designed for males, while home economics was included to provide education for homemaking and for occupations relating to homemaking.[10]

With this beginning, vocational education programs were intentionally sex-typed. This separation of training for males and females continued with no legislative direction for change until the Equal Pay Act of 1963 was passed. This act, considered the first significant legislation relating to vocational sex equity, called for the end of discrimination on the basis of sex in the payment of wages for equal work. This law was soon followed by Title VII of the Civil Rights Act of 1964, prohibiting discrimination in employment on the basis of sex, race, color, religion, and national origin.

Title IX of the Educational Amendments of 1972, the landmark legislation banning discrimination in education on the basis of sex, continued the legislative direction for change. Title IX provided that "no person in the United States shall, on the basis of sex, be excluded from participation in, be denied the benefits of, or be subjected to any educational program or activity receiving federal financial assistance."[11] In addition, the Women's Educational Equity Act of 1974 (Public Law 93-380) provided for funding of projects to advance educational equity, specifically including expansion and improvement of programs for females in vocational and career education.[12]

Despite passage of Title IX and the Women's Educational Equity Act, sex bias and sex-role stereotyping remained evident in vocational education. Because of this, the Education Amendments of 1976 made sex equity an overt issue for the first time in federal vocational legislation. These amendments required the development and implementation of programs to eliminate sex discrimination, sex bias, and sex-role stereotyping. To comply with the 1976 directives, each state was required to employ a full-time sex equity coordinator to provide leadership in eliminating barriers that inhibit equal access to vocational education, to offer technical assistance to local educators, and to develop a public relations program to promote vocational sex equity efforts.

More recently, in 1984, with the passage of the Carl D. Perkins Vocational Education Act, increased emphasis was placed on gender equity efforts. This law, in effect until 1989, contained the largest amount of federal dollars ever set aside for vocational training for women and girls.[13] According to this law, in addition to fulfilling the requirements of the 1976 amendments, states were required to expend a percentage of federal vocational education money to provide vocational education and training which led to marketable skills and support services for single parents, homemakers, and displaced homemakers. With the expiration of the Perkins Act, congressional reauthorization of federal mandates affecting vocational education maintains a focus on improving vocational programs and increasing access to these programs for populations who typically can't or haven't participated in them. Thus, unlike programs in most other educational areas, vocational education programs continue to be provided with federal money to aid sex equity efforts.

Vocational Education and Feminism

At a time when increased federal dollars are available to encourage change in gender perception within vocational education, vocational educators benefit from analyzing their efforts from a feminist perspective. This analysis is easily made since a feminist perspective, like the vocational education perspective, derives much of its view from the experience of being subservient, second class, or unnoticed.[14] Vocational education has traditionally served those in need of training and skills in our society: the minorities, the poor, and those with intellectual and physical handicaps. Though participation in vocational education is nearly universal, with students of all ability levels represented,[15] vocational training is still often associated with students who are seen as somehow "deficient" or "second class." Vocational education and its students have been looked down upon because the field has historically focused on training for manual and skilled labor, and Americans have traditionally undervalued such labor.

In Kathleen Weiler's discussion of teaching intended to change gender, class, and power structures, she describes feminist teachers as doing something very similar to what vocational educators are doing, with assistance from Perkins Act funding. Weiler writes that feminist teachers "challenge sexist assumptions and call into question accepted definitions of gender. . . . They challenge sexist notions of appropriate behavior and work for women and men . . . " (125). There is a variety of feminist approaches to the many injustices in our society, but feminist strategies that include wide social and economic analyses fit best with the purposes and clientele of vocational education. Just as vocational equity efforts should include both females and males, so too feminist vocational education should not be exclusionary. In *The Skeptical Feminist*, Janet Radcliffe

Richards describes the feminist perspective as one that should not be concerned with women per se but that should focus on the type of injustice it wants to eliminate, an injustice which causes women to suffer only because they are female.[16] Vocational educators have extended this definition to include any person who suffers because of gender. Hence, barriers to males enrolling in nursing programs should be as much a concern of feminist vocational educators as barriers to females entering nontraditional fields.

Weiler points out that teachers with feminist ideologies often teach in women's studies courses, which are constructed to address issues of sexism directly; such courses are usually taught on the postsecondary level and in disciplines labeled "humanities" or "English." Thus, their audiences are typically small and dominated by "white middle-class" women (131). The audience for vocational education equity work is more heterogeneous, including both males and females and the low, middle, and upper classes, since these are the traditional groups served by vocational education. Thanks to monies provided by the Perkins Act, this audience now includes more teenage parents, single parents, homemakers and displaced homemakers, and women and men who are unemployed or underemployed but wish to advance in the workforce. The focus for this expanded audience is feminist in that vocational education genuinely includes issues pertinent to women's lives, experiences, work, and aspirations—issues such as sex discrimination, sex stereotyping, sexual harassment, career choice, self-efficacy, and economic self-reliance.[17]

The majority of vocational equity efforts have feminist objectives, regardless of whether they are so labeled. They focus on the underlying theme of freeing females from "the feminization of poverty."[18] Shirley Dennis has noted that 90 percent of persons on welfare are women and children.[19] The poverty of women becomes an increasingly critical factor in our society as the number of female-headed households increases. Data from the U.S. Census Bureau documents increases over the last decades, and leading family experts predict continued growth of this family type.[20] A profile of these families shows that they already make up over 25 percent of all American families and that they are at a consistently disadvantaged position relative to other family types.[21] They are characterized by a high rate of poverty, a high percentage of minority representation, and relatively little formal education. As a group, they generally have little equity or stature in society and constitute a major population with unusually pressing social and economic needs.

Since this nation's poor are mostly women and their children, vocational education's analysis of labor market inequities that perpetuate this condition is a helpful step in determining solutions. Sex segregation of occupations is certainly a major barrier for women. Women typically offer fewer working skills, sometimes because they have been trained only for work inside the home or for a narrow spectrum of home-related occupations. In spite of the presence of the women's movement, most adult women have been taught traditionally feminine traits of dependence, nurturance, and helplessness, with emphasis on physical attractiveness and finding a mate. These traits do not prepare them well for serious career choices and career training.[22] And according to a United States Civil Rights Commissions study, if a woman's education has not prepared her for employment, she and her children may be destined to live in poverty.[23]

To compound the injustice, most women continue to be paid less than men for the skills they do possess. Recent marketplace analyses indicate that, overall, women earn between 60 and 70 percent of every dollar men earn in most full-time, year-round occupational categories.[24] These wage differences arise from the amount of labor market preparation and experience attained by women and from discrimination against women.

Other more subtle factors prohibit most women from sharing the social and economic power that comes from participating meaningfully in the marketplace. Women's lack of a positive self-image is linked to their inability to support themselves or their families financially. For women, obtaining an education for work is more difficult because, while the system has openly valued this pursuit for males, it has not done so for females. Additionally, women have been expected to provide child and elder care for family members unable to care for themselves, thus becoming further trapped in the home sphere. Finally, even if women can find jobs, since they are often paid so little, their work is not seen as a significant contribution to the family. As with other feminist concerns, equity issues in vocational education extend beyond the immediately obvious factors. Thus, vocational education's training for work necessarily incorporates into its scope women's views of themselves and of the workplace as well as concerns with the family—child care, elder care, power and worth within the family unit, and financial support.

Target Audiences for Feminist Vocational Efforts

Feminist theory is always involved in at least an indirect critique of society; feminist literary criticism, for example, indirectly criticizes society as it interprets and evaluates literary texts produced and valued by the society's members. Many vocational education programs also entail a critique of society, though the critique may not always be stated overtly. Vocational education's gender equity programs implicitly reject the social status quo as they challenge the gender biases built into the workplace and prepare people to move into higher paid, more prestigious positions. Of course, vocational education programs do more than offer a critique; they actually change the structure of society. For special segments of the population, vocational programs designed with a feminist perspective and intended to open the society to their participation are essential. Such programs enable families to avoid public assistance altogether or to leave the welfare roles and be self-supporting. Vocational education also provides a means for those in low-paying, low-prestige areas to qualify for better jobs. Target groups for whom vocational education is particularly beneficial are single parents, teenage parents, homemakers, and displaced homemakers. These students require programs that offer a full range of services, from occupational exploration to job search assistance. With a well-developed total educational and family-designed program, the barriers to obtaining job skills encountered by these groups are no longer overwhelming.

The 1984 Perkins Act provided for the establishment of high school and college education programs intended to help some women break the poverty cycle. Specifically, the Perkins Act required each state to expend 8.5 percent of the basic grant under Title II, Part A, to provide, subsidize, reimburse, or pay for vocational education and training activities that furnish single parents and homemakers with marketable skills; make grants to eligible recipients for providing single parents and homemakers with marketable skills; make grants to community-based organizations for the provision of vocational education services to single parents and homemakers; make vocational education and training more accessible to single parents and homemakers by assisting them with child care or transportation services or by organizing and scheduling such programs so that they are more accessible; and inform single parents and homemakers of vocational education programs and related support services.[25] In Virginia's community colleges, for example, in response to the Perkins Act, during the 1987–88 school year there were twenty regional centers available to serve the needs of single parents, homemakers, and displaced homemakers.

Within the group of women bound to second-class status by poverty and in extreme need of government-supported vocational (feminist) education efforts is the subgroup of teenage mothers. The United States has a higher teenage birth rate than almost any other developed nation, with nearly one-fifth of all births being to teenagers in 1986.[26] Each year, more than one million—that is, one in ten—teenage women become pregnant in this country. The association between single mothers and a continuing state of deprivation is greater and continues longer for women who are young and single at the birth of their first child.[27] In most cases, diminished educational and vocational achievement is the norm for the teen mother.[28]

With about 80 percent of teenage mothers currently leaving school, a logical program emphasis for vocational educators becomes dropout prevention;[29] Carlos Azcortia and Philip A. Visa found students enrolled in career vocational instruction less likely to drop out of high school and college than those not enrolled in such programs.[30] Especially effective are programs that offer instruction in basic academic skills as well as in marketable skills. Teenage parents, like all other young people, also need sexuality and family planning information and guidance. Adolescent parents often report feeling caught between their own needs and those of their children. They commonly have poor self-images that inhibit long-term goal setting and contribute to guilt about parenting abilities. For these parents to take advantage of vocational opportunities, all of these issues must be addressed.

Vocational sex equity programs have had enormous impact on education for teenage parents in all regions of the country. Ohio, a leader in vocational consumer and homemaking training, offers a noteworthy example. It provides a unique high-school-based program to meet the needs of pregnant teens and adolescent parents. Graduation, Reality, and Dual-Role Skills (GRADS) is a program for pregnant students and/or young parents that has one overriding goal: to keep teens enrolled until they graduate. The GRADS program provides individualized instruction and counseling, and it shows teens how to network and make decisions that will lead them to economic independence. In the 1987–88 school year, about sixty-five GRADS programs were functioning throughout the state of Ohio (Ferguson & Reed 8). These and other programs are meeting the needs of some young parents—and the requirements of the 1984 Perkins Act—but many more teens require assistance beyond what current funding permits.

Strategies for Vocational Programs

Educational programs such as GRADS, which respond to governmental mandates for increasing vocational sex equity and which seek to empower females, must address a variety of issues. Whether offered on the high school or college level, they must include components which (1) encourage nontraditional occupational choices, (2) improve recruitment of girls and women, (3) establish support systems, and (4) analyze the relations between the workplace and the home.

Promoting nontraditional occupational choice is necessary because, despite the gender equity efforts within the vocational curriculum over the last decade, women tend to enroll in business (clerical) courses or in other female-intensive programs. They avoid the trade-skills programs which could prepare them for work with pay sufficient to support a family or provide for most alternative aspirations.[31] However, when women are recruited and retained in job preparation areas nontraditional for their sex, their earning power is enhanced and they gain a wider range of job selections with which to match their interests, abilities, and talents. Increasing the range of job selections includes improvement *within* occupations, getting more women at all levels of an occupational hierarchy, and improvement *across* occupations, getting more women into areas still dominated by men and getting men into areas still dominated by women. This notion of "spreading the wealth" benefits all of society by increasing the pool of talent for any job. A 1980 report prepared by the National Science Foundation and the Department of Education suggests that "women still remain the largest pool of talent available for increasing the size and quality of the science and engineering labor force."[32]

Unfortunately, such occupational movement is prohibited by several barriers. Nontraditional students are very much in the minority, have few role models and mentors, and still must face traditional prejudices.[33] Even as they begin training for nontraditional work, they often have to deal with negative attitudes of educators when attempting to find support for their occupational preferences.[34] The passage of the Perkins Act and its recent reauthorization, however, made money available to help nontraditional students pursue careers of their choosing.

Virginia Polytechnic Institute and State University, for example, administers a statewide Access & Equity network—made up of teachers, counselors, and administrators from elementary, middle, and senior high schools, and community colleges and four-year universities—that provides in-service and educational materials on equity, nontraditional careers, and reduction of sex discrimination. Materials used in Access & Equity training sessions include the Illinois State Board of Education's "Think Purple" campaign (purple is a mix of half pink and half blue)[35] and the Mid-Atlantic Center for Sex Equity's *Communications Gender Gap* quiz.[36] This twenty-item true/false quiz helps audiences challenge myths about how men and women communicate with each other. The newsletter, *Access & Equity*, with a national circulation of over 7,000, also provides helpful information: bibliographies of sources related to equity, progress reports by equity project directors in Virginia, teaching tips for achieving an equitable atmosphere in the classroom, and pointers for counselors on how to help students make career choices that are not tied to gender.[37] These resources help teachers and counselors become aware of the limitations inherent in traditional attitudes about sex-appropriate jobs and behaviors. Participants in the Access & Equity network are encouraged to inform parents, students, and other groups, such as the PTA, Jaycees, Lions, and Elks, in their own local school districts. During 1987–88, over 2,000 persons across Virginia attended at least one presentation on equity conducted by one of the forty Access & Equity network members.

Other programs, such as Freestyle, Opening the Doors, and Project HEAR, have been targeted at elementary schools and are aimed at reducing sex-role stereotyping before it becomes firmly entrenched in young minds; these programs are operated around the country by universities and state boards of education. Parallel programs, using a variety of equity materials, are aimed at middle and high schools. The Girl Scouts of America, with federal funding, has developed sex equity career education materials, called *Careers to Explore*, for use by Brownies and Junior Scouts. These materials encourage investigation into many different career areas and development of positive attitudes toward self (Farmer 356–58).

Improving the recruitment of women and girls, the second component of programs intended to increase vocational sex equity, is needed in order to encourage single heads of households and displaced homemakers to use project services. Recruitment efforts are most effective if the initial contact establishes the benefits prospective students can receive through program participation. As Carlene Robinson Whited, a single mother returning to school, points out: "I was very confused and unsure of myself, but [the director] went out of her way to help with my schedule and assured me I would make it. She literally had to hold my hand."[38] By using bias-free statements and photographs in course catalogues, posters, and other recruitment materials, program directors can show that women are welcome in all vocational programs.[39] Effectiveness is also enhanced if the information reaches prospective students in familiar, accessible ways. Printed announcements using appropriate reading levels as well as radio or television announcements are effective means. Concerned educators can display information in such places as supermarkets, laundromats, hairdressers, clinics, churches, and schools.[40] Tom Dunn reports that the best recruiters for special programs are disadvantaged students who are currently enrolled or recently graduated. He also suggests recruiting through other agencies that serve similar target populations.[41] Setting up advisory councils that include persons from the county mental health center, the YWCA, the local adult learning centers, local banks, and counselors from the middle and high schools also ensures the development of a wide-ranging network for recruitment.

Once recruitment efforts are completed and the women have enrolled in a vocational education program, the third component—support services for women—must be put into place. American educational institutions were originally founded by men for the education of other men. Most public schools today are controlled by male administrators and are, hence, designed and organized by men. Women have often felt alienated in academic settings and have experienced formal schooling as either peripheral or irrelevant to their interests and development. For many women, the "real" and valued lessons learned did not necessarily grow out of academic work but out of relationships with friends and teachers, life crises, and community involvement.[42] Support services help women gain a positive sense of self in a system which devalues work done by women and denies the importance and uniqueness of female experiences.[43] Formal, structured-informal, and informal support systems can enable women to overcome these barriers and to remain in vocational education programs.[44] Formal support consists of the services of professionals, such as counselors or agency workers. Structured-informal support is a by-product of involvement in group activities such as religious organizations, the PTA, and Parents without Partners. Informal support is provided by relatives, neighbors, friends, and romantic relationships.

Examples of support are as diverse as the needs of the target populations. One method of support is the established linkage with business, industry, and community agencies that allows school personnel to monitor and advise students as they proceed through occupational exploration, goal-setting, interviewing, and employment. Another important support group is made up of fellow students or program participants who meet formally twice a week, and informally more often, to discuss problems ranging from child care, abusive boyfriends or husbands, and transportation to professional goals, new-found feelings of self-worth, and the possibility of being economically independent for the first time.

Unfortunately, encouraging nontraditional occupational choices, improving recruitment of women, and establishing support systems are not sufficient for programs designed to overcome sex equity barriers. As women gain educations that will enable them to support themselves financially or contribute to the support of families, the overlapping roles of work and home must be analyzed. In order to fulfill this final component, career educators preparing students for occupations in today's workplace need to explore work-family interactions in both instruction and counseling.[45] Traditional career development programs have not placed much emphasis on constraints imposed by the expectations of work and family roles.[46] Too often, career education has been viewed as an individual activity—a view that clearly lacks validity for single parents.

Such exploration is necessary because of shifting roles for men and women. Women especially must face these issues, since staying at home with the children and not developing job skills can be economically crippling if divorce, death, or a change in aspirations creates a change in the family structure. The "myth of separate worlds" must be dispelled.[47] For both women and men, the supposed separateness of work and home implied by traditional value systems provides an inaccurate picture of both work and home participation. Most women work outside the home to satisfy psychological as well as economic needs, and men are recognizing their own failure in not contributing directly to day-to-day family life. As vocational educators plan programs to assist women to obtain workplace roles, this myth must be challenged.

Whether or not flextime, job sharing, and on-site child care become readily available to facilitate commitment to both family and work, women are entering the work force in increasing numbers and are shifting from being solely homemakers to being wage earners as well as homemakers. In March 1987, 52 percent of mothers with children one year old or younger were in the labor force. In 56 percent of married-couple families, both husband and wife were earners at some time in 1987.[48] Men are also moving from being primary wage earners to becoming both wage earners and homemakers. Counseling and training for these roles is imperative as women and men train for new jobs in the workplace and new roles in the family.

Those who complete vocational programs with home/family counseling and support as an integral part of their training can become advocates for better workplace policies that respond to human needs. Examples of these needs include permanent part-time work, shared jobs, revised maternity and paternity leave regulations, industry-sponsored child and elder care, altered nepotism rules, and an expectation that moving and promotion may be dependent on family needs.[49]

Conclusions

As William Camp has pointed out, vocational education grew out of the necessity to train workers in smokestack industries.[50] However, just as American economic and social systems have changed since the late nineteenth century, so too has vocational education expanded its mission and clientele. Though training for the workplace is still an essential part of vocational education, the scope and complexity of training has expanded. Included are concerns about basic skills preparation, entry-level job preparation, and preparation for occupational movement. Aptitudes and abilities are still developed, but concerns with the workplace are supplemented by concerns with issues such as sex roles and family structure. Incorporated into this expansion of mission and clientele have been federal mandates for gender equity and feminist perceptions of education.

There is substantial evidence to suggest the social utility of sex equity in our society. The society gains if women and men prepare for occupations for which they have aptitude, knowledge, and desire, not just for those dictated by traditional gender assignments. Society gains if women achieve the economic freedom that allows them to contribute as central characters rather than from oppressed, powerless, second-class positions. Through the unique perspectives of vocational education— a field whose purpose is to link education and work, a field that has had to respond repeatedly to political initiatives, and a field that is applying a feminist perspective in education—this pragmatic view of equity can be achieved. Vocational education, supported by the power of federal legislation, is helping women break the bonds of poverty through supplying nontraditional work training and through improving the quality of lives of girls and women. A feminist perspective in vocational education helps women and men enter freely into nontraditional occupational areas, helps business and industry take into account the home and family responsibilities of their employees, and helps all employees receive equitable pay for their work. Vocational education has enabled thousands of single parents, teen parents, homemakers, and displaced homemakers to receive their G.E.D. diplomas and obtain further training and schooling, often in nontraditional areas that offer higher pay and greater economic security. Like Carlene Robinson Whited, many would agree that, because of such programs and the support networks created to enhance them, "My life has been given new meaning."

Nevertheless, while it is important to recognize contributions made by existing vocational education programs designed to achieve gender equity, it is critical to note that the number of people served by these programs represents only a small proportion of those in need of services. Currently, most states have made exemplary use of Perkins funds to help women and girls contribute to the economy. However, as projected economic conditions mandate increased participation of women in the workforce, it is increasingly important that employment education be designed to meet their needs. Clearly, advocates of vocational education targeted to assist females must continue to lobby for other funds, besides those provided by the Perkins reauthorization, to be set aside specifically for equity programs.

NOTES

1. Jean Stockard, "Sex Inequities in the Experiences of Students," *Sex Equity in Education,* ed. Jean Stockard et al. (New York: Academic, 1980) 13.

2. Rosemary Deem, *Women and Schooling* (Boston: Routledge & Kegan Paul, 1978) 20.

3. Aaron Benavot, "The Rise and Decline of Vocational Education," *Sociology of Education* 56 (1983): 68.

4. Although no official standard exists to establish with which sex an occupation is identified, many researchers consider a field to be sex-intensive if one sex makes up 70 percent or more of the workers employed nationally. Carol Yuen, "Internal Barriers for Women Entering Nontraditional Occupations: A Review of the Literature," *Occupational Education Forum* 12. 2 (1983): 2.

5. Rupert N. Evans and Edwin L. Herr, *Foundations of Vocational Education* (Columbus: Merrill, 1978) 4.

6. *Statement of the National Coalition for Women and Girls in Education* (Washington, D.C.: National Coalition for Women and Girls in Education, 1983) 4.

7. Project on Equal Education Rights (PEER), *The 1986 PEER Report Card: A State by State Survey of the Status of Women and Girls in America's Schools* (Washington, D.C.: NOW Legal Defense and Education Fund, 1986) 21.

8. Richard N. Adams, *Equity from a Vocational District Administrator's Perspective,* Research and Development Series no. 214A (Columbus: National Center for Research in Vocational Education, 1982) 4.

9. *A Compilation of Federal Education Laws as Amended through June 30, 1977* (Washington, D.C.: GPO, 1977) 520.

10. *U.S. Statutes at Large,* vol. 39, pt. 1 (Washington, D.C.: GPO, 1917) 929–30.

11. *U.S. Statutes at Large,* vol. 86, pt. 1 (Washington, D.C.: GPO, 1972) 374.

12. William Fishel and Abe Potter, *National Politics and Sex Discrimination in Education* (Lexington: Lexington, 1977) 67–69.

13. *Working toward Equity: A Report on the Implementation of the Sex Equity Provisions of the Carl D. Perkins Vocational Act* (Washington, D.C.: National Coalition for Women and Girls in Education, Vocational Education Task Force, 1988) 1.

14. Kathleen Weiler, *Women Teaching for Change: Gender, Class, & Power* (South Hadley: Bergin & Garvey, 1988) 57–58.

15. *First Interim Report from the National Assessment of Vocational Education* (Washington, D.C.: U.S. Department of Education, 1988) 1–5.

16. Janet Radcliffe Richards, *The Skeptical Feminist: A Philosophical Inquiry* (London: Routledge & Kegan Paul, 1980) 271.

17. Jane R. Martin, *Reclaiming a Conversation* (New Haven: Yale UP, 1985) 4.

18. "Playing Both Father and Mother," *Newsweek* 15 July 1985: 42–43.

19. Shirley Dennis in "Women's Bureau Director Discusses Welfare Reform, Economic Status of Women before House Subcommittee," *Women and Work* (Washington, D.C.: U.S. Department of Labor, Office of Information, Publications, and Reports, 1987) 2.

20. Shirley M. H. Hanson and Michael J. Sporakowski, "Single Parent Families," *Family Relations* 35.1 (1986): 3.

21. Arthur J. Norton and Paul C. Glick, "One-Parent Families: A Social and Economic Profile," *Family Relations* 35.1 (1986): 9.

22. Diana Hulse and Diana Sours, "Multiple Mentoring with Single Mothers," *Journal of Employment Counseling* 21.1 (1984): 32.

23. Marsha Levick, *Facts on Women and Poverty* (New York: NOW Legal Defense and Education Fund, 1986) 2.

24. Carol J. Jacobson, "Women at Work: Meeting the Challenge of Job and Family," *AFL–CIO Report* 3 (1986): 23.

25. U.S. Cong., House, *The Carl D. Perkins Vocational Act of 1984*, 98th Cong., 2nd sess. H. Rept. 98-1129 (Washington, D.C.: GPO, 1984) 19.

26. Alice G. Pecoraro, Faye B. Robichaux, and Judy G. Theriot, "Teen Pregnancy: Effect on Family Well-being," *Journal of Home Economics* 79.1 (1987): 27.

27. Rachel Filinson, "Illegitimate Births and Deprivation: Recent Findings from an Exploratory Study," *Social Science and Medicine* 20.4 (1985): 308.

28. Frances A. Campbell, Bonnie Breitmayer, and Craig T. Ramey, "Disadvantaged Single Teenage Mothers and Their Children: Consequences of Free Educational Day Care," *Family Relations* 35.1 (1986): 64.

29. Judy Ferguson and Joan Reed, "To Graduate or NOT to Graduate," *What's New in Home Economics* (March, 1988): 8.

30. Carlos Azcortia and Philip A. Visa, "Dropout Prevention, Chicago Style," *Vocational Education Journal* 62.2 (1987): 33.

31. Paul Campbell et al., "What Vocational Education Can Do for Women, Minorities, the Handicapped, and the Poor," *Facts and Findings* 4.8 (1986): 3–4.

32. National Science Foundation and the Department of Education, *Science and Engineering: Education for the 1980s and Beyond* (Washington, DC: GPO) 64.

33. Linda H. Evans, "Problems Encountered by Nontraditional Students Enrolled in Secondary Vocational Education Programs," diss. Virginia Polytechnic Institute & State University, 1979: 2.

34. Helen S. Farmer et al., "Sex Equity in Career and Vocational Education," *Handbook for Achieving Sex Equity through Education*, ed. Susan S. Klein (Baltimore: Johns Hopkins UP, 1985) 343.

35. *What Color Is Your Language?* (Springfield: Illinois State Board of Education, 1987) 1–2.

36. Myra Sadker, David Sadker, and Joyce Kaser, *The Communications Gender Gap* (Washington, D.C.: The Mid-Atlantic Center for Sex Equity, 1983) 4–5.

37. Steven M. Culver, ed., *Access & Equity* 1.1 (1985): 1.

38. "Carlene Robinson Whited at SVCC," *Access & Equity* 3.4 (May 1988): 1.

39. Louise Vetter and Delina R. Hickey, "Where the Women Are Enrolled," *Vocational Education Journal* 60.7 (1985): 28.

40. Marjorie A. Pett and Beth Vaughan-Cole, "The Impact of Income Issues and Social Status on Post-Divorce Adjustment of Custodial Parents," *Family Relations* 35.1 (1986): 111–12.

41. Tom Dunn, "Connecting with the Disadvantaged," *Vocational Education Journal* 62.2 (1987): 33–34.

42. Mary F. Belenky et al., *Women's Ways of Knowing: The Development of Self, Voice and Mind* (New York: Basic, 1986) 4.

43. Adrienne Rich, "Taking Women Students Seriously," *On Lies, Secrets, and Silence: Selected Prose, 1966–1978* (New York: Norton, 1979) 78.

44. Mary M. Wiberg and Marie Mayor, "The Special Needs of Women Students," *Vocational Education Journal* 60.7 (1985): 34–35.

45. Penny L. Burge and John Hillison, "Facilitating Sex Equity in Vocational Education," *Southern Journal of Occupational Education* 1.1 (1987): 11.

46. Juliet V. Miller, "The Family-Career Connection: A New Component for Career Development Programs," *Journal of Career Development* 12.1 (September 1985): 9.

47. Rosabeth Moss Kanter, "Productivity and the Quality of Life," *J.C. Penney Forum* (May 1983): 14.

48. *Women & Work* (August 1987): 1.

49. Amanda J. Smith and Charlotte J. Farris, *Pioneering Programs in Sex Equity: A Teacher's Guide* (Arlington: American Vocational Association, 1982) 33.

50. William Camp, "Social Efficiency and Vocational Education: An Examination of Our Changing Philosophies," *Journal of Vocational Education Research* 8.3 (1983): 11.

MYRA SADKER & DAVID SADKER

Confronting Sexism in the College Classroom

"Finding . . . that the young women did no manner of harm, we very cautiously admitted them to some of the recitations of lectures in the university building itself, providing always that they were to be marched in good order, with at least two teachers, one in front of the other in the rear of the column as guards."[1]

Only a little more than a century ago, women were not allowed to enter most college classrooms. In the latter half of the nineteenth century, the debate over women's academic place was often acrimonious. When deciding whether to admit women, the president of the University of Michigan charged, "we shall have a community of defeminated women and demasculated men. When we attempt to disturb God's order, we produce monstrosities."[2]

Today the status of women in postsecondary education seems light years away from this inauspicious beginning, but subtle problems remain. Although the last decade has witnessed a significant increase in the number of women attending postsecondary institutions, often the needs of these students are not met. Low enrollment of females in traditionally masculine fields continues, as does the lower level of confidence felt by college women. Women experience an actual decline in academic and career aspirations during their college years.[3] These findings take on even greater significance today as females comprise the new undergraduate majority in higher education. Given this enrollment trend, the education of women should become a central concern to postsecondary education.

Many social institutions other than education erect barriers to equity for women. However, the practices of the postsecondary community can serve to reduce or reinforce these barriers. Unfortunately, as Alexander Astin notes: "Even though men and women are presumably exposed to a common liberal arts curriculum and other educational programs during the undergraduate years, it would seem that these programs serve more to preserve, rather than to reduce, stereotypic differences between men and women in behavior, personality, aspirations and achievement."[4]

Several factors in the higher education environment contribute to this problem. Content analysis studies of college textbooks document the omission and stereotyping of women and their contributions.[5] Assessments of staffing patterns reveal that not only do men outnumber women at all professional ranks and in administrative positions, but the higher the rank or position, the more dramatic the imbalance.[6] On the pages of their books and in the halls of their buildings, female students encounter few role models.

Despite the bias found in the curriculum, staffing patterns, and society at large, most faculty members try to treat all their students fairly. However, a new and important area of research suggests that the teaching act itself, the very heart of the educational process, is the source of significant, if inadvertent, sex bias. At the elementary, secondary, and postsecondary levels, the differential treatment instructors give to male and female students has been documented.

Inequality in Classroom Interaction

At the elementary and secondary levels, research indicates that direct instruction appears to be very important in increasing student achievement. Direct instruction involves active teaching; it includes setting goals, assessing student progress, making active and clear presentations, and giving instruction for both class and individual work.[7] Yet a review of recent research shows that elementary and secondary teachers give far more active teaching attention to boys than girls. They talk to boys more, ask them more lower- and higher-order questions, listen to them more, counsel them more, give them more extended directions, and criticize and reward them more frequently.[8]

This pattern of more active teacher attention directed at male students continues at the postsecondary level, and female students often find it difficult to interact with their professors.[9] While postsecondary instructors provide male students with detailed instructions on how to complete academic and technical assignments on their own, they are more likely to complete these assignments for their female students.[10] In general, women are rarely called on; when female students do participate, their comments are more likely to be interrupted and less likely to be accepted or rewarded.[11] The research suggests that, in postsecondary classrooms across the nation, female students are more likely to be "invisible" members in teacher-student interactions. Postsecondary instructors, however, report that they are generally unaware of these biased patterns in student-teacher interaction.

Sex Segregation and Classroom Interaction

Children learn early to value the opinions of their peer group. The importance placed on this opinion increases as children mature, resulting in a high degree of conformity during the pre-adolescent and adolescent years. In his classic study of students in ten urban and ten rural high schools, James Coleman found that students typically valued popularity more than academic success.[12] This peer group pressure for social rather than academic success was shown to be especially potent and stressful for the adolescent female. Lynn Fox has found that the adolescent peer group can have a negative effect on female participation in math and science. Many young women in high school perceive strong peer pressure against enrolling in advanced math courses, and mathematically gifted females show reluctance to skip grades due to peer disapproval and rejection.[13]

Peer groups that are segregated by sex characterize the elementary school years. Sometimes teachers create this segregation by grouping students on the basis of gender; they may form separate boy-and-girl lines, teams for contests, and groups for various classroom tasks and assignments. However, even when this teacher interference does not occur, children tend to self select into same-sex groups. D. Clement and M. Eisenhart found that ten- to-twelve-year-olds sorted themselves into gender-segregated groups whenever the opportunity arose. Within these sex-segregated groups, girls stressed the importance of being "popular," "cute," and "sweet." Boys' groups placed higher value on being "strong," a "good student," and a "good basketball player."[14]

Same-sex interactions are more common than cross-sex interactions among elementary school children; children are more likely to cross racial lines than sex lines in classroom interaction. L. Grant conducted ethnographic observations of urban first-grade classrooms and found that girls often fulfilled a caretaker role for boys (helping with academic work, tying shoes). Boys were far less likely to demonstrate these behaviors for girls. In contrast, girls received more hostile remarks in cross-sex interaction and were more likely to be the victims of criticism and sexist remarks.[15]

At the postsecondary level, sex segregation is often solidified through the curriculum. Classes in education and nursing are primarily or totally female; in advanced mathematics and physical science the gender gap is also apparent, since boys fill most of the seats in these classrooms. Even when classes are coeducational, including fair representation of women and men, more informal gender segregation takes place as all-male and all-female work and social groups form.[16] This gender segregation has an important effect on classroom interaction. Teachers gravitate to male sections of the classroom, and these become action zones where most of the discussion takes place. Consequently sex segregation adds to the invisibility of female students during class discussions.[17]

Sex Differences in Evaluative Feedback

When female students do become active participants in teacher-student interaction, other forms of sex bias emerge. Research studies conducted in elementary schools reveal that male and female students receive different kinds of evaluative feedback. Boys are more likely to be praised for the intellectual quality of their ideas, while girls are more likely to receive praise for attractiveness of their work and general appearance. Girls are also more likely to have their intellectual competence criticized, while boys are more likely to be criticized for lack of neatness and failure to follow the rules of form.[18]

When this evaluative feedback is examined more closely, another more subtle but significant difference emerges. As teachers criticize boys, they tend to attribute their academic inadequacies to lack of effort. However, when teachers criticize girls, they seldom attribute intellectual inadequacy to lack of effort. Male students who perform poorly are led to believe that, with a greater effort, they can achieve success. As researchers point out, "the pattern of evaluative feedback given to boys and girls in the classroom can result directly in girls' greater tendency to view failure feedback as indicative of their level of ability."[19]

Other studies of teacher interactions conducted at elementary, secondary, and postsecondary levels reveal four types of evaluative feedback that have important implications for the achievement of female and male students. These forms of feedback are as follows:

1. Criticism—explicit indication that a response is wrong. Responses such as "No," "That's not correct" and "You're not paying attention" would be classified as criticism. Criticism need not be punitive and harsh, but it explicitly indicates that a student comment is inaccurate. Less than 5 percent of evaluative feedback at all levels of education is critical in nature.

2. Praise—positive evaluation and reward for successful accomplishment. Comments like "That's a fantastic insight" or "Good" are classified as praise. Praise constitutes less than 10 percent of instructor feedback.

3. Remediation—corrective comments designed to improve a student response. "Try this formula, Linda" or "Remember—the rule is *i* before *e*

except after *c"* are classified as remediation. About a third of instructor reactions are remedial.

4. Acceptance—nonevaluative reaction which recognizes that a student has responded. Fairly typical acceptance responses would include "OK," "Uh-huh," "Yes," or silence. More than 50 percent of responses made by teachers at all levels of education fall into this category.

From grade school through graduate school, instructors use more acceptance than praise, criticism, and remediation combined. This heavy emphasis on acceptance indicates that teacher feedback is diffuse and imprecise, creating a placid and flat classroom climate. While there are appropriate times to use nonevaluative reactions, there are also reasons to view this heavy reliance on acceptance as a problem. Teacher effectiveness research indicates that specific feedback is important for student achievement. While male students receive more than their fair share of all evaluative feedback, the gap is greatest with praise, criticism, and remediation, the reactions which provide the student with the most valuable and precise evaluation.[20]

In summary, patterns of sex bias in teacher-student interaction are prevalent in classrooms at all levels of the educational process—elementary, secondary, and postsecondary. These interaction patterns may result in lower levels of achievement, career aspiration, and self-esteem for women. Although girls start out ahead of boys in most academic areas, as they progress through school their achievement as measured by standardized tests declines.[21] Males score well ahead of girls on all subsections of the Scholastic Aptitude Test (SAT) and the American College Testing Program Examination (ACT). On tests for admission to professional and graduate schools, males outperform females on the Medical College Admissions Test (MCAT), the Graduate Management Admissions Test (GMAT), and the Graduate Record Exam (GRE).[22] Girls enter school at a higher achievement level and leave at a lower achievement level.

Research indicates that instructors at the elementary and secondary levels are unaware of classroom bias but that with resources and training they can learn to interact on a more equitable basis with their female and male students.[23] While patterns of inequity characterize higher education as well as the early years, far less has been done to enable postsecondary faculty to become aware of and to eliminate sex bias in their teaching. The next section of this article reports on a faculty development program that succeeded in achieving gender equity in the postsecondary classroom.

Training for Equity and Effectiveness in College Teaching

Supported by the Fund for the Improvement of Postsecondary Education (FIPSE), a recent intervention involving forty-six professors in an urban university determined that faculty development in sex equitable and effective interaction can have a significant impact.[24] Twenty-three faculty members from a variety of departments including business, communications, chemistry, mathematics, computer science, biology, education, economics, anthropology, government, and American studies participated in the equity training program. An additional twenty-three faculty members matched by race, sex, age, and academic discipline constituted the control group. All forty-six faculty members agreed to have their teaching observed as part of a classroom interaction study.

The two-and-one-half-day training program consisted of didactic, interactive, and microteaching sessions. On the first day of training, the twenty-three professors in the experimental group reviewed classroom interaction research and learned to detect various forms of gender bias. A quiz illustrating the differences in male and female communication styles was administered and explained by the project staff.[25] Participants next viewed a five-minute videotape of a classroom teaching scene and were asked to assess the degree of bias in the instruction. Most professors rated the instructor as fair; after a second, more analytical viewing of the tape, they were amazed to find that the instructor asked three times as many questions and gave four times as much praise to male than to female students. After a discussion of the tape, project staff conducted role plays demonstrating blatant forms of sex bias in classroom teaching. Day one concluded with faculty viewing "Sex Bias in the College Classroom," a thirty-minute videotape summarizing the research on sex bias in postsecondary instruction; the tape also included several classroom scenes showing bias and strategies for making instruction fair for all students. Participants were asked to prepare brief lessons for the next day's training. The lessons were to emphasize discussion rather than lecture, and instructors were to focus on equitable participation for male and female students.

On the second day of training, the twenty-three faculty in the experimental group participated in a microteaching clinic. Since its inception in 1964, microteaching has been a much-researched and widely used approach to teacher training. Microteaching enables teachers to concentrate on one teaching skill at a time. Research indicates that this reduction of the complexity of the teaching act enables teachers to incorporate specific teaching skills into their behavior in a rational and sequential manner.

In a microteaching clinic, instructors try out the specific teaching skills in a clinical setting. Each instructor teaches a group of postsecondary students a brief lesson in any content area, the instructor focuses on mastering the designated teaching skill, and the lesson is videotaped and observed by colleagues and by a supervisor. When the lesson is over, the instructor discusses skill mastery with colleagues, the supervisor, and the students being taught. The instructor also has an opportunity to analyze the videotape of his or her teaching demonstration. When competency in one skill is attained, the instructor focuses on mastering a new skill.

During the microteaching phase of this faculty development project, instructors concentrated on mastering two skills: demonstrating equitable distribution of teacher attention, and demonstrating precise responses to student comments, rather than responses that are vague and unclear. Faculty taught ten- or fifteen-minute lessons in their content areas to small classes of five or six students. They were supervised by a group of two or three of their colleagues as well as by a project staff member. Their lessons were videotaped, and faculty viewed the videotaped lessons as part of the supervisory process.

On the final morning of training, individual problems were discussed and questions answered. Other equity issues, such as assuring a nonbiased curriculum, using nonsexist language, the importance of female administrators as role models, and distributing wait time[26] equitably were discussed.

This training program was unique because college faculty not only discussed teaching but actually practiced a variety of teaching skills and received feedback from their colleagues. Reactions were very positive. One professor commented, "I've been teaching for twenty years and no one has ever evaluated my teaching before. It's thrilling." Many found the experience insightful. A professor who had won national awards for his dynamic teaching style was stunned to find out he spoke primarily to male students. Other faculty accustomed to using only lecture were surprised at how challenging it was to change to an interactive approach to instruction.

After the completion of the faculty development program, trained raters visited the classrooms of experimental and control group professors and conducted systematic observations using a modification of the INTERSECT Observation Instrument (Interactions for Sex Equity in Classroom Teaching). The INTERSECT Observation System includes coding categories which allow a trained observer systematically to record behaviors that are significant in determining the degree of gender bias in the ways teachers interact with students. The classrooms of all forty-six faculty members were coded three times for a total of 128 fifty-five-minute observations. Significant differences emerged between trained and control group faculty in the frequency of interaction, the specificity of teacher feedback, and the degree of sex bias in instruction. To attain a clearer sense of the differences between trained and untrained faculty instruction, it is useful to compare the typical control group and the typical experimental classroom.

In the typical control classroom, males dominated discussion. Ten percent of the students were involved in approximately 25 percent of all interactions with the professor. Forty-five percent of the students interacted with the professor one or two times; the remaining 45 percent were silent. Salient students were usually male and silent students were usually female.

Classrooms of trained faculty were 38 percent more interactive than control group classrooms. Females and males were equally likely to be either salient or silent in classroom discussion. Only 7 percent of the students were silent; 66 percent participated in one or more teacher-student interactions, and 77 percent were salient.

Training also increased the range and specificity of professor reactions to student comments. The untrained professors in the control group responded primarily with acceptance, with heavy use of words such as *uh-huh* and *OK*; in fact, acceptance comprised over half of professor reactions in the control group. And since male students dominated classroom discussion, they received more praise and acceptance, as well as remediation and criticism, from their professors. Female students, mostly silent and invisible, received far less feedback. In contrast, the twenty-three professors in the experimental group gave more precise and clear responses, used less acceptance and more remediation, and achieved virtual equity in their interactions with female and male students in their classes.

Thus, this faculty development program resulted in more effective and more equitable postsecondary teaching. Training increased the frequency of classroom interaction as well as the precision of faculty reactions to student comments. Male and female students participated equitably in the classrooms of faculty members who had received training.

Recommendations for Attaining Equity and Excellence in the Classroom

Based on the literature review as well as the successful sex equity intervention described above, the following recommendations can be used to attain equity in postsecondary instruction. Some of the recommendations require organizational support, while others can be accomplished by individual faculty sensitive to the bias that frequently, if inadvertently, occurs in classrooms.

1. *A program of systematic observation and feedback is the key to attaining both equity and excellence in the college classroom.* Most faculty spend their entire professional lives working in classrooms in isolation from colleagues. Many have never seen a videotape of their teaching or received feedback from a colleague on the quality of their instruction. Postsecondary institutions should provide faculty development to acquaint instructors with the research on effective teaching. Further, these faculty development programs should go beyond "talking about teaching." They should offer instructors the opportunity to try out new teaching skills in clinical settings and to work with their colleagues for instructional improvement.

2. *Faculty development should focus on equity as well as excellence.* The issue of equity in postsecondary education is one that most faculty have never considered. When faculty development programs do deal with gender equity, they typically focus on curriculum and not instruction. Research showing that many faculty inadvertently give male students more instructional attention should be disseminated along with strategies for eliminating biased teaching patterns. Faculty should also be made aware of the achievement gap between male and female students that is reflected in standardized measures such as the Scholastic Aptitude Test and the Graduate Record Exam.

3. *Even without organizational support, individual faculty can determine whether there are differences in the amount of instruction provided to female and male students.* Although faculty development programs on gender equity may not be available, individual faculty can focus on the issue in their own classrooms. One of the first steps is to determine the level and nature of inequity that may be present. Systematic observation can be accomplished in a variety of ways. Faculty can video or audiotape sessions for later analysis; they can appoint students to observe and record classroom interactions; or colleagues can provide assistance.

The first step is to draw a seating chart that indicates placement and gender of students. Each time a student is asked a question, the observer should make a tally on the seating chart, indicating the student who was asked the question. Comparing the distribution of questions to the actual attendance of males and females in the class will indicate whether there are gender inequities in the allocation of teacher time and attention. This procedure will reveal not only whether males or females receive more attention but also which individuals are silent and which are monopolizing classroom discussion. The observer can also note whether the students who were asked the questions volunteered responses by raising their hands or calling out, or whether the teacher called on them when they did not volunteer a response. This information will indicate whether it is the instructor or the students who determine who gets access to classroom interaction.

4. *Even without organizational support, individual faculty can also analyze whether there are differences in the quality of instruction provided to male and female students.* Systematic observation can reflect qualitative as well as quantitative inequities. Keeping a tally on a seating chart can indicate whether males or females are asked more difficult and thought-provoking questions. Although most questions asked in classrooms are factual or lower order, relying on memory, those questions that call for higher-order reasoning are the most vital to advanced levels of achievement. Instead of recording a tally mark on the seating chart to note which students are asked questions, the observer can mark an *L* for each lower-order question and an *H* for each higher-order question asked. This procedure will reflect whether there are gender inequities involved in who receives the most challenging and thought-provoking questions.

Information recorded on the seating chart could also reflect whether males or females are getting the more precise and valuable teacher feedback. Every time a student responds to a question, the observer can indicate the type of teacher reaction. If the student is praised, the observer will mark a *P* in the appropriate box on the seating chart; likewise *A* will indicate instructor acceptance ("Uh-huh," "OK," "No Comment"), *R* notes remediation, and *C* indicates criticism. An analysis of the notations on the seating chart will indicate any inequities in the way evaluative feedback is distributed.

5. *Faculty can develop skills to interact fairly with all students.* Professors are the gatekeepers providing or denying students access to classroom interaction. They have the power to allow volunteers to dominate the discussion or to designate any student to participate in class discussion. Sometimes professors worry that calling on quiet or shy students will embarrass or upset them, so they allow these quiet students— usually female—to remain invisible spectators to the educational process. In this gesture of benign neglect, they forget that active participation is related to achievement and confidence, and that education is not a spectator sport. By assessing instruction and then taking assertive measures to call on and involve all students, professors can attain equity in class instruction.

In *College: The Undergraduate Experience in America*, Ernest Boyer says: "Students go to college expecting something special. Their parents share this hope. Only in America is the decal from almost any college displayed proudly on the rear window of the family car."[27] For too many female students, hope does not become reality. Although they pay full tuition, they do not receive their fair share of the most valuable resource in the classroom—professor time and attention. Only when professors take steps to close the gender gap in classroom interaction and student achievement will quality and equality in postsecondary education be attained.

NOTES

1. Quoted in Nancy Frazier and Myra Sadker, *Sexism in School and Society* (New York: Harper, 1973) 144.

2. Quoted ibid.

3. Roberta Hall, *The Classroom Climate: A Chilly One for Women* (Washington, D.C.: Association of American Colleges, 1982).

4. Alexander Astin, *Four Critical Years: Effects of College on Beliefs, Attitudes and Knowledge* (San Francisco: Jossey-Bass, 1977) 216.

5. Myra Sadker and David Sadker, *Beyond Pictures and Pronouns: Sexism in Teacher Education Texts* (Washington, D.C.: U.S. Department of Education, 1979).

6. *The Half-Full, Half-Empty Glass*, Report of the National Advisory Council on Women's Educational Programs (Washington, D.C.: U.S. Department of Education, 1981).

7. Thomas Good, "Teacher Effectiveness in the Elementary School," *Journal of Teacher Education* 33 (1979): 55–61.

8. Myra Sadker and David Sadker, "Sexism in the Schoolroom of the '80s," *Psychology Today* (March 1985): 54–57.

9. S. Sternglanz and S. Lyberger-Ficek, "Sex Differences in Student-Teacher Interactions in the College Classroom," *Sex Roles* 3 (1977): 345–52.

10. C. Safilios-Rothschild, *Sex-Role Socialization and Sex Discrimination: A Synthesis and Critique of the Literature* (Washington, D.C.: National Institute of Education, 1979).

11. Candace West, "Female Interruptions in Cross-Sex Conversation: Seldom Seen, Soon Forgotten," paper, annual meeting, American Sociological Association, 1979.

12. James Coleman, *The Adolescent Society* (New York: Free Press of Glencoe, 1961).

13. Lynn Fox, "The Effects of Sex Role Stereotyping on Mathematics Participation and Achievement of Women in Mathematics: Research Perspectives for Change," Papers in Education and Work no. 8 (Washington, D.C.: National Institute of Education, 1977).

14. D. Clement and M. Eisenhart, *Learning Gender Roles in a Southern Elementary School* (Chapel Hill: U of North Carolina P, 1979).

15. L. Grant, "Sex Roles and Statuses in Peer Interactions in Elementary Schools," paper, American Educational Research Association, New York, 1982.

16. Dawn Thomas, "An Analysis of Sex Differences in Teacher/Student

Interaction in Elementary/Secondary and Postsecondary Mathematics/Science, Composition/Literature/Language Arts Classrooms," diss., American U, 1983.

17. Joan Long, David Sadker, and Myra Sadker, "The Effects of Teacher Sex Equity and Effectiveness Training at the University Level," paper, American Educational Research Association, San Francisco, 1986.

18. Carol Dweck, W. Davidson, S. Nelson, and B. Enna, "Sex Differences in Learned Helplessness: II. The Contingencies of Evaluative Feedback in the Classroom. III. An Experimental Analysis," *Developmental Psychology* 14 (1978): 268–76.

19. Ibid., 270.

20. David Sadker and Myra Sadker, "Is the O.K. Classroom O.K.?" *Phi Delta Kappan* 66.5 (January 1985): 358–61.

21. Myra and David Sadker, *Report Card: The Cost of Sexism in School* (Andover: New England Center for Equity Assistance, in press).

22. S. Dauber, "Sex Differences on the SAT-M, SAT-V, TSWE and ACT among College-Bound High School Students," paper, American Educational Research Association, Washington, D.C., 1986.

23. David Sadker and Myra Sadker, *Promoting Effectiveness in Classroom Instruction: Final Report*, Report no. 400-80-0033 (Washington, D.C.: National Institute of Education, 1984).

24. Myra Sadker and David Sadker, *Final Report: Project EFFECT (Effectiveness and Equity in College Teaching)* (Washington, D.C.: Fund for the Improvement of Postsecondary Education, 1986).

25. Myra Sadker, "What's Your Gender Communications Quotient?" *The Communication Gender Gap*, ed. Myra Sadker, David Sadker, and Joyce Kaser (Washington, D.C.: Mid-Atlantic Center for Sex Equity, American University, 1983).

26. *Wait time* refers to the amount of time an instructor waits after asking a question. Research shows that typically teachers wait less than a second. If the student response is not immediate, the teacher rephrases, calls on someone else, or answers the question for the student. If teachers can increase wait time to three to five seconds, the quality of classroom interaction improves.

27. Ernest Boyer, *College: The Undergraduate Experience in America* (New York: Harper, 1987).

NOTES ON CONTRIBUTORS

LINDA LAUBE BARNES is a linguist and composition specialist in the Department of English Language and Literature at Southern Illinois University at Edwardsville. She has conducted research in the areas of collaborative learning, teacher commentary, and gender and writing. She teaches graduate courses in the sociolinguistics of writing in addition to undergraduate and graduate composition theory and practice courses.

NINA BAYM is LAS Jubilee Professor of English at the University of Illinois at Urbana-Champaign. She is the author of several books, essays, and reviews about American literature, American culture, and American feminism. She has published in journals such as *American Literature, Nineteenth-Century Studies, Texas Studies in Language and Literature,* and *Tulsa Studies in Women's Literature.* She has edited Kate Chopin's *The Awakening* for the Modern Library and Maria Susanna Cummins's *The Lamplighter* for the Rutgers University Press American Women Writers series. Among her books are *Women's Fiction: A Guide to Novels by and about Women in America, 1820–1879,* and *Novels, Readers, and Reviewers: Response to Fiction in Antebellum America.*

PENNY L. BURGE is Associate Professor and Program Area Leader, the Division of Vocational and Technical Education, in the College of Education at Virginia Polytechnic Institute & State University. Her research includes several articles focusing on gender roles and family structures. She has authored an information analysis paper, *Career Development of Single Parents* (Columbus, OH: The National Center for Research in Vocational Education, 1987), which has been widely used in equity programs in a number of states. Most recently she has served as a gender equity consultant for the National Center for Research in Vocational Education, Berkeley, CA.

STEVEN M. CULVER is Director of Student Assessment Programs at Radford University in Virginia. He has lectured to diverse groups on nonsexist language and unbiased communication in the classroom. As editor of *Access & Equity,* a newsletter funded by the Gender Equity Office, Virginia Department of Education, he has been involved in communicating the efforts of equity projects around the state to teachers, counselors, administrators, and state department personnel across the country. He has published articles and presented papers and workshops concentrating on gender equity and the needs of pregnant teens, single parents, homemakers, and displaced homemakers.

ROBERT CON DAVIS teaches American literature and critical theory at the University of Oklahoma. He has published many articles on fiction and contemporary discourse, and he is co-editor of a book series titled the Oklahoma Project for Discourse & Theory. He has edited and co-edited a number of books, including *Lacan and Narration: The Psychoanalytic Difference in Narrative Theory; Intertextuality and Contemporary American Fiction; Contemporary Literary Criticism: Literary and Cultural Studies;* and *Literary Criticism and Theory: The Greeks through the Present.* Recently he finished *The Paternal Romance: Zeus, Yahweh, and Oppositionalism* and co-authored another book titled *Criticism as Critique.*

ELIZABETH A. FLYNN is Director of the Institute for Research on Language and Learning at Michigan Technological University. She is co-editor (with Patrocinio Schweickart) of *Gender and Reading: Essays on Readers, Texts, and Contexts* and has published articles in *College English, College Composition and Communication, New Orleans Review, The Writing Instructor,* and other journals. She edits the journal *Reader: Essays in Reader-Oriented Theory, Criticism, and Pedagogy.*

SUSAN L. GABRIEL is Director of the SIUE Corporate Writing Program and a technical writing instructor at Southern Illinois University at Edwardsville. She has presented numerous workshops on gender equity in the classroom, gender and pedagogy, and gender and writing for elementary, secondary, and university instructors. She co-edited (with Isaiah Smithson) a special issue of *Papers on Language and Literature,* "Gender, Text, and Meaning."

CAROLYN HEILBRUN is Avalon Foundation Professor in the Humanities at Columbia University, where she teaches modern British literature, the novel, and feminist studies. She has published many articles in *PMLA, Twentieth Century Literature, Critical Inquiry,* the *ADE Bulletin,* and other journals. Her books include *The Garnett Family, Christopher Isherwood, Toward a Recognition of Androgyny, Reinventing Womanhood,* and *Writing a Woman's Life.*

CHERIS KRAMARAE teaches courses in language and gender and in language and social control in the Speech Communication Department at the University of Illinois at Urbana-Champaign. She is the author of many articles on language and gender, and she is the author, editor, or co-editor of nine books, including *Women and Men Speaking; Language, Gender and Society; A Feminist Dictionary; Language and Power;* and *Technology and Women's Voices.* She is the co-editor (with Paula Treichler) of the periodical *Women and Language.*

DAVID SADKER is professor of education at American University. He has conducted training programs concerned with teacher effectiveness, supervision, and educational equity for teachers and supervisors in over forty states. As co-director of projects funded by the National Institute of Education, The Fund for the Improvement of Postsecondary Education, and other sources, he has conducted and managed numerous training and research efforts on equity for women in education.

His articles have appeared in *Psychology Today, Phi Delta Kappan, Harvard Educational Review,* and *Journal of Teacher Education.* He has co-authored several books (with Myra Sadker), including *Now Upon a Time: A Contemporary View of Children's Literature.*

MYRA SADKER is professor of education at American University in Washington, D.C. She has written many articles and given many presentations dealing with gender equity in education. She is co-author (with David Sadker) of *Sex Equity Handbook for Teachers; Teachers, Schools and Society;* and other books. She has co-directed several projects funded under The Women's Educational Equity Act, Title IV of the 1964 Civil Rights Act, The National Institute of Education, and The Fund for the Improvement of Postsecondary Education. In 1980 the American Educational Research Association awarded Myra and David Sadker the Women Educator's Award for research making the greatest contribution to women in education.

PATROCINIO P. SCHWEICKART is associate professor of English at the University of New Hampshire. She is co-editor (with Elizabeth Flynn) of *Gender and Reading: Essays on Readers, Texts, and Contexts.* Her essays on feminist criticism and gender and reading have appeared in *Signs, Modern Fiction Studies, Canadian Journal of Political and Social Theory,* and *Reader.* She is currently working on a book-length study of a feminist theory of discourse.

ISAIAH SMITHSON is Chair of the Department of English Language and Literature and a faculty member in the Women's Studies Program at Southern Illinois University at Edwardsville. He teaches courses in women and language, feminist research methodology, literary theory, and composition theory. His articles have appeared in *Studies in English Literature, College English, Journal of the History of Ideas,* and other journals. He has edited several special issues of journals, most recently issues of *Papers on Language and Literature,* "Gender, Text, and Meaning" (with Susan Gabriel), and *Computers and Composition,* "Computers and the Teaching of Writing: An Overview." He is presently engaged in studies of metaphor in scientific discourse.

PAULA A. TREICHLER has been a teacher and administrator at the University of Illinois at Urbana-Champaign; she is now associate professor in the College of Medicine's Medical Humanities and Social Science Program, the Institute of Communications Research, the Unit for Criticism and Interpretive Theory, and the Women's Studies Program. She has published many articles on feminist theory, language and gender, and language and medicine. She is co-author of *A Feminist Dictionary* and *Language, Gender, and Professional Writing: Theoretical Approaches and Guidelines for Nonsexist Usage.* She is co-editor of *For Alma Mater: Theory and Practice in Feminist Scholarship* and of the periodical *Women and Language* (with Cheris Kramarae). She is presently working on a cultural and linguistic analysis of AIDS and a second book with the working title *Feminism, Medicine, and Cultural Crisis: Current Contests for Meaning.*

INDEX

DATE DUE

AP 18 '06			
SE 20 '06			
AP 11 '08			

DEMCO 38-296